The Voice:

How The Bible Reveals Reincarnation

Large Format Edition

A Spiritual Voyage to Enlightenment.
History. Science. The Bible.

Captain L. Edward VanHoose, MA

United States of America

Copyright © 2004 by L. Edward VanHoose. All rights reserved. No part of this book may be reproduced in any form, except for brief review, without the express permission of the publisher (with exception of biblical and Cayce quotations.) For further information, please contact:

KDP is a division of Amazon.com

You may contact the author at
www.reincarnationworld.com   or   www.capnlarry.com

Library of Congress Cataloging in Publication Data:
VanHoose, L. Edward
The Voice: How The Bible Reveals Reincarnation
Includes bibliographical references and index
Printed in the United States of America

Edgar Cayce Readings © 1971, 1993, 1994, 1995, 1996, 2009, by Edgar Cayce Foundation. All Rights Reserved.

The Voice: How The Bible Reveals Reincarnation

Body, Mind, Soul - Reincarnation

ISBN: 9798366227957

First Printing, May 2004
Second Printing June 2004
Third Printing June 2009
Kindle E Book Version 2011
Large Format Edition 2022

Prologue

Elijah's Return

Saint James, the brother of Jesus, reminded the world that the Prophet Elijah led a remarkable life. So much so, that marvelous metaphors were made depicting his being taken bodily to heaven. In a like manner, this same honor had been bestowed, as a matter of custom, upon the deaths of other ancient luminaries. Some included Romulus the founder of Rome, Mithra of Persia, and Caesar Augustus.

They were not deities; nor was Elijah.

In the final analysis, he would stand equally before his Creator, and as do all God's children, receive the wisdom of Divine justice. James was correct in concluding that Elijah was a human being:

"Like ourselves." (James 5:17)

(Unless otherwise noted, Bible quotations are translated from Aramaic, the language spoken by Jesus.)

The Prophet Isaiah predicted that, the very human, Elijah would return to prepare the way of the Messiah:

"The voice of him that cries in the wilderness *prepare the way* of the Lord, make straight in the desert a highway for our God."

(Isaiah 40:3.) (All Italics are added)

The Prophet Malachi concurred. He wrote, in the closing prophecy of the Old Testament:

"He shall *prepare the way* before me…the messenger of the covenant, in whom you *delight* Behold I will send you Elijah the Prophet."

(Malachi 3:1 - 4:6)

Jesus said of such prophesies:

"The Scripture cannot be broken."

(John 10:35)

He said of Elijah's return to fulfill such Scripture:

"Elijah will come first so that everything might be fulfilled."

(Matthew 17:11)

He said of John the Baptist's work in a fulfillment:

"For all the prophets and the law prophesied until John."

(Matthew 11:13)

Jesus also said a lot about Elijah's - a human being *like ourselves* - reincarnation as John the Baptist:

1.   "For this is he of whom it is written, behold I will send my messenger before your face to ***prepare the way*** before you."
(Matthew 11:10)

2.   "And if you wish to accept it,
   He is Elijah who was to come.
   He who has ears to hear, let him hear."
(Matthew 11:14-15)

3.   "But I say to you Elijah has already come...
   Then the disciples understood that what he had told them was about John the Baptist."
(Matthew 17:12-13)

4.   "He said to them, Elijah does come first to prepare everything… But I say to you that Elijah has come."
(Mark 9:12-13)

5.   "This is he of whom it is written, Behold, I send my messenger before your face to ***prepare the way*** before you."
(Luke 7:27)

6.   "He was a lamp which burns and gives light; and you were willing to ***delight*** in his light for a while."
(John 5:35)

These words of the New Testament's highest authority are clear: Elijah returned. This prepares the way, a highway of certainty - at least for followers of Jesus - in answering a fundamental question concerning the actuality of life after death: If Elijah stood equally before God, as a human being *like ourselves* - and returned - then cannot we all?

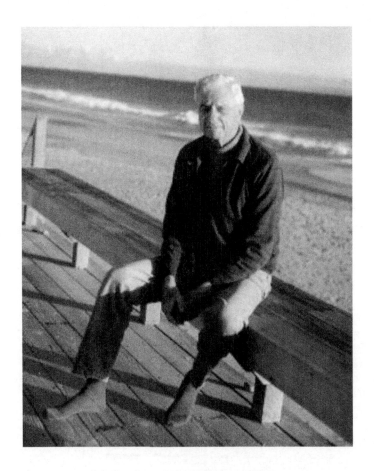

Foreword

"This will be a best seller. I'll even write the foreword!"

I met *Captain* Larry when he was a student in my creative writing class. I found his work warm, probing, and enlightening. His, *The Voice: How The Bible Reveals Reincarnation* represents years of extensive research in the exploration of a very exciting subject. Its universal message merits the reader's attention. This is a highly personal adventure, which may change one's life.   Jess Stearn Malibu, California

There is more to follow. Unfortunately, Mr. Stearn passed away before the rest of the final draft could be completed in his own words. However, his sentiments will continue throughout portions of the text, as recorded in my notes, which will also include the moving circumstances of his passing.

A memorial message appears on page 9.

The Preparation.

Contents

		Page
Prologue	Elijah's Return	i

Chapter

1	The Search for Bridey Murphy	1
2	Evidence	11
3	A Guide to Navigation	47
4	The Cayces	55
5	The Work	59
6	The Research	63
7	The Dialogue	65
8	Saint Paul	89
9	Saint Peter	95
10	Voices: Hear O Israel	99
11	Others	125
12	The Holy Spirit	145
13	The Procedure	147
14	Shore Leave	169
15	The Grand Slam	175
16	Conclusions	193
17	Other Cases / Other Lessons	199
18	Back to the Case	209
19	Appendix	245
20	Some Closing Remarks	263
21	Bibliography, and Index	269
	How The Bible Reveals Reincarnation (A short synopsis for Sharing)	279

List of Tables

Comparisons of Spontaneous Cases of the Reincarnation Type and the Biblical Case of John the Baptist   193

Table 1
Direct Statements of Jesus Identifying John the Baptist as Elijah:
Aramaic Bible Version   245

Table 1a
Jerusalem Bible Version   246

Table 1b
King James Bible Version   247

Table 2
Twenty Cases Suggestive of Reincarnation in the Scriptures   248

Table 3
Summary of Behavior and Statements Concerning John The Baptist's Identity With Elijah   249

(Unless noted otherwise, all photographs have been rendered by the author.)

Chapter 1

The Search for Bridey Murphy

Before beginning, you might want to know about my past. I was sixteen years old when I first read about reincarnation. The local Baltimore paper had serialized a book titled, *The Search for Bridey Murphy*. According to the works late author, Morey Bernstein, *Bridey* was born in Cork, Ireland in 1798 and died sixty-six years later. Bernstein's rather detailed information had been obtained through the hypnosis of Ruth Simmons, a Boulder, Colorado housewife. When hypnotized, she claimed to have been Bridey Murphy in a previous life. I avidly read each installment and was first in line when the movie came to town. My family seemed content with their traditional beliefs and showed no interest. While religious, they were not regular church goers. This might explain they're having little concern that such an alien concept could so fascinate their young teen. They probably figured it was something I would just outgrow. It never occurred to me to seek out our pastor's opinion, on those Christmas and Easter Sundays, when we got to church. Phoning him about reincarnation was not an option. Kids my age just didn't do such things.

I was already a philosophical type, though I seldom shared this with my rough and ready peers. They thought "snagging" fly balls of more import. That I was a lousy ballplayer didn't help my status in the schoolyard. I overcame this deficiency in overtly proclaiming a like-minded disinterest in things academic and followed through with appropriate grades as evidence. This maintained my status as a regular guy.

It was a tough school and, as I had few friends who were big, I felt it best to keep my growing interest in Plato, classical music, and art, in particular photography, to myself.

As for things theological, reincarnation made sense. I believed, as I do now, in a just God. Thus, I understood that there were reason and purpose behind the experiences of my life. As a human, I was an eternal soul. What I experienced on earth was surely some aspect of that eternity.

No one needed to be a rocket scientist, or even a precocious teenager, to understand that eternity lasts for a long time and can cover a lot of territory, both within and beyond the earth. That souls could make future returns didn't seem at all outlandish. And so much the better that humans received rewards for their previous life's behavior.

For the most part, I was content with this understanding. I could accept that I would not get out of the human condition alive. However, I could also accept that I would pull through to survive in some rational form. My future life would exist and would reflect both the virtues and shortcomings of all that I had become, since creation. Such was my concept concerning the reality of eternal life.

The Search for Bridey Murphy would never prove to be a case establishing the realities and virtues of reincarnation, nor would be the escapades of my youth. While I inwardly yearned for the scholarly life of a writer and artist, my family - being a family of practical entrepreneurs and salesmen - was quick to look at my grades and quick to overlook that I had once been published at age eight. In noting my more obvious innate skills as a talker, they thought it best that I continue the family tradition. My first year out of high school was spent learning about the home improvement industry. I started as a door-to-door canvasser, setting appointments and otherwise "preparing the way" for salesmen, including my father, who were selling aluminum siding. I worked with integrity and I worked hard. After a year, I was able to buy a very used *Alfa Romeo* roadster and begin classes at the University of Maryland. My lack of academic preparation proved problematic. However, I hung on.

The economics of fast cars and faster motorcycles forced aside a fast academic track. And so did the even faster vehicles of feminine pulchritude, which I found so elusive.

Dad's searches for a family fortune lead us into the mobile home business. With mom running the office, and dad and myself in sales, we soon became one of Maryland's more successful dealerships. Though the operation stayed open seven days a week, I still found time for study. An opportunity for a new dealership opened in Fort Lauderdale. I didn't like the proposition, but we went south anyway.

Business was good. Though too busy for a scholarly life of contemplation, I possessed an XKE Jaguar, two sailboats, several fine cameras, girlfriends, and lived in a nice place. Then my sister sent dad a book by Jess Stearn. It concerned the life of Edgar Cayce. Dad had always been of a spiritual bent, though he seldom talked about religion. The Cayce story had fascinated him. Edgar Cayce was a fellow Kentuckian and had developed an ability, while in trance, to speak with amazing accuracy, on most any subject. He died in 1945. Though both a Christian mystic and psychic, he offered erudite discourses on reincarnation. The bottom line was dad's changed life. He relaxed and became less driven by the fears of failure, which had so pushed him. I would learn that his high school class had voted him the least likely to succeed. We became closer in our shared beliefs. It came as no surprise in his wishing to get out of our mega-stress business and my wishing to return to Baltimore and get on with my own life. We never worked together again. Mom didn't like the idea, reminding us both that we could not live on "moonbeams." Dad went on to a career selling resort property. He seemed happier and years later, upon his death, he died a contented man.

    Having no regrets in leaving my life as a Fort Lauderdale workaholic and playboy, and nearing thirty, I yearned to discover my life's purpose and make my mark doing what I had come to earth to accomplish. The first step was to formally finish my studies. Over the years, I had amassed quite a few college credits, though I had been bounced out of the University of Maryland, when I foolishly enrolled in their engineering school. There had been this certain coed. Beautiful, but she only dated engineers. When I flunked something called Pythagorean Trigonometry, the dean's farewell words went something like, "you'd have had better luck getting her fingers in your hair, with a little dab of Brylcreem®, rather than with the little dab of 'trig' you're lack of study has gotten you this semester. Good day sir!" Banished, I changed colleges and wound up at the fine, and forever forgiving, University of Baltimore.

(Photo by E. C. Gregory)
Toga Time!
A certain playful Pythagorean participates, with diligence, in preparation for the next day's exam.

I had remained in good standing and, having long achieved senior status, could quickly graduate. The plan was short lived.

Just before Christmas, though hardly the marrying type, I got married. A few weeks later, the fine Arabian horse I was riding reared and lost her footing. Awakening, encased in a body cast, I was to learn patience. That the event probably prevented me from getting killed on a motorcycle, or might have had some causation from a past-life problem, offered some solace. While it was a politically correct "all natural" accident, my "all natural" bones still hurt a lot. So much so, that I received countless injections of "all unnatural" synthetic morphine and other nasty painkillers. But balanced with a prescription of beer and marijuana ("all natural") which my friends smuggled into the hospital, life was at least bearable. I managed to complete my courses and even "Aced" the trigonometry of the ancient Pythagoreans. I began to walk at about the time my son was learning to do likewise. Once out and about, I never felt the need for drugs of any nature. Purchasing an old Baltimore townhouse, I restored it to her 19th century elegance, during my rehabilitation.

With a degree in the social sciences, I found a job in one of the "helping professions" as a worker in a mental institution for adolescents. I had a lot of problems with the behaviorist approach of B. F. Skinner, then in vogue. While the kids made progress, I thought a lot of it came from hugs by staff, and other indications of caring, as much if not more, than from the dictates of Dr. Skinner. He didn't acknowledge the soul's place in bringing about healing.

Frustrated, I served a short stint as a tugboat deckhand. I had always found solace in things nautical. Years later, I sat for the difficult U.S. Coast Guard captain's exam. As a seafarer, my most exciting experiences have probably occurred in past lives. This time around, my most memorable maritime adventure was as captain at Virginia's Norfolk Marine Institute. I counseled and taught citizenship skills - presented as seamanship skills - to troubled teen delinquents. They learned to handle boats and how to fish. The sea soothes souls, and these kids - long deprived of the fruits of life, liberty, and the pursuit of happiness - found life, liberty, and pursued happiness in pursuing Chesapeake Bay striped bass! With angered egos quieted, their soul's needs were easier to access.

One young man revealed his anger over the burning of Norfolk during the civil war. He vividly remembered a past life as a southern soldier, but was afraid to tell anyone. Assured that he was wasn't crazy, for having such a remembrance, he was able to get a lot off his chest. A few weeks later, he went back to high school and become an automobile mechanic. To date, he repairs cars instead of stealing them.

Of course, not all the students faired so well. The point is that therapy must recognize the reality of the soul, and stress its issues, which sometimes - but not always - include past-life problems. I suspect soul issues motivate human behaviors more so than do factors of heredity and environment. That sums up my differences with Skinner and the behaviorists.

I'm getting ahead of myself. Off the tug, my next job was as an advisor to Baltimore City's famous "Dollar House" program. People could buy an old house, for a dollar, and fix it up with low interest city loans. It was interesting and the same newspaper, which had featured Bridey Murphy, wrote a story about my work. By then, I had divorced and remarried. With two more children, mom's admonition that no one can live on "moonbeams" struck home. So I came full circle and started in the home improvement business again.

I had also become active in the Edgar Cayce work. I joined the Association for Research and Enlightenment, which had been founded to study psychic and spiritual phenomenon. I met Cayce's son, Hugh Lynn, and grandson, Dr. Charles Thomas, in Virginia Beach. I felt like I had known the Cayce family for a long time. My wife and I started a weekly spiritual study group in our home. It was here that I developed an interest in the Bible. I trimmed my beard and became a card-carrying Episcopalian. The priest had some problems with reincarnation and asked why I had joined. I explained my membership in that, as I felt no one church had every answer, I would choose a church based on how it might best magnify the good work I put into it - whether in money or time. Memorial Episcopal Church was noted for its feeding the poor and Father Farnham accepted my explanation. I did not tell him that my reasoning came from an Edgar Cayce discourse. I later learned that the Church's tradition, concerning theology, was quite open and no bishop, or higher authority, could silence individual viewpoints or kick someone out because of them. Bishop James A. Pike of the California diocese was one of my heroes. Before his death, he believed in reincarnation and had been in Israel studying early Christianity. Early Christianity held the same belief. While he had given up his title, he had remained an Episcopalian. I felt quite at home and even gave several lectures, always to a filled audience, in our small parish house.

But Father Farnham invariably nailed me on how the subject was handled in the Bible. I could point out one verse and he, or someone else, could point out another verse which seemed at odds.

The experience taught me that reincarnation would need a strong biblical justification, before it would ever be taken seriously in the West. As I could never find a book, which properly addressed the issue, I hoped someone would write one soon.

Mom passed on at about this time. She had been diagnosed with terminal cancer. Three days before dying, she demanded a pain prescription, checked out of the hospital, and drove home. Her choice had been to die with dignity. While she never fully accepted reincarnation, nor the role of organized religion, her faith stood tall. Just before passing, Father Farnham, with sister Sandy and myself as assistants administered her the church's last rites.

Mom awakened from her coma and gave all a broad smile. Her last words were, "thank you, I love you."

Most stories like mine end, with all leading happy lives of middle class bliss. Another divorce and resulting bad business decisions, aimed at reducing stress rather than solving problems - the business of business is business - changed that scenario. In due time, I found myself sailing south to, again, start over again.

The destination was Virginia Beach. I had enrolled as a graduate student at Atlantic University. The school had been established by Edgar Cayce in 1930, and though long dormant, had resurrected itself in offering a serious master's degree in transpersonal study (parapsychology, comparative religion, and the like). The endeavor culminated in a hard won diploma and the research backing this book.

Surprisingly, my writing teacher was Jess Stearn - the same biographer of Edgar Cayce, who had so moved my father. I submitted my stuff, as did the other students. Though jovial, they were a tough bunch and a surprising number held scientific degrees in psychology, physics and engineering. A few already had doctorates. My B.A. degree seemed puny by comparison. Being a licensed sea captain, I thought the playing field might be leveled in introducing me as *Captain* L. Edward VanHoose. I figured the title and lofty "*L*" would lead these astute folks to think I had brains. Most wound up calling me Captain Larry or just plain "Cap'n." We struggled, as equals, through each class as Jess critiqued our work.

I girded up my loins when my turn finally came.

"He's a big guy," I thought, as I watched him size me up. As a savvy reporter with the hard boiled New York Daily News, he had listened to the greatest of the greatest generation: Eleanor Roosevelt, Dwight Eisenhower, Carl Sandburg, Frank Sinatra, Mae West, Clark Gable. He'd heard it all! Authoring thirty-five books and, for a time, a contributing editor with the no-nonsense Newsweek magazine, he'd told it all. His best-selling book on Edgar Cayce, *The Sleeping Prophet*, prompted Jess' familiarity with greatest of the greatest story ever told: Adam and Eve, Mary and Joseph, Jeremiah, Jesus and Mary Magdalene, John the Baptist, Solomon.

Good News: and Mr. Stearn had read all about it!

I sat, sweating out what I feared would be an inquisition. Pacing back and forth, in front of the class, he mulled over my submission. He snorted a few times, and as each page was completed, he would utter a loud, "Harrummph!"

With each "Harrummph," I inched deeper into my seat. I try to use humor in writing about the Spiritual. Its tough, because not everyone agrees that such a tack is appropriate, especially in addressing the Bible, though there are more than four hundred sixty –two (count em!) mentions of happiness, happy, joy, joyfulness, laugh, laughter, laughing, glad, gladly, and gladness!

But despite this insight I caught, as I sometimes still catch, a more often polite (but jaundiced) raising of eyebrows. Back then, I wasn't sure how Jess was going to react.

By the third "Harrummph," I knew I was in deep trouble, even deeper, when his next utterance was the dreaded "H" word! But he quickly added, I thought you were just a captain! Snort, snort - Har-rummph! Hell man, you're a writer! Stay on course captain!"

And so I did.

It's been a while since that class and Jess Stearn's kind words of encouragement. Today, I find myself making an appearance, through miraculous means in the desert of Palm Springs California, announcing the completion of this work. Many have helped. Among them are the numerous teachers, who might find their patience rewarded in its pages. Others are my children and certain angels - both seen and unseen: the A.R.E. library staff, Charles Thomas Cayce, June Case, Susan Galloway, Ray Houserman, Marion Kincaid, Dr. Rhonda Clifton Lyons, Laura Miller, Norfolk Marine Institute, Nancy Riner, sister Sandy, Allen Smith, Virginia and John Smith, Barbara Tautz, the Brother/Sisterhood, Van and Peggy, and the rogues and rascals of Willoughby Harbor.

Memorial

Jess Stearn transitioned to spirit, March 27, 2002. The day previous, I was fortunate enough to have been with him. Though I knew he had been ill, I had no realization of the extent. Naively I entered his modest beachfront home, by Malibu standards, carrying in a copy of this manuscript. We had remained friends over the years.

He had just awakened and his caretakers were attending his needs. Bedridden, Jess lay surrounded by books, art, and a panoramic view of the Pacific. Numerous birds flew about and occasionally a big gull or two would strut about the back deck, like sentries, and stare inside. Soon, the doctor dropped in.

I excused myself as one of the aids led me to the small dining room and lunch. In a while, the doctor began to leave and I went with him. A pleasant fellow, he turned out to be Jess's godson. The tears in his eyes revealed Jess's condition. We talked about his remarkable life. Our parting words were that the best was yet to come.

Returning, south California's Mexican/American versions of "Harrummph!" "Snort!" and "Capeeetaaan" echoed excitedly throughout the house. An aide was reading to Jess from the pages I had given her. I had shown them to her previously, and when she saw his picture, had asked for copies. I promised to send her some. But in fidgeting through my disheveled manuscript case for a pen, to write down her address, some unexpected duplicate pages popped out. They described the classroom scene you have just read.

Jess was drifting off for his afternoon nap, and in knowing that all authors love to hear words read about themselves, she had been keeping him awake long enough to have made a proper farewell.

Back at his bedside, I grasped his hand. Without forethought, I spontaneously began reciting the Lord's Prayer!

I don't kiss guys and I don't cry. But I kissed him and I cried anyway. I tried to remember the last rites Father Farnham had recited at my mother's passing. All I could remember was the reminder: "your sins have been forgiven" and to "look for the light." Then I asked Jess to look out for his students: "When you get to the other side, see that they get published." It made me feel selfish. Then I remembered the writing class and his reminder, "Stay on course captain."

"Thank you," was all I could say. Then I lost it.

In the meantime, the aides had placed a crucifix nearby and a large picture of Jesus at the foot of the bed. Rendered from the image on the *Shroud of Turin,* and though Jess had been born Jewish, it had long been his favorite.

My parting remembrance was the woman reminding Jess to, "look for the light!"

At five, that next morning, he found it.

Look for the Light.

Chapter 2

Evidence

Rising.

Tombs, pyramids, religions, and the comment by prominent 20th century psychiatrist Carl Jung, that he never saw a patient over forty, whose problems didn't stem from spiritual concerns, attests to humanity's need for answers about life after death. Jung sought his own answers and studied reincarnation. He wrote in his memoir, *Memories, Dreams, Reflections,* which was published after his passing: "I had to be born again - because I had not fulfilled the task that was given to me. When I die, my deeds will follow along with me, that is how I imagine it."

Reincarnation is but one consideration concerning humans surviving death. However, as we'll see, it is the one consideration which is supported by such compelling evidence, that one can accept it for rational reasons, rather than for reasons based upon faith alone! This is not to diminish the role of faith, quite the contrary, it is only to say that faith, which stands in harmony with rationality, stands securely. Albert Einstein addressed the issue with these words: "science without religion is lame; religion without science is blind."

Long ago, Plato recorded Socrates' belief in reincarnation: "The soul is immortal, and at one time has an end, which is termed dying, and at another time is *born again* - but is never destroyed." Some hundreds of years later, the Bible's Saint John (Chapter 3: Verse 3) said Jesus, as we have seen in Jung, also employed the phrase - *born again*. I'll offer like Plato, Socrates, and Jung - *reincarnation*, was what Jesus had in mind.

Defining Terms

Simply stated, reincarnation declares that aspects of the human personality survive bodily death and retain potentials for future returns in physical form. Today's terminology, aspects of the human personality, was what the ancients might have described with the word *Soul*. I submit we are immortal Souls, that is, *Spiritual Beings* undergoing a human experience.

I'll also submit that a major problem in defining words like reincarnation is that the concept is very old and that ancient authors assumed their reader's would always understand what such terms meant. The assumption might have been well founded during those times, as meanings tended to remain constant for longer periods of time. But with improved technologies having long surpassed oars, sails, stirrups, and domesticated camels - civilizations, through commerce, military adventure, and just plain curiosity now impact each other to a far higher degree. Though, subtle at first, languages are among the factors most impacted.

Today, new words and changes in old meanings proliferate from all sides of the globe and they do so very quickly. If the long venerated unabridged dictionary gathering dust in the corner of your local library is more than a generation old, it's essentially obsolete, much to the delight of the dictionary industry. Words like *ninja, byte,* and *CD-Rom* won't be found and the common usage's of *disco* and *floppy* will appear as laughably outmoded, as are the tastes and technology that appeared and disappeared before local librarians everywhere could lug in new and pricey dictionary editions.

Reincarnation, as a phenomenon, has been understood around the world for a long time. But back in time, another word was more commonly coined in its description.

This was perceived as a problem for some, then a minority, in the early churches and will more than likely again present problems for some, now in the majority, among today's denominations. A sensitive and healing discussion and reevaluation needs to come about, not only because of some astounding revelations in science, but because that other word had been *Resurrection*. Even today, the words are so closely related that they can, as seems to have been the case back then, be used interchangeably. The bottom line is that what many of the ancients meant when they mentioned *resurrection,* other than the *Resurrection* of Jesus, was also *reincarnation!* The key is in the prefix *re*. Found in both words, it's generally mentioned in dictionaries as not only signifying *back* and *backward*, but also *again, anew,* and *over again.*

The following two sentences illustrate just how much ambiguity two little letters can introduce into two big words: *Re*incarnation has *re*surrected into the forefront of western thought. *Re*incarnation has *re*incarnated into the forefront of western thought.

Also in the forefront of everyday western thought is the *Reader's Digest.* That it more or less speaks for our mainstream is beyond debate. Nor is it's mentioning (on page 1287) the two words as synonyms. You can see this in the 1996 American edition of the *Reader's Digest - Oxford - Complete Wordfinder!*

The Bible is like a highway: a magnificent highway. Though built on words, like all highways, whether their foundations rest on the concreteness of *The Word of God,* or on the concrete of cement, sand, and gravel, their travelers must navigate them carefully. If not, breakdowns, delays, and detours result. On word highways understanding a word's individual usage is important. In the Bible, because it was written in times and tongues far different than our own, understanding its language is not only critical, but requires a great effort. Never forget that words change in form, usage, and meaning. These factors are often called *semantics.*

Semantics becomes the tough issue they often are, when the specific meanings of the words, and their linguistic derivations, are not clearly defined. For this reason, accounts of specific actions, as recorded in biblical history, must be emphasized over semantics in seeking evidence of reincarnation. In theory, because such accounts reveal past life events and their consequences convincingly, a reincarnation hypothesis can be established.

The phenomena will be revealed in the corresponding actions of those living them and in referencing any good biblical concordance. You'll find neither *R* word appearing in the Old Testament. In the Gospels and Saint Paul, while resurrection appears, it is not defined. "Reincarnation" is never mentioned nor condemned. Had there been a conflict, it would surely have been reported. This strongly suggests that the biblical authors assumed their readers were on the same page - in agreement - when it came to describing a basic aspect of humanity, that today's science strongly suggests is *reincarnation*. Misunderstandings among mainstream religious sects arises from those, often writing hundreds of years after Jesus, who mistake resurrection to mean something other than what its original users had intended.

The Wordsmith

Though a discussion of loaded words and missed meanings must ultimately, of necessity, take a back seat, the *wordsmith's* insights are still worth considering.

Ancient theologians often studied and communicated in *Greek,* as they often do today. While Greek influenced their language, the movers and shakers of the early churches, who would grow throughout Europe and here, got started, not in Greece or even in Palestine, but in *Rome*. Romans spoke *Latin* and as a lot of our English language is derived from that tongue, its influence is critical.

Incarnation derives from two Latin words. The first is *in.* It translates into English as *in.* Got it? The second word, *carnation,* is a derivative from, *carnatio,* which evolved from *carnis.* It means *flesh.* Recall that *re*, also from Latin, means *again.* Thus, to a Roman *re in carnation* meant *again in flesh.* Back in Miss Frazier's 9th grade Latin class, such a submission might have earned a scholarly scowl. *In flesh again* would have been more to her liking. She made us look up ten English words derived from Latin every day. Old time dictionaries note them in abundance. I remember little Latin, but I've never forgotten its influence on our language. Bless Miss Frazier's sweet soul and those of all such dedicated teachers.

As for resurrection, *surrection* derives from *surrectus* and means *rise* or *appear* Add *re* and again you get *again*. The result is *again rise* or *again appear,* or Miss Frazier's *rise again* or *appear again.* Again argues that whether we appear in flesh, or in some unnamed state, be it spiritual or otherwise, we do it *again* and *again.* I wouldn't be surprised if the foundation for such ambiguity had been purposely prescribed as an act of enlightened compromise. Christianity, from even its earliest times, was never a unified movement. Popular Princeton professor of religion, Elaine Pagel's notes: "the 'real Christianity' - so far as historical investigation can disclose it - was not monolithic, or the province of any one party or another, but included a variety of voices, and an extraordinary range of viewpoints, even among the saints." [4]

After church, in services which they'd often shared, divided parishioners sometimes pointed angry fingers back and forth as each side accused the other of drifting off course, and in doing so, differed in their ideas from that accepted by the mainstream. Such differences were labeled as *heresies.* There were many issues, reincarnation being but one. The factions sincerely sought a unified theology, but before that could be accomplished, they needed to reach unanimity in creating an official source documenting the history of the life and teachings of Jesus. These accounts, called the *Gospels*, and commentaries of others, principally Saint Paul, made up what would be called the *New Testament.* When combined with the *Hebrew Bible,* which Christians revered as the *Old Testament,* the result would be the official (or *Canonized*) version of the *Christian Bible.*

The task took some doing over a long period of time. The actual date and place is shrouded in controversy and often open to debate among the many denominations calling themselves Christians. Catholics assert the Council of Trent canonized their *Vulgate* Latin translation sometime between 1545 to 1547C.E.[5] A quick cruise on the Internet sees sources proclaiming *Gospel Truth* in listing 375c.e. as the earliest date. Other than the *Vulgate,* determining who canonized what and when aren't always clear.

Princeton University and Harvard Divinity School scholarship suggest the essentials of the document, as we generally know it today, were displayed at the *Counsel of Nicea* in 324. [6]

Initiated nearly three hundred years after Jesus, the event was understandably tumultuous, not only for the faithful, but for the empire itself. Though long persecuted, literally overnight, Christianity had become Rome's religion. Emperor Constantine converted as the result of a dream he experienced on the eve of a major battle. Supposedly, Jesus told him that painting images of the cross on the Roman army's shields would result in a great victory.

Victorious in war, he would prove equally adept in the art of diplomacy. At the council, he prominently placed fifty elaborate copies of what was held to be the Bible back then. While the delegates might have seen passages with which they might have disagreed, they had no disagreement as to what was the emperor's official outlook. In encouraging them to minimize their many differences and to maximize the issues upon which they agreed, Constantine could hopefully, get momentum going, to achieve something of great value.

While a fully canonized Christian Bible didn't result, the long venerated *Nicene Creed* was to come about. Revered, it's recited by both the Roman and Eastern churches of Italy, Spain (and its former South American and Asian empires), France, Africa, Greece, and Russia, as well as their many divergent *Protestant* outgrowths, which include German and Scandinavian *Lutherans,* American *Episcopalians* and England and its former empire's *Anglicans.* Today on any given Sunday, before the sun sets, throughout much of the world's happier places, the Nicene Creed will have been heard.

Though Constantine moved the Roman capital to Byzantium which became Greek speaking *Constantinople*, so named in his honor, he insisted Latin would be spoken in the western church. That this played some part in minimizing the divisiveness the usage the two loaded **R** words would have created, when the inevitable question of life after death came up at Nicea, stands evidenced in the outreach to unity seen in the creed's closing words.

"We look for the **_re_**surrection of the dead, and the life of the world to come."

Constantine's considerable skills, and the *Holy Spirit's* presence, presided and a pathway to the coming New Testament was prepared. Though not an easy route it lead to what would become for many - as **the Voice** of John the Baptist had once proclaimed:

"A highway for our God."

What I would like to believe is that Constantine's efforts had been aimed at allowing a positive outcome at Nicea and that dancing around word issues was unavoidable. Interestingly, he was hardly a theologian, and spoke almost no Greek. What he knew about his adopted religion probably came from his mom. She had become a hard working member following his dream. That she might have taught him good deeds matter more than good creeds and *isms* and to simply stick to the *Ten Commandments* and *love your neighbor as yourself* accounted for his spiritual evolution. The Eastern Church sainted both he and his mom.

We'll later look at how the stumbling blocks, which impaired the *Highway of our God,* got placed. I suspect, despite the sincerity of the *Highway's* workers, that because totalitarian politics prevailed, as they often did then and even now, and as these must ultimately maintain themselves through fear, they are doomed to failure. Human beings, as reincarnation makes clear, are immortal and as such are *Godlike*. Godlike beings respond to love, rather than to fear. It doesn't matter whether its fear of government imposed concepts of one God, one Lord, one Faith, one Church, one Empire and one Emperor, as many in Constantine's time had understood, or fear of today's one manifesto, one party line, one dictator, and one state. Fears of either eternal damnation for most, or eternal obliteration for all just don't cut it!

Semantics aside for now, that we make returns as human beings is secondary. The primary issue is our returning to *Spirit*, which is our normal state. What we call death is a misnomer. In reality, only physical bodies die, souls don't. They return to normalcy - surely the <u>consciousness</u> called *Heaven* - and having achieved this, they need never come back to become, "<u>*born again,*</u>" <u>*anew,*</u>" <u>*over again.*</u>" or to "<u>*again appear*</u>."

It may be that the condition called *Heaven* (or *Normalcy*) is what should be meant by the term *Resurrection*. *Reincarnation* might then be better understood as being the process souls use in achieving the heavenly *Estate* Jesus called a *Mansion!*

Forgiveness

Regardless, the catch is that returning to such *Normalcy* can take some doing. Ideally, we visit earth to pursue happiness. Some arrive for family type experiences, others as students like Plato, or teachers such as Jess Stearn, entrepreneurs as were my parents, and healers as was Dr. Jung. More, maybe most, show up for the innocent merriment of champagne, sex, and old time rock-n-roll! Free will allows choices, which, thank God, includes frivolity. However, we must create no harm. Earth's cause and effect nature requires that our thoughts and actions set up reactions, which must be met. If we mess up and try to wiggle free of our consequences, in overusing earthly ways, trouble results. The overuse of earthly ways risks forgetting our divine nature and our divine methods of problem solving through *forgiveness*.

Forgetting forgiveness leads to entanglements, entrapment, and unwanted returns. These can be *Hell!* Einstein's brain isn't needed to see evidence, as close as your newspaper headline, that Hell is here! Reincarnation theories often follow this logic. In the East, escaping entrapment motivates many to practice virtuous lifetimes of spiritual discipline, to awaken the soul's higher memory. When the proper pinnacle is reached, as in *Resurrection*, returning becomes unnecessary.

Middle Eastern/Western ideas offer similarities, though utilizing rigid caste systems as *carrot and stick* awakening devices is mistrusted as politically exploitable and while past-life behaviors may impact our future social positions, gauging soul growth in material ways risks diverting one's eyes from a prize which is spiritual. (Edgar Cayce's universal mind gauged growth in those striving to "smile oft, speak gently, and be kind."[7]) Hindu views that humans return as animals are also unpopular. Our bodies are held as uniquely created vessels for the soul. Some see the biblical Adam and Eve as having been the first *homosapien* couple.

While animals may reincarnate and physically evolve as earthly entities, separate from us, I cannot imagine heaven without Labrador retrievers, cats, pelicans and striped bass! I'll term as Western thought, thought that's more typical West of India. Thus uniquely Western, is the Christian concept of the Divine's active intervention through Jesus.

Repentant souls can be freed through a forgiving *Grace*.

In all this, free will allows the forgiven to forego a most welcomed prodigal return and, despite the risks, come back to help the world through *Saintly* ways. Knowledge about being "born again," in the context of reincarnation, though enlightening, is not the key to salvation. Salvation lies in being "born again" in the spirit of God's goodness. If you're not born again in this spirit, you'll need to become born again, and again, and yet again, until you get it. There are no short cuts to Heaven.

Beings believing reincarnation's emphasis on choice and situation ethic somehow allows us an unbridled freedom to rationalize rules and behaviors, which circumvent the common norms of human kindness, are in grave error. Two who made such errors were General Togo, of Japan's World War II Imperial Army, and the Third Reich's infamous Heinrich Himmler. Both believed in reincarnation, but forgot that God will not be mocked!

(The Third Reich's founder, Adolph Hitler, had been an atheist. His *Nazi* socialist system was based upon the "survival of the fittest" teachings he, and the many *Social Darwinist's* of his time, saw in the evolution theories of Charles Darwin, when applied to race and/or social systems such as Communism.)

Heady Stuff

This is heady stuff. Unfortunately, a sad past of *inquisition* has left a tradition having long driven reincarnation considerations from mainstream debate concerning the nature of humankind. Today's mainstream debate focuses on materialists claiming humans have no souls, especially since Darwin's theorizing that we have descended from monkeys, and as monkeys don't have souls, we don't either, and religions claiming that while we have souls, these face an after death salvation for a few and damnation for the majority.

But as seen in Plato, arguably Jesus, Jung and other luminaries in the past and present, reincarnation is neither new in Western thought, nor outmoded. At present, dramatic scientific research, which we'll soon see, is making new inroads and a resulting revival of interest. So much so, that the debate between materialistic proponents of Darwin's genetics and environmental-based positions, such as that seen in Dr. Skinner's behavioral psychology, and main line religious factions, is soon to take a back seat. Reincarnation is to return "born again" as the foundation stone - concerning the soul - of Western thought. The perennial nature of such thought, for it has been rejected and returned numerous times, might have been that as predicted by the Psalmist, "the stone which the builders rejected has become the headstone of the corner" (see Psalm 118).

However, the contributions of genetics and environment will not be set aside in understanding the human condition, for indeed, such factors are important. What will happen is the establishment of the *Soul* - based upon evidence outside philosophical and religious constraints, as a major player in all this. Thus genetics, environment, and reincarnation will be recognized and integrated into new understandings (which will include religion) from which, hopefully, humanity will benefit.

Obviously, I am a proponent of reincarnation. How I personally feel won't matter; I'm not a Socrates, Saint John, or a scientist. What will matter is the biblical contribution these pages will make. For it is precisely because these contributions are biblical, that the West will find reincarnation's return easier to accept as a welcomed event. Western reincarnation will become a welcomed event in the East as well, for it will lead to unity.

This is an important book on an important subject. Of necessity, it will demand something from both of us. I have attempted to do the best that I can in researching and presenting the findings in as readable and as accurate a form as my mental and creative capacities can offer. As for your part, please read on with an open and patient mind. I ask only that whatever conclusions you reach, even if in opposition, be directed in constructive dialogue with those who might share an interest.

Translation

The King James Bible lists Yahweh as Jehoveh and, in its New Testament, spells Elijah as Elias. To lessen questions on translation, I have utilized Aramaic. The earliest Bible's are in Aramaic. It was the language spoken by Jesus and the prominent translator, the late Dr. George Lamsa. His first hand grasp of regional customs and linguistics has long offered unique biblical insights. On critical issues, the primarily Protestant *King James* and the primarily Catholic *Jerusalem* versions are most often compared. Others are submitted when an increase in clarity is in evidence.

Bible translations abound. I recently purchased a nifty CD disc containing thirty-one. The local Wal-Mart offered it for less than Ten Dollars! You might do even better on the net. My experience has been that while the world's words vary over time in usage and meaning, *The Word* - that God loves us - remains the same.

Forever!

Gertrude Cayce, Mr. Cayce's wife, once asked her husband which translation was nearest to the truth. His conscious choice had long been the venerable *King James.* He generally read it through at least once a year! His response to Mrs. Cayce, while in a trance, appears in his archives numbered (2072):

"The nearest true version is the version that ye apply in your life."

Much of his work was couched in the Elizabethan English of the Bible he so loved: "There have been many versions that have been written and changed from all those versions, but remember the whole Gospel of Jesus Christ is 'Thou shalt love the Lord thy God with all thy mind, thy heart, and thy body, and thy neighbor as thyself.' Do this and thou shalt have eternal life. The rest of the book is trying to describe this."

In this context, his conclusion stands: "It is the same in any language, any version." Before continuing, you might want to place, as a handy reference, a copy nearby of, "the version that ye apply in your life."

In this chapter, as it's so critical, I'll keep references to the various verses prominently placed for your convenience. Additionally, they will be annotated with a small numeral listed at the end of the reference and throughout the text when appropriate. These correspond with additional information located in the Appendix.

Hopefully, this will make the material flow more easily for the general reader. At the same time, it will allow researchers an easy access to whatever areas they might wish to scrutinize. Note well: While references to the Cayce insights will be made, they are not to be construed as the primary source in establishing the case for biblical reincarnation. His work will be but one among many. I will more formally introduce these as the voyage continues. Keep in mind; the most persuasive evidence will be in science and the Scripture itself.

John the Baptist

From among the Bible's personalities who might have experienced a past life, John the Baptist is one of the best known. Biblical evidence suggests he had once been the prophet Elijah. The first issue of such evidence is that John's appearance fulfilled major Old Testament prophesies that Elijah would return to proclaim the Messiah. The 40th chapter of *Isaiah the prophet* opens with such a prediction. Elijah is referred to as the one who will "prepare the way of the Lord." The fiery book of Malachi closes on the same subject. It prominently reveals Elijah's coming return as the final promise of the Old Testament:

> "Behold I will send you Elijah the prophet before the great and dreadful day of the Lord. And he shall turn the heart of the fathers to the children and heart of the children to their fathers before I come and smite the earth to ruin."

(Malachi 4:5)(2)

About a year before "the great and dreadful day of the Lord" arrived and the promised Messianic age metaphorically smote "the earth to ruin," in displacing the old covenant with that of the new, an angel appeared (Luke 1:17)(3) to Zechariah. A temple priest, he was told that his wife, Elizabeth, would bear him a son. (8) He was to be named John (9)(17):

> "He will not drink wine and he will be filled with the Holy Spirit, while he is still in the womb of his mother.
>
> And he will go before them in the spirit and the power of Elijah to turn the hearts of parents to their children."

The experience would leave Zechariah speechless until after the birth. (4)(10) Six months into her pregnancy, Elizabeth received a visitor:

> "And she entered the house of Zechariah, and saluted Elizabeth.
>
> And when Elizabeth heard the salutation of Mary, the babe leaped in her womb; and Elizabeth was filled with the Holy Spirit.
>
> And she cried in a loud voice saying to Mary, Blessed are you among women, and blessed is the fruit of your womb.
>
> How does it happen to me that the mother of my Lord should come to me?
>
> For behold, when the voice of your salutation fell on my ears, the babe in my womb leaped with great joy."
>
> (Luke 1:40-44)(7)

The earliest New Testament editions began with Saint Mark. In introducing John the Baptist, Mark (1:2) opened his Gospel in addressing Elijah's return:

> "As it is written in Isaiah the prophet, Behold I send my messenger before your face, that he may prepare your way."

That the Old Testament ends with the promise of Elijah's return, and the New Testament begins with the issue, would seem significant. Saint Luke's first chapter devoted seventy verses (out of eighty) in his account of John's nativity. The other Gospels likewise address the return as their first order of business, except for that of Saint Matthew. He addressed it in his third chapter, with this introduction of John the Baptist:

> "For it was he of whom it was said by the prophet Isaiah, **The voice** which cries in the wilderness, Prepare the way of the Lord, and straighten his highways."
>
> (Matthew 3:3)(5)

Not every scholar is aware that the New Testament once began with Mark. However, most accept as historical fact, as will be shown that significant numbers and even a majority of early Christians believed in reincarnation. Matthew's later placement, before Mark, has been criticized as clouding the dramatic connection between Elijah and John the Baptist. I cannot comment on whether such a distraction was deliberately attempted by misguided authorities opposing reincarnation during the dark ages, as I found no hard evidence to support such an accusation. However, those not familiar with the Gospels, or wishing to reread them, might want to start with Mark. Reading all four books uses about as much time as it does to take in the annual American Sunday "Super Bowl" football game. If you want to take in a real super Sunday, try the Gospels. There are no commercials, save the message that we love one another!

But back to biblical prophecy. Persons of faith cannot get around the promises of biblical prophecy. Nor can this statement by Jesus. He proclaimed that the Old Testament prophecies, concerning Elijah's return, came true in John the Baptist:

"For all the prophets and the law prophesied until John.
And if you wish to accept it, he is Elijah who was to come.
  He who has ears to hear, let him hear."
(Matthew 11:13-15)(1)

Additional reincarnation evidence is indicated in Elijah and John's similar skills and behaviors: Elijah was an eloquent orator. Isaiah addressed this characteristic utilizing but two words. He honored Elijah as - ***The Voice***:

"***The voice*** of him that cries in the wilderness, prepare the way of the Lord, make straight in the desert a highway of our God."
(Isaiah 40:3)

Saint Mark honored John the Baptist in a similar manner:

"***The voice*** which cries in the wilderness: make ready the way of the Lord and straighten his highways."
(Mark 1:3)(14)

Elijah had an impish side and tales of his wiles are still the delight of Jewish folk tradition. John reacted with similar minded mischief, when he was faced with an investigation by the temple police. They had the authority to arrest him, and as it would have been politically risky for anyone to have said he was Elijah returned, John, in facing this "no win" situation, pretended to be crazy. David had once used the same ploy:

"So he changed his behavior." (1stSamuel 21:13)(20)

While the fourth Gospel, like Mark and Luke, began with Elijah's return, it differed in that the author was, highly likely, an actual eyewitness to its events. He was quite candid concerning Elijah's playful performance, in avoiding arrest:

"This is the testimony of John, when the Jews sent to him priests and Levites from Jerusalem to ask him, 'Who are you?' And he confessed and did not deny it; but he declared, 'I am not the

Christ.' Then they asked him again, 'What then? Are you Elijah?' And he said, 'I am not. Are you a prophet?' And he said, 'No."
(John 1:19-21)(21

That the ruse worked, is seen in many saying of John:
"He is crazy." (Matthew 11:18)(27)

John the Baptist was, and still is, famous for his verbal articulation. At no other time, except for his last days in prison, did he ever offer such evasive and convoluted testimony. When sure he had convinced the cops he was harmless, and feeling sure the danger had past, in sharp contrast to his previous words, he would issue this precise statement of Scriptural eloquence:

"I am *the voice* of one crying in the wilderness, Straighten the highway of the Lord, as the prophet Isaiah said."
(John 1:23)(14)

Elijah possessed unusual wilderness skills:
"The ravens brought him bread and meat in the morning and bread and meat in the evening; and he drank from the brook."
(1st Kings 17:6)

John the Baptist also possessed such skills:
"His food was locusts and wild honey." (Mark 1:6)(16)

Elijah was a "big guy" and wore distinctive clothing:
"He was a hairy man of girth with a girdle of leather about his loins." (2nd Kings 1:8)

John was also impressive and was the only New Testament figure who wore a similar dress:
"John wore a dress of camel hair with a girdle of leather fastened about his loins." (Mark 1:6)(15)

Herod

John the Baptist was not the only one who exhibited past-life characteristics. Another biblical figure was Herod Antipas (he should not be confused with his infamous father, Herod "the great" – *Herod*, is a royal title meaning *Hero*). The trail of evidence begins with the understanding that individual souls possessing unfinished business between them, often return during the same time period, to iron out they're leftover issues. Clues to Herod's former existence are seen in the complex political and personal relationship between himself and John. It was similar to that seen in the past-lives of Elijah and the Israelite king of that era. His name was Ahab.

King Ahab generally gets bad biblical press, though the scribes occasionally concur with secular history, which regards Ahab as a very able Middle Eastern monarch. An example of both biblical and historic agreement, on his more positive qualities, is the depiction of Elijah's preparing the way of the king, by running before him.

"And the hand of the Lord was on Elijah; and he girded up his loins and ran before Ahab till he entered Jezreel."
(1st Kings 18:46)

The act indicates Elijah's respect for Ahab and his position as the duly anointed king, according to the distinguished Old Testament scholar, I. W. Slotki (1977). He noted that "running before a king" is a metaphorical indicator that the runner is offering homage.

At their last encounter, Ahab and Elijah's relationship had changed tragically. Naboth, the owner of a vineyard, had been executed on a trumped up charge of treason and his estate confiscated by the crown. Ahab's wife, Jezebel, allegedly devised the plot and stole the land. Ahab failed to intervene:

"But there was none like Ahab, who thought to do evil in the sight of the Lord, whom Jezebel his wife incited."
(1st Kings 21:25

After the event, Elijah and Ahab were to part. Ahab heroically died defending Israel (see 1 Kings 22:35-40) and Elijah's passing saw him honored - as we've seen so honored in others such as Mithra of Persia, Romulus, the founder of Rome, and Caesar Augustus.

They were recorded as being taken bodily to heaven.

The Bible's evidence suggests that when Elijah and Ahab next met, it would be as John the Baptist and Herod Antipas. Like Ahab, Herod generally receives bad biblical press, though the press of secular history regards him as a very able Middle Eastern monarch. And as it was with Ahab, occasionally, good things were recorded about Herod's more positive qualities:

"For Herod was afraid [respectful] of John, because he knew that he was a righteous and holy man, and he guarded him; and he heard that he was doing a great many things, and he heard him gladly." (Mark 6:20)(24)

Like Elijah and Ahab, John and Herod had also seen their relationship reach a tragic turn. It was a tragedy which Herod's "wife incited." She had threatened the Baptist's life, after he had publicly demeaned her recent marriage to Herod. This forced Herod, because of

John's popularity, to place him in protective custody.

The Saga of a Certain Three

Herod's wife was named Herodias. In the same manner that John had exhibited past-life similarities with Elijah, and Herod showed similar links with Ahab, Herodias would resemble Jezebel. And like Jezebel and Elijah, who had grappled, Herodias and John would also be in conflict. The saga had begun some 850 years before the trio - Elijah, Ahab, and Jezebel - had returned, "born again."

As to where they were between lives, I found the Bible saying little about such abodes, other than in metaphorical figures of speech open to a broad interpretation. Nor did I find views, as in some Hindu sects that humans return as animals. Thus, while *the three* didn't continue their feud as lions and tigers, they may have reappeared individually in non-biblical settings, and at other times, surely saw realms outside this world. Jesus spoke of such places in John 14:2:

"In my father's house are many rooms."

The vastness of God's universe explains why we can have so many varied experiences and why the number of souls existing elsewhere doesn't effect earthly population variances. Consider Virginia Beach summers: while tourists' tan and traffic snarls fume the locals, the basic U.S. population tally stays constant.

I feel between life biblical cases don't appear because histories of the living best address and instruct those who are alive, rather than do case histories of the so-called dead.

On his previous visit, Elijah had staged a mighty feat on Mount Carmel, in miraculously returning to dominance, the worship of the traditional God of Israel, known as Yahweh.

Elijah's deed was accomplished in winning a contest with his religious rivals. Elijah challenged them to have their god, Baal, produce a flash of fire and precipitate rain to end a three-year drought. When Baal failed to answer, Elijah's turn was next. He poured vast amounts of water on the altar, in *Baptizing* a bullock, to be burnt as an offering.

The source of 1 Kings (18:37-39)(30) goes on to record Elijah's famed eloquence:

"Answer me, O Lord, answer me, that all this people may know that thou art the Lord God in Israel and that thou hast turned their perverse heart back again.

Then the fire of the Lord fell, and consumed the burnt offering and the wood and the stones and the dust, and licked up the water in the trench.

And when all the people saw it, they fell on their faces; and they said, 'The Lord he is God; the Lord, he is God."

While grand, the event was flawed by Elijah. Forgiveness and an opportunity for the religious conversion of his rivals would have seemed, at least to the more compassionate minded, the appropriate action. But by his own will, Elijah, in a not so eloquent manner, there being no eloquent manner in which human beings can be killed, executed them in cold blood. 1 Kings (18:40)(26) continues:

"And Elijah [not God] said to them, seize the prophets of Baal, and let not one of them escape. And they seized them; and Elijah brought them down to the brook Kishon and slew them there."

Baal worship honored the nature deities, collectively called the Ballim. Vestiges still stand expressed in contemporary concerns with ecology and a reverence for *Mother Earth*. Practitioners of Native American religions, and those of other indigenous peoples, would find its principles familiar, especially the prominent place of dance. Another Baalist practice involved rituals of sacred sexuality. Similar sentiments and rites exist today, often called Tantra, in both East and West. Though volunteers, usually revered ministers, offered themselves in sacrifice, Baalism was an essentially benign belief.

I'll catch some heat for having said this. However, Hebrew practices praising abuses of women: "cut off her hand"(see Deuteronomy 25:11-12); Joshua's penchant for crucifying unarmed prisoners of war: "crucified on a tree, and thus put to death" (see Deuteronomy 21:22-23 & Joshua 10:24-27); racism: "above all the peoples" (see Deuteronomy 14:2), slavery: "take an awl and thrust it through his ear to the door" (see Deuteronomy 15:12-18); and the stoning of troubled children: "our son is stubborn and rebellious" (see Deuteronomy 21:18-21); requires that the region's historic realities be evaluated with impartiality, rather than seen through the "holier than thou" eye of popular myth and unbridled use of verse to support sectarian suppositions.

My purposes are not to step on the toes of anyone's belief system, but simply to examine biblical history, in an accurate and open-minded fashion, to see if returns by human beings have been recorded. This same practice of impartiality is seen in today's mainstream Bible historian, though few, if any, presently pursue reincarnation research. As researchers, they are not required to shoulder a particular Judeo-Christian/Islamic religious bias or apology for the lack of such. Their task, like mine, is historical accuracy.

This task also includes the distillation of *The Word of the Lord*, from words, which, arguably, were merely intended to reveal religious beliefs of the biblical era and the history of those of us who lived it. To illustrate: an example of *The Word* might be seen in Psalm 82:6, which Jesus (John 11:34)(6) had quoted concerning, not only *His* divinity, but the divine nature of all humanity:

"I have said, you are gods; all of you are children of the most High."

Contrast this with words whose purpose seems simply to convey history. The horror they describe here, was that observed by Jezebel, now grown to old age, in the murder of her youngest son: "And Jehu drew a bow with his full strength, and smote Joram in his back, and the arrow went out at his heart."

(2 Kings 9:24)(29)

Historical Approaches to Bible Study

I used these extremes to point out the especial need for discernment in Bible study. Hopefully, such discernment will result in correct conclusions concerning the nature of God.

Another reason, why I studied the Bible from a historic perspective, was that most of the biblical books, where evidence of reincarnation occurs, were written during some very tough times in the world's Spiritual evolution. The Elijah tales occurred in the hard *Iron Age*, which would see Israel's people dispersed. The saga's continuance climaxed under Roman occupation and similar upheavals. These were hardly "the good old days," and as fragmented myths and propaganda ploys of both victor and vanquished may have unavoidably found expression, I wanted to be sure that as many aspects could be covered, as was possible, in maintaining a correct course. This can be seen in the *Bibliography*. Most of my sources are pretty much over the counter, in terms of availability and mainstream scholarship. The result has been that, while these pages may not always seem suitable in Sunday school settings, they stand as the product of some considerable effort in maintaining factual history. This effort was doubled, when evidence began to reveal reincarnation.

The concluding rationale in taking a historical approach was that, as will be shown, the scientific study of reincarnation utilizes a similar tack. It followed that the more my approaches matched those seen in science, the better the case could be made that a significant correlation exists between biblical and scientific studies of the reincarnation type. The beauties, in this, are that such scientific studies reveal, scientifically, what proper past-life links and characteristics look like. When these same links and characteristics are seen in the Bible, the resulting biblical and scientific agreement makes for a strong persuasive position regarding reincarnation. My hope is that this persuasive position will establish a smoother highway for our God, in the new millennium.

Edgar Cayce

The work of Edgar Cayce, as has been noted, is to play a role. Some readers might have difficulty with such sources, and in an effort to reach a broader spectrum, I have purposely not utilized Cayce, as has been demonstrated in this chapter, in establishing biblical reincarnation. Establishing reincarnation in the Bible will be left to the hard-nosed historic and scientific methods of today. Cayce's work will provide, along with other sources, the sweet spiritual beacons of faith and open-minded common and uncommon sense, that will be needed, in this voyage through the storms and calms of the Scriptures.

But some may still have an especial difficulty with Cayce's material. Typically, such difficulties stem from certain verses found primarily in the Old Testament's *Book of Deuteronomy,* (18:10-11):

"There shall not be found among you anyone who makes his son or his daughter pass through the fire, or who practices divination or black magic, or is an enchanter or a witch.

Or is a charmer or a consulter with familiar spirits or a sorcerer or a necromancer."

Mr. Cayce was none of these. He was a pious person of faith helping others by hypnotizing himself. But even if he were a sorcerer or a "consulter with familiar spirits," the laws would not apply. Moses, the accepted author (though this is highly unlikely as we'll later see) had been very specific as to whom he had restricted. He carefully prefaced these directives at the beginning of the chapter. They applied only to:

"The priests and the Levites."   (Deuteronomy18:1)

Five verses later, the inclusion was reduced to just Levites:

"If a *Levite*."

Cayce's critics have harshly, on occasion, applied numerous names in certain comments concerning him. Trust me on this; while he's been called unchristian, he's <u>never</u> been listed as a *priest* or a *Levite*!

The Scriptures, quite rightly, warn against the misuse of any of God's gifts, which includes the paranormal. In contrast, as in all things, when paranormal processes are applied properly, praise follows!

Saint Paul said that abilities should used as gifts of God, praising both the normal and the paranormal. He made no distinction between the two:

"But the manifestation of the Spirit is given to every man as help to him.

For to one is given by the Spirit the word of wisdom; to another the word of knowledge by the same Spirit;

To another faith by the same Spirit; to another gifts of healing by the same Spirit;

To another the working of miracles; to another prophecy; to another the means to distinguish the true Spirit; to another the interpretation of different languages.

But all of these gifts are wrought *by that same Spirit*, dividing to every one severally as he will."

(1Corinthians' 12:7-11)

So, as Dr. Jung's and Dr. Einstein's scientific knowledge was "by that same Spirit," and the many biblical translator's abilities, in the interpretation of language, was "by that same Spirit," and the fundamentalist's faith is "by that same Spirit," it is submitted that Edgar Cayce's abilities were by *"that same Spirit."*

Through the same means of clairvoyance, precognition, and telepathy used for the good by Edgar Cayce – "by that same Spirit" - Zechariah (Luke 1:13) received knowledge from an angel that his wife, Elizabeth, would become the mother of John the Baptist: "Fear not Zechariah; for your prayer has been heard, and your wife Elizabeth will bear you a son."

The Baptist, as recorded in John 1:32, (31) envisioned the Holy Spirit descending upon Jesus. It was seen as a dove, and heard as a voice:

"And John testified, saying, I saw the Spirit descending from heaven like a dove, and it rested upon him."

Saint Luke (1:45) recorded predictions regarding Jesus were made by Elizabeth to Mary:

"And blessed is she who believed; for their will be a fulfillment of the things which were spoken to her of the Lord."

Another observation by Luke (1:22) saw a psychokinetic phenomenon in Zechariah's speech being affected by the vision of an angel:

"When Zechariah came out, he could not speak with them. They understood that he had seen a vision in the temple."

As these are seen as praiseworthy, then Cayce's work - obtained from the same Spirit and used for the same good - must surely be seen as a valid tool for Scriptural study! Cayce's demonstrated help to others and personal life of faith offer ample evidence of *that same Spirit*. In regards to Spirit, Cayce voiced:

"Be willing to be led; not by spirits, but by the Spirit of God."

In any examination of Edgar Cayce, these words of Jesus in Matthew 7:16 stand as the final benchmark:

"You will know them by their fruits." (11)

An Additional Perspective

If there still remain ruffled feathers, over the issue of the Yawest's and the Ballist's, I'll try to smooth the highway a bit more in declaring that ancient humanity's concept of God was not yet fully realized, as it is not yet fully realized today. The creators of the United States Constitution expressed this same sentiment. It was their top concern. So much so, that the document's first amendment guaranteed religious freedo

Some feel, as do I, that the Constitution's principles were divinely inspired. Those involved in its creation were mostly Freemasons. Many Freemasons, as you'll soon see, embraced reincarnation. One was George Washington. Another was Dr. Benjamin Franklin, a person of unquestioned intellect. He left not only his genius, as a major architect of the Constitution, but as seen in his humorous epitaph, the genius of his personal persuasion, and that of enlightened others throughout the World, regarding reincarnation as an expression of eternal life:

**The Body of B. Franklin, Printer,
Like the Cover of an Old Book, It's Contents Torn Out
And Stripped of its Lettering and Guilding,
Lies Here Food for Worms,
But the Work shall not be Lost, For it Will as He Believed
Appear Once More
In a New and more Elegant Edition
Revised and Corrected By the Author.**
(The Papers of Benjamin Franklin, p. 310)

Benjamin Franklin would not have been one to have lived on *moonbeams* nor one to have embraced some far out cult. He was one of the world's first scientists and, despite his epitaph, generally kept quiet, as did his fellow Freemasons, concerning their beliefs. Well-founded fears of religious persecution prompted such secrecy. Most good libraries, however, offer reference materials about them, including the library of the George Washington Masonic Shrine in Alexandria Virginia. No Masonic secrets are being betrayed here (I am not a Mason).

They saw God as the great architect of the universe and often depicted His/Her presence, symbolically, as an all seeing eye. This *eye* still appears on the reverse side of the Great Seal of the United States. The design has long been attributed to Dr. Franklin. Franklin Roosevelt, himself a Mason of high rank, decreed - as president - that the image appears on the U.S. dollar bill. It still stands. (Freemason and Mason are essentially synonymous.) Had they been so inclined, many of the Constitution's framers, like both *Franklins,* could have proclaimed reincarnation as American as apple pie, baseball, and *Harley-Davidson!*®

The Reverse Side of the Great Seal of the United States, as it appears on the Dollar Bill.

A Sermon

Long attributed to Benjamin Franklin, Franklin Roosevelt saw to the prominent placement of the "Great Seal of the U.S." The upper motto translates, "God Prospers Our Undertaking," the lower, "New Order of the Ages." The president often discussed destiny and a national *rendezvous with destiny*. His confidence, during dark days of hardship and war, might have come in believing the seal prophesied an expeditious event of great magnitude.

As a Mason, he would have observed God, symbolized as all seeing, appearing within a smooth sided triangle. This hovers over a four-sided pyramid made of 13 courses of rough edged blocks. The base is dated 1776 in Roman numerals. Thirteen is significant in Masonic lore and if each course represented 13 years into the future, then the founding father's work (seen symbolically as the unfinished pyramid) would reach the Logos 169 years later (i.e., 13 years times 13 levels is 169 with 169 + 1776 being 1945). Thus, a *rendezvous with destiny* was to occur in 1945.

Coincidence or prophesy, 1945 saw the U.S. literally become the "New Order of the Ages" in "Undertaking" global leadership and ending histories worst world war. It became the *super power* of today, a super power which - despite its rough edges - so long as it stands under God, is to stand for the good!

That such a wise and beloved president, he was elected to four terms, so honored the founding fathers and mother's spiritual beliefs, encourages us as beneficiaries, to honor them with a similar wisdom and loving respect.

In respect, Cayce made this loving prediction for the future: "For, with the changes that will be wrought, Americanism - the ism - with the universal thought that is expressed and manifested in the brotherhood of man [and woman] into group thought as expressed by the Masonic Order, will be the eventual rule in the settlement of affairs in the world. Not that the world is to become a Masonic Order, but the principles that are embraced in same will be the bases upon which the new order of *peace* is to be established." [8]

(Captain *L.*)

The Voice

As astute scholars of the Scriptures, the founding fathers (and mothers) would also have seen reincarnation as biblical as Isaiah, Matthew, Mark, Luke, and John. Like the first Christians, the founders could easily have grasped reincarnation's hidden presence in but two catch words - *the Voice*. Recall that Isaiah had identified Elijah as *the voice*. That the Gospels repeat these in linking him and the Baptist, could have been the first step toward their convictions:

"The voice" (Isaiah 40:3)
"The voice" (Matthew 3:3)
"The voice" (Mark 1:3)
"The voice" (Luke 3:4)
"The voice" (John 1:23)

Confirming that Elijah was no different from other human beings would be next. This would be a stepping stone in establishing that his reincarnation experience was not unique and, as we are equal, all could do the same. The *Word of the Lord* revealed such a confirmation in James (5:18). Saint James was the brother of Jesus. He said Elijah was: "like ourselves!" This prepared the way and made the highway straighter, in understanding more about God's love, which stands behind the creation of the immortal human soul.

This might displace Abraham Lincoln's favorite theory, "God loved the common people because he made so many of them." However, I doubt if Mr. Lincoln (where is he, now that we need him) would mind his keen observation being set aside, with the reasoning that God made so many of us, because we are not at all common! Consider: Mary, Elizabeth, George, Ben, Abe, the potentials of children, and your own unique self!

Jesus, as you recall, had been literal in putting it this way - "you are gods [the lack of an apostrophe mark before s, is not a misprint] all of you are children of the most High."

The Constitution's creators, in grasping this understanding, knew that the *government of the people by the people and for the people*, had to be more than just another secular contrivance of control, if it were to succeed. Free-willed souls, as history has shown, don't do well when they feel they're being manipulated to conform to someone else's behavioral expectations, especially when the cost of such manipulation is to be paid to the manipulator's taxman, by those who are being manipulated.

While practicality is paramount, governing *gods* requires the wisdom of an enlightened theocracy - an enlightened theocracy which differs from the norm in that no one people or *ism* is recognized as a spiritual authority to govern the citizenry. What makes the American approach unique is that it recognizes the divinity of each individual, and acts accordingly, to determine his or her collective will through the voting process.

While history books seldom mention these insights, such a theocracy was what the Constitution was designed to maintain. It does this in addressing secular issues through an ingenious formula of political checks and balances, religious freedom, and the handling of things Spiritual in subtle ways, such as imprinting money with, *In God We Trust!*

The U.S. Constitution now stands as the world's oldest written governmental guideline, and body of law, which is still in daily use. As to its success: that the *land of the free and the home of the brave* is also home to so many of the world's happiest people - a people who have the highest rate of voluntary compliance with their nation's tax code, but whose most frequently used commemorative postage stamp simply reads *Love*, says a lot.

The Voice: How the Bible Reveals Reincarnation

George Washington in Masonic Regalia.
This mural, at the Masonic Shrine in Alexandria VA, depicts the president placing the cornerstone of the nation's capital. Note the Master Mason's apron and sash. When the cornerstone of his faith becomes better understood, a new era of fair play and joy will surely manifest throughout this land and the globe.

A Sermon

He owned slaves. But slavery wasn't invented here. The foul practice had long been a product of the *Old World*. Never forget that within a few short generations after the world of the *New Order of the Ages* had been established and allowed to assert itself, Emancipation, at great sacrifice, came about.

As America's foremost founding father, Washington, along with his founding brother and sisters, were perplexed. The revolutionary war took thirteen bloody years and freeing the remaining *We the People* - without additional bloodshed - had yet to be resolved. Thomas Jefferson would make twelve legislative attempts.

No, he never made improprieties toward slave Sally Hemings. (see Ch 3) This is slander best forgotten. Better remembered are the thundering debates Jefferson sparked among the later politicians. Unfortunately, they failed. Washington worked in quieter ways. Actions spoke louder than words. Acutely aware his acts would set standards for the nation's future, he was careful in setting precedents. Many stand to this day. One, though circumvented by Roosevelt, was that presidents serve only two terms. But the most profound, and often overlooked, was that set in his will, emancipating Mt. Vernon's slaves. Mrs. Washington was to retain them until after her death. But in sharing her husband's sentiments, as the foremost founding mother, she quietly bestowed them their freedom. This action by the first family stands among the many firsts for human rights that, despite still lingering "Old World" prejudice, characterized the mainstream of those first calling themselves, *Americanly*. (Captain *L*.)

Faith of Our Fathers, Mothers, Sisters, and Brothers

This also says a lot about those who understood the logic of reincarnation. The insights of a President and Mrs. Washington, Benjamin Franklin, and Franklin Roosevelt cannot be dismissed; neither can the need for us to understand the rationale behind their prodigious faith.

When you hear the old hymn, *Faith of Our Fathers*, remember reincarnation!

The Constitution insured Spiritual evolution, I believe, by encouraging religious freedom. Each citizen was to learn more about the Divine in living lifetimes as Jews, Christians, Moslems, Buddhists, Hindus and everything else, including atheists. The lesson: "*Love your neighbor*."

Though when learned, reincarnation becomes unnecessary, many might opt to return and, hopefully, help out. Mary, Elizabeth, George, Martha, Abe, Ben, Frank - get back here. We need you!

While religious freedom would be cherished, this would not allow anyone to break duly established laws through such beliefs. Both Baalism and Yahweh worship would have, as a result, found some of their practices prohibited. Any reasonable attorney, as today, could have argued, before the Supreme Court, that the Baalist's concept of combining sexuality and spirituality was protected by the first amendment. However prostitution, as practiced in ancient times by congregational members, as a way of raising funds for Baal, would be illegal. Likewise, *Yawest* practices of slaughtering cattle and spewing such unfortunate beasts' blood over congregates, would not get by any congressional investigation concerning cruelty to animals.

Back to the Saga

This gets us back to the thesis that, like most religions, Baalism and Yahweh worship did not have all the answers and had their rough spots. Both were benign and that while Elijah was a saintly *good guy* - he had made an *unsaintly* bad mistake. Personally, I side with him and the Hebrews in their developing concept of *Yahweh* as the cosmic God of the universe. I believe, as I believe the founding fathers and mothers believed, that we are extraterrestrial and, as such, must understand that our true abode lies in inner and outer heavens - and not the earth. As for Baal worship, it had existed for centuries and was seen in countless Mediterranean and Middle Eastern communities. This included Israel. About half its population, according to archaeological finds, worshiped these gods in some capacity. A considerable portion prayed to Yahweh in times of war and honored the Ballim when planting.

Most were fertility figures, though such illustrious entities as *Poseidon,* the god of the sea, and his wife, the patroness of mariners everywhere, were included. Today we know her as *Venus*. She was also the goddess of love. And among those honoring love in Israel was a young Queen Jezebel. Like Herodias, she had just recently married before encountering Elijah. Unlike Herodias, Jezebel had become her religions holy high priestess. Upon hearing of the murders of her beloved men of the cloth, she sent Elijah a death threat:

> "So let the gods do to me and more also, if I do not make your life as one of them [Baal's prophets] by tomorrow about this time. And Elijah was afraid, and he arose and fled for his life."
> (1 Kings 19:2-3)(25)

The Voice cried in the wilderness:

> "O Lord, take away my life; for I am no better than my fathers." (1 Kings 19:4)

His remorse was real. So was his fear. As an evolved Avatar, he would have felt, from the innermost levels of his heart, that committing murder in the name of God was a sacrilege. No divine protection would be forthcoming and Jezebel's curse was to remain written in the Scriptures:

> "As it is written of him." (Mark 9:13)

Elijah would also use *fire of the Lord*, in the subsequent deaths of two captains and one hundred additional souls. They had been Israelite servicemen, whose loyalty was rightly with the king (see 2nd Kings

1:9-12). Elijah would have to be confronted with the consequences of his errors. For if he were to remain unaccountable, following generations of Bible believers could continue to construe such actions, as sanctioning the killing of others over religious and political differences.

That the Divine disapproved of Elijah's murderous behaviors, despite their often being overlooked by bigots, is glaringly revealed in these words of Jesus. Seen in Luke 9:54-56 - upon returning from what must have been a hard day at the office in soul saving - the disciples reported they had been kicked out of the town that the Master was to have visited. Chased away by an angry mob, their first question put to Jesus was: "Would you be willing that we command fire to come down from heaven and consume them, just as Elijah did?"

Without hesitation Jesus responded:

"You do not know of what spirit you are. For the son of man did not come to destroy lives, but to save." (22)

End of conversation!!!

And so it would be that John the Baptist's powerful voice, as had Elijah's, was to *cry again,* in the wilderness:

"Prepare the way of the Lord."

(Matthew 3:3)(12)(17)(18)(19)

The positive aspects of his past life would see him rewarded in baptizing yet another offering and *preparing the way* for a new King of Israel. This time it was to be the Messiah. This is a title bearing similarity to that of *Mahatma*, which is the preferred term for Master Souls seen in Eastern religious traditions. The Greeks favored the word, *Christ*. His baptism made straight the highway for a forward step in humanity's spiritual consciousness. Jesus said this fulfilled what:

"All the prophets and the law prophesied until John."

(Matthew 11:13)(23)(31)

It is important to remember that, as John was born before Jesus and Jesus named John as Elijah, the Old Testament pronouncements clearly concern first century events. This negates theories that the prophecies refer to a Messianic *Second Coming*. As to that event, Revelation 11 notes the presence of two heralding prophets. In sharp contrast to the Gospels, Elijah is not specifically mentioned, though the prophets are to have similar abilities such as calling upon fire and one is described as a messenger who can control the weather, as had been said of Elijah (See 1 Kings 17:1). Of course, he could make yet another return, though the issue would seem settled in these words of Jesus:

"Elijah has already come." (Matthew 17:12)

The future will unfold in due time. As for now, our focus must concern history and how *all the prophets and the law*, addressed both Elijah's positive behaviors and his shadow side, seen in the bloody events at Mount Carmel and the deaths of the two captains and their men. The *Big Picture* must be seen in all its ups and downs, for Jesus had also said:

"The Scripture cannot be broken." (John 10:35)

Mark's macabre depiction of John's death (see Mark 6:21-28) reveals that the highway was made straight. Mark must have felt that certain of its small details were important, seen in their inclusion. (Matthew 14:7-11 includes similar minutiae). The scene opens with a seeming unnecessary mention of the persons who were witnesses:

"Then came a state occasion, when Herod on his birthday gave a banquet to his officials."

Mark was not one to waste words, so why were such minor figures mentioned? Reincarnation rationale offers that, as these had been the prophets slain by Elijah, their presence provided a picture of perfect poetic justice that was fitting.

"And captains and the leading men of Galilee."

Listing captains would seem superfluous. Again, reincarnation submits an answer: They were included, because two had been, along with their men, the same souls' Elijah had killed!

Did the prominent place of dance reflect rituals, which the devotees of Baal had so revered?

"And the daughter of Herodias [named Salome] entered and danced, and she pleased Herod and the guests who were with him."

If such minute details did not relate to issues of Elijah's past life, which were now to be confronted in his execution as John the Baptist, then why their mention? Another question concerns John's harassment of Herodias. Not even Jesus derided her. John surely knew it would result in his arrest. Did he deliberately place himself at Herodia's mercy - in the same attitude of self sacrifice (though not so humble) as would have a minister of Baal - and thus heroically act to bring about a Scriptural fulfillment? Such questions will long be debated, as reincarnation returns to the forefront of Western thought. As for now, one thing is certain, Jezebel's oath came to pass:

"And the king said to the little girl *[Salome]*, Ask me whatever you wish, and I will give it to you.

And he swore to her, whatever you ask me, I will give you, as much as half my kingdom.

She went out and said to her mother, 'What shall I ask him?' She said to her, 'the head of John the Baptist."

The Lessons

Another certainty is that, while Elijah was a remarkable personality, as a human being, he was no different from us. And as humans, *like Elijah*, we must acknowledge numerous biblical lessons of hope, when reincarnation becomes a factor. One lesson is that we are immortal beings living in a Cause - Affect world. As such, we are always accountable for our own actions. It is not that we are rewarded or punished because of them - but by them. They are free willed situations, which we have self-created. And as we have created these situations, we can change them. The deeper we study this concept, the better we can appreciate that the actions of others, either for or against us, are really responses which often had their beginnings, at some time in a past life. In the East, this is understood as the law of *Karma*.

Accordingly, when things go well, we should give thanks. And when trespasses are put upon us, not only must we still give thanks, but offer forgiveness. For as we forgive, in reality we are forgiving events which we have had some part in bringing-about. Theoretically, such events are gifts, in that they call to our attention, something within ourselves which needed work. Jesus offered in *The Sermon on the Mount* (see Matthew 5-7) the proper perspective to be kept in such matters: "Love your enemies, bless anyone who curses you, do good to anyone who hates you."   (Matthew 5:44)

This passage, to someone not familiar with the Gospels, could easily be attributed to an Eastern sage such as Gandhi or the Dalai Lama. It reminds us that the borders of the *Holy Land* stand closer to India than they do to most Western Christian centers. This is not to say that Christianity is an Eastern religion, though some have termed it as such. The point is that the great religions of the world, when reincarnation reveals itself within their Scriptures, provide a united message of appeal.

A second united message of appeal provides the biblical insight, seen in the case of Elijah/John, that no matter how righteous our personal persuasions about the ways of God might seem, the Bible clearly calls us to respect the religious beliefs of others.

A third revelation offers that, until we learn to forgive, "all the prophets and the law" (as in law of karma) apply equally and justly to everyone, whether to an Elijah, saint, sinner, male, female, commoner, or *big shot*.

Ahab and Jezebel were big shots. And so it followed, that like Elijah, they would receive appropriate rewards for their karmic pluses and minuses. Secular history reveals Ahab/Herod's pluses: Retaining Ahab's prodigious diplomatic skills, he sought peace in the Middle East, through his actions as a major mover and shaker, in bringing the quarreling Roman and Persian empires to the negotiating table. He built cities, as had Ahab. And like Ahab, he was one of the most powerful and wealthiest of men. He had about as much money as God and Herod's generosity resulted, among other blessings, in the building of the synagogue at Tiberius. This was a synagogue where Jesus had undoubtedly once preached. Had not Herod's wise rule maintained Galilee's relative peace and prosperity, in a region often characterized by turmoil, it's doubtful that John and Jesus could have established their ministries. Seen in this light, despite his bad press, which often overlooks his attempt to save Jesus, as we'll see - Herod's final plus was in being honored among those chosen to help, *prepare the way*.

Jezebel had been a *King's Daughter*. This was about as high a position that women in those times could reach. Her pluses saw her return with the same title. As the daughter of a king, Jezebel/Herodias had all the prestige, luxury, and material comforts that the age could offer.

However, the powerful pluses and minuses of Herodias and her husbands roles in John's execution raise questions. As free-willed souls, what had been their option? Had they been destined to act as agents of Divine justice? On the other hand, had Herod blundered in not asserting himself and was his wife so blinded by past-life bitterness, that she failed both unconsciously and consciously, to offer Elijah/John forgiveness?

What would have been the repercussions had he been freed? Remember, Elijah had committed criminal acts which, today, would be labeled as crimes against humanity and the execution took place before Jesus offered the *New Covenant* of forgiveness. Many parts of the world - long before the events of *911* - settle religious differences with the sword and can cite Elijah's example as biblical, in sanctifying their excesses. Had he been set free, would not an important message have been forever lost?

The Herod's acts have undoubtedly long been settled without recourse to human judgment. I see this in the words Jesus offered about our place in this area:

"Judge not, that you may not be judged. For the same judgment that you judged, you will be judged, and with the same measure with which you measure, it will be measured to you."
(Matthew 7:1-2)

The theory is that what we think we are judging in others is, in reality, only the judgment of our personal perceptions and feelings. As for the future, Matthew 18:7 reveals *His* directive to those thinking they can judge themselves as divine agents and dish out their own brand of karmic consequences,

"Woe to the world because of offenses. Offenses are bound to come; but woe to the man [women] by whose hand the offenses come."

Human judgment seldom errs, when it acknowledges that *offense* happens for the right reasons. Though judged as holding high positions, Ahab/Herod and Jezebel/Herodias saw the inevitable *offence* hit the fan, changing their situations in about a *New York minute!* They were to die in exile, after seeing their lands confiscated by the crown. The calamity resulted over a trumped up charge of treason, as had happened to Naboth! Remember him? The recipient of the Herod family land was King Agrippa. Like Naboth, whose family vineyard Jezebel and Ahab had likewise confiscated, Agrippa had a similar fondness for wine!

The case of Naboth/Agrippa offers this final message of biblical certitude. The lesson stands, as certain as death and taxes, that in the end (as in heaven, so on earth) nice guys finish first!

Our voyage will explore these, and other cases, in greater detail and explain how they were derived. Each case will offer its unique lesson. Together, they will lead to some surprisingly upbeat and positive conclusions, concerning the sometimes strange and mysterious ways the Lord uses, in bringing about human spiritual evolution. Until then, keep in mind that as these upbeat and positive words of Saint Paul suggest - *life is fair*:

"For whatever a man [woman] sows, that shall he [she] also reap." (Galatians 6:7)

Notes

1. See Head & Cranston (1977) p. 447
2. Einstein 1950 p. 39
3. Meno
4. Pagels (1988) p. 152
5. The Cayce insights are called *Readings* and are customarily referenced numerically in parenthesis. This particular insight is numbered (262-109). Those receiving readings were assigned a number. Names weren't revealed to insure a recipient's privacy. The numbers following the dash indicate the actual reading. In this case, the subject's information had come on they're one hundred - ninth visit! See chapter 4 for more information.
6. New Catholic Encyclopedia (1972)
7. See Pagels (2003) Ch. 3
8. (952 - 11)

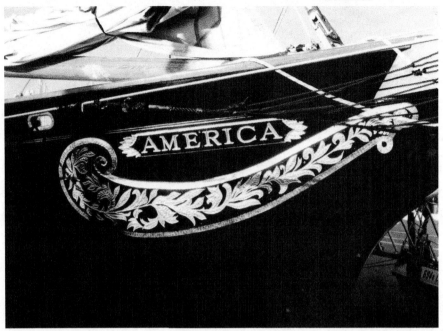

In God We Trust.

Cayce predicted America would see times of internal trouble and turmoil. But through it all, he held that the nation would continue as the beacon of hope for a coming more spiritually evolved world, so long as the principles of the American Constitution were upheld.

"The principals that are embraced in same [the American Constitution] will be the basis upon which the new order of *peace* is to be established." (952-1)

Chapter 3

A Guide to Navigation

By now, you should have a good idea of how straightforward past lives and reincarnation rationales present themselves in the Bible. I hope you have found the information priceless and well worth your investment. If you still remain unconvinced, hang on. Much more is to follow. A few fearful storms, especially for the more fundamentally minded, will be experienced in encountering new approaches to biblical and Spiritual study. Occasional currents and calms, of seeming tedium, may discourage those looking for simple answers on a complex subject. This undertaking involves a step-by-step, precept-by-precept, here a little, there a little, navigational approach. I cannot promise that the going will always be easy or make for a relaxing weekend read.

I use a threefold approach embracing metaphysical, philosophical and scientific inputs. Each of these is gone over at least three times. This is because most, like ourselves, get more out of essentially new material when the one doing the telling tells what it is they're going to tell, tells it, and then tells what it was that they had told us. Starting with the metaphysical, the next few chapters concern Edgar Cayce, Atlantic University, and the uniqueness of this type of research as an invaluable beacon, in approaching reincarnation from a Western Judeo/Christian and Islamic perspective.

Chapter Seven discusses the major issues, both for and against reincarnation. These involve ideas from the finest minds of philosophy, biblical history, and science.

As for philosophy, the vast numbers and quality of Western thinkers supporting reincarnation will surprise those not familiar with the subject.

Reincarnation has been, and still is, a very much alive and familiar concept, among the learned in our part of the world.

As for biblical history, in the past, approaches attempting to discover evidence of a reincarnation phenomenon have proven arduous. The material was difficult to find and evaluate as indicative of previous life evidence of specific personalities. Also, a deep-rooted disinterest among most Scriptural scholars has resulted in little for new research to build upon. Unfortunately, a lot of this disinterest has resulted from a sordid past history of suppression during the *Dark Ages*. But the terror of those methodologies, through inquisitions, have long been abated (as will be discussed) and replaced with the methods of scientific archaeology and the more recent historic approaches of theologians (though these do not directly concern themselves with reincarnation). The result, however, is that a new freedom of inquiry has been opened and new vistas of information on biblical personalities and events made available. A literal new age of opportunity now exists for investigation and dialogue. Hopefully, this new opportunity will lead to reconciliation among mainstream Western religions, with one of the most fundamental premises of original Christianity: the premise of reincarnation. Sensible logic points out that this premise was that as taught by Jesus to His first followers, for as we will see, His first followers embraced reincarnation.

As for science, the scientific study of reincarnation essentially began with the work of the late University of Virginia psychiatrist, Ian Stevenson. Through years of research, he developed a model for obtaining evidence of past lives, seen in verifying the memories of young children claiming such experiences. The fruit of his research has been that we can now observe a general pattern of frequently occurring characteristics, which can then be used to better understand the workings of reincarnation phenomenon's and verify its existence outside the norms of religious and philosophical speculation.

Stevenson's techniques for gathering and assessing data, though intended for the secular researcher, makes the task of biblical past-life research much easier and, while complex, relatively straightforward. Numerous correlations will be shown to exist between Stevenson's scientific cases and those seen in the Bible. When these are placed alongside the Bible's own unique evidence, as well as that seen in the rich support of the metaphysical and philosophical literature of both Western and Eastern thought, a formidable case can be made for reincarnation as a verifiable understanding. This, points to the welcome realization that human consciousness survives bodily death!

That the Bible, philosophy, and science stand united in confirming such a prospect, is a wonderful discovery. I have long wanted to share this with you, despite taking so long to bring it out in book form.

A Guide to Navigation

I hope your patience is rewarded. You might wish to share the information with a loved one, especially a loved one who may be short on faith and getting up in age or gravely ill. Your Pastor, Rabbi, local Imam, or other religious mentor, might also benefit. At the least, they won't think you're crazy because you believe in, or wish to learn more about, reincarnation. In sharing, you could copy this publication's prologue, which contains the statements of Jesus identifying John the Baptist as having been Elijah, and/or what you have just read in Chapter Two. You will probably find the last chapter: *How The Bible Reveals Reincarnation*, the most persuasive for this purpose Although these are copyrighted, such limited use isn't going to upset anyone, least of all myself: *Freely received, freely given!* On the other hand, you could purchase additional copies of the whole book and present them as gifts. I'm sure those benefiting from such purchases will, as will my creditors, receive them gladly.

Chapter Eight addresses Saint Paul. The varieties of controversy surrounding Christian concepts concerning life after death, is generally attributable to the many interpretations of the Apostle's biblical letters. In magnifying areas of often overlooked Paulian agreement with the classical Greeks, Gnostics, and the free thinkers use of allegory - new insights and aids in unraveling and making clear his many misunderstood pronouncements will be seen.

These won't be the traditional *hell and damnation* presentation of Paul still prevalent in many churches. The result will show he favored reincarnation and, surprisingly, a lot of today's thinking. This is because he purposefully wrote, which many haven't yet learned, for readers of varying levels in spiritual development: *Greeks, barbarians the wise and the unwise.* (Romans 1:14) He also maintained an oral tradition in which a more esoteric side of his belief was imparted: "*We discuss wisdom with those who have the comprehension.*" (1st Corinthians 2:6) His allegorical notions using loaded words like *fornication* and *unnatural acts,* as in sexual acts, were to be understood by inner initiates as references relating to *ignorance. Ignorance* of the natural nature of one's oneness with God is *unnatural*.

Can natural natures be sinful?

He was also careful in prefacing his views on conscience concerning social convention as being personally his and not necessarily that of the *Divine:* "For I would that all men [women] were like <u>*myself*</u> in purity. But every man [woman] has his [her] <u>*proper* gift</u> from God, one after this manner and one after that. (1st Corinthians 7:7) But the conscience of which I speak is *not yours."* (1st Corinthians 10:28)

As citizens of the universe, aren't we to openly seek after the heavenly ways of loving immortals, rather than submitting, without question, to the blind bondage of materialism's many sad strictures and taboos from a time of lessened evolutionary development?

Custom and taboo wasn't Paul's focus. Discretion and honesty, as in all things, were the issues: "*Everything is lawful for me,* but not everything is expedient; *everything is lawful for me;* but everything does not edify." (1st Corinthians 10:23)

Chapter Nine features Saint Peter. Close to Jesus and labeled *the rock* of the disciples, the fisherman's down to earth and simple straightforward insight concerning reincarnation is refreshing. Some down to earth and straightforward definition of the *"R"* word and how commonly held was its belief, between the rank and file of those like Peter, will also be noted.

Ten concerns the *Greeks* who embraced Paul's position on pre-existence and its corollary, reincarnation. Other Saints, including those labeled as Gnostics are to be seen. While Gnostic thought is anathema, to most *mainline* denominations, Gnostic's best and brightest looked to Paul as their leader. We'll explore why. We'll delve further into the *voices* of the founding mothers, fathers, sisters and brothers and especially brother Thomas Jefferson. The *man of light's* importance still stands in modern times, despite some serious *politically* correct (but *historically* incorrect) accusations about his religious views and the alleged affair between himself and slave, Sally Hemings. Answering attacks from a long time ago, upon his religion, can wait. Answering attacks, seen in today's slander, cannot.

Briefly as noted in the *Wall street Journal's* July 4, 2001 coverage of the, *Scholars Commission on the Jeffeson-Hemings Issue,* the distinguished panel ranged in their conclusions that the allegations against the then sixty-four year old retired president were: "almost certainly false…Thomas Jefferson was simply not guilty of the charge…and evidence was either factually false or was explained on other grounds." As to those *other grounds,* DNA evidence likely links one of two dozen Jefferson males as having fathered the youngest of Ms Hemings six children, Eston.

A Guide to Navigation

Eston maintained - <u>to his dying day</u> - as his mother had maintained - <u>to her dying day</u> - that his father had been the president's brother.

The scholars (made up of varying ethnic, racial, and political backgrounds) after some five hundred and fifty pages of overwhelming hard evidence and personal touching testimony from the past, believed both mother and son in concluding that Randolf Jefferson, the president's substantially younger brother, had been the father.

As a people united in the long trek toward social justice, which since its inception has been so much a part of our national destiny, we must continually keep on keeping on in believing, from deep within our hearts, that one day: *We Shall Overcome!*

Three full follow up cool sermons - *count-em* - though off the record, will be included at no extra charge.

Paul's finest *voice* will follow. He's always been a controversial commentator. Divisive at times, but his healing and unifying ultimate wisdom, concerning love for centuries, has found no finer expression.

Better batten down the hatches and rig for some heavy weather during Chapter Eleven. A review of early church history and the shabby treatment of those professing reincarnation will make for a rough ride.

Chapter Twelve addresses the important role of the *Holy Spirit* in all this.

Establishing the case for biblical reincarnation was a difficult personal journey. I've included, because of this, a number of my experiences and emotions in Chapter Thirteen. If you are among the many who will encounter similar problems in exploring the Scriptures from an historic and scientific perspective, you'll benefit. My confessions of bias and feelings are formally bared, warts and all, in an effort to make sure that the playing field was kept level, in the presentation of all sides of the evidence. This is an accepted norm for works of this nature.

Trust me! The issues are important! On the other hand, if you're like me, an impatient *meat and potatoes* type, and prefer to jump into the *meat and potatoes* of things, you can skip and jump to Chapter Fourteen entitled *Shore Leave*. Check it out before going on ahead to the next chapter. But before you leap, ask yourself if you're already a pretty good metaphysician, know all there is to know about psychic phenomena in the Bible (especially the parallel prophetic abilities of the Old Testament's Jeremiah and the Twentieth Century's Edgar Cayce) and are

Spiritually secure in confronting the *Good Book* as history.

Further, you might miss more good stuff and risk the wrath of your local literary society in skipping around in the text. A knock on the door from the *book police* isn't a pleasant experience. To avoid such *knocks,* be sure to read chapter fourteen later.

If you stick aboard for the coming tough two back-to-back chapters, the fun chapter titled *Shore Leave* will be well deserved and welcomed. But before departing, a *pop quiz* will be presented to make sure you've been paying attention. You might find it helpful in better defining for yourself where you stand, either for or against, regarding reincarnation.

You'll be turning on the television or reading the newspaper as soon as you disembark: The Captain *knows*. So as a way of preparing for the media's daily onslaught of some very ugly realities, you'll also have been given some insights on the *911* crises. Unfortunately, it will be with us for some time. Hopefully this book will contribute in some portion towards its peaceful resolution.

Religion is important and magnifying areas of agreement is critical. Muhammad was not a biblical figure. But Islam, the religion that he established some six hundred years after the Gospel events, is based upon the Bible's many teachings. That over a billion souls embrace the *Prophet,* makes it critically important that his positive persuasions concerning reincarnation are presented. *Nine-Eleven* - it must be made clear - resulted from the ignorance of misguided cults, who in being unaware of the Elijah/John lesson, created actions, which stand as an insult on the faithful of Islam and the truly spiritual throughout the world.

Solomon, in his wisdom, pointed out (Ecclesiastes 1:9): "*there is nothing new under the sun.*" Concerning cults, history has long proven his correctness. It will be noted that in the same manner as have certain Islamic cults shamed their religion, the cults of Jerusalem's King Josiah misguided ancient Judaism, the cults of the heresiologist crippled Christianity, the cults of Hitler and Himmler hoodwinked the German Christian community, and in a like manner, the cults of Japan's militarists' brought Buddhism down! Truly, *there is nothing new*: be it in human souls or in human misbehaviors.

As soon as you get back, we'll *shove off* with Chapter Fifteen: *the Grand Slam*. A metaphorical home run, of sorts, is made in establishing biblical reincarnation. All the bases are covered in sixteen quick pages. A major chapter concerning Conclusions follows. Normally, a collection of data section precedes such chapters. Here, that area has been placed near the end of the text in Chapter Nineteen as the *Appendix*. The rationale is that this book has been intentionally rigged as a *reader friendly* vessel in an effort to better deliver, to a broad cross section of persons, a serious and profound cargo of information. As the data's complexities might be a distraction to the general flow of the material, at this juncture, they were placed at the end for later study and absorption.

The hope is that mainstream seekers will be less distracted while scholars will still remain served. The appendix itself is readable on its own, in providing insights. Two indexes are included in the Bibliography and Suggested Reading final chapter. The first covers general subjects and the second deals with major personalities.

Don't be surprised if you find some of the time periods and personalities studied more inviting than did others. None of us can overlook that we might have lived back then and were associated with such beings - or even were such beings! If you find it necessary, read and reread whatever section appeals to you first and do so at your own pace. There is a lot to be studied and absorbed. If you can make better headway by underlining points, making notes in the margins, and *dog-earing* pages, then underline points, make notes in the margins, and *dog-ear* the pages. Extra pages for notes have been included, should you find yourself in need.

You might also want to get hold of a Bible. Choose the translation you find of most appeal. I checked out three and all three confirmed the same conclusions.

Other Cases / Other Lessons examines still more lives. One dramatic case concerns the brutal assassination, at the city of Meggido, of Samaria's king Joram, Jerusalem's king Ahaziah and of Queen Jezebel herself. The two kings had been her respective son and grandson. Returning as an Egyptian Pharaoh, Joram avenged the past-life murders of himself, his beloved nephew, and their grandmother. You'll not forget Joram: "And Jehu...smote Joram in his back." Nor Jehu (often pronounced as yahoo)!

Jehu was a religious bigot and murderer. He had worn a sheep's skin of phony piety and fooled many in his time. Today's archaeologist pegs him as having been the world's first *yahoo* and the sleeping Edgar Cayce ranked him with Adolph Hitler! The unrepentant Jehu returned, as Josiah. The cult, which he established, proclaimed him as Jerusalem's most pious king. In reality, he was still a *yahoo*: "so Pharaoh smote him at Meggido." (2nd Kings 23:29).

Another case concerns an incarnation of Jesus. As Joshua, the proud *Prince of War,* he had humiliated his prisoners and crucifixion sometimes followed. Humbled as the *Prince of Peace*, He willingly confronted crucifixion. His reward was *Resurrection!*

Chapter Eighteen, *Back to the Case*, reveals more on the personalities, but in a less formal setting. You get to see them as I saw them. Some twenty cases will be seen and biblical people's present whereabouts considered.

Chapter twenty brings all to an end with some surprisingly positive closing comments, concerning humanity's hopeful future.

The coming voyage will be one of exploration, and discovery. New ideas and concepts are to present themselves, on a very old subject.

Welcome aboard mate.

Chapter 4

The Cayces

As the decade of the roaring twenties neared its close, Edgar Cayce was asked for advice on the then booming stock market. His answer was a resounding but disturbing, "Sell all that thy have...sell, sell, sell!" For six solid months, like the unerring prophesies of Jeremiah, Cayce would predict, in the eloquent Elizabethan English of the King James Bible, a disaster. Though Wall Street's sharpies urged their fellow bulls to, "buy, buy, buy," the crash saw such urgings reduced to the "bears, bears, bears," of a panic.

A few years later, on November 29, 1932 to be exact, and at a little past noon, Gertrude Cayce sought her husband's same sure-sighted accuracy on a far more important subject. In the soft-spoken voice of a well brought up genteel lady of Kentucky, she asked, "What part of the New Testament definitely teaches reincarnation?"

Mr. Cayce, now motionless on his comfortable couch would soon, as he had done for many years, respond. He lay in a self-induced trance, and would not know what he had said until he saw a typed transcript.

Renowned as the foremost psychic of the Twentieth Century, Edgar Cayce was also a Sunday-schoolteacher and devout student of the Bible. He had read its pages from cover to cover - once for each year of his life – such that by the time of his death in 1945, he had read those pages 67 times!

He is seen by some as a Christian mystic and possibly a saint. But the reincarnation issue has led most Western religionists and the scientific mainstream to regard him with trepidation, despite mountains of corroborating research validating psychic phenomena. This must be weighed, in evaluating Edgar Cayce.

However, so must the love expressed by those helped through the uncannily accurate information he revealed while asleep. The metaphysical, or transpersonal, process was called a *Reading*.

(With Permission)
The Cayces.
**This modern work was painted by artist Harriet Kornick.
The Bible rests on Mr. Cayce's lap.**

By 1932, at age 52, he was in dire straits. He had never charged for a "reading," which he felt was God's Work. He had supported his family as a photographer. The readings suggested he move to Virginia Beach and build a hospital devoted to holistic health. The same investors, who would so disastrously ignore his advice, were to supply the funds. Their philanthropy was to allow Cayce a full time devotion to helping people. But, the market's demise saw the hospital, which had held such promise, lost.

Atlantic University, founded to promote in education what the hospital proposed to accomplish in medicine, also seemed doomed.

Penniless, the Cayces confined themselves, and the thousands of pages the readings had now amassed, to their small lakeside cottage. But, despite the time's turmoil, it would be business as usual when Mr. Cayce went to sleep.

His devotion to *God's Work* knew no bounds.

The old Cayce cottage has long been leveled and a tiny playground for children now occupies the site. However, The Work, as the readings' researchers affectionately term their calling, continues and Atlantic University stands:

"Realizable, plausible, feasible." (254-48)

(The numbers in parentheses identify specific readings as catalogued in Cayce's archives. His general advocacy of free market economies, when compassion and ethics were implemented – despite his personal poverty and the pitfalls of the stock market of his day – makes for lively study in the voluminous 254, 257, and 900 series.)

Edgar's and Gertrude's conversation, regarding reincarnation and the Bible, is now housed by the Association for Research and Enlightenment - which oversees Cayce's Work - in a proper library and on the internet at www.edgarcayce.org:

"(Q) What part of the New Testament definitely teaches reincarnation?

(A) John. Six to eight. Third to fifth. Then the rest as a whole."
(452-6)

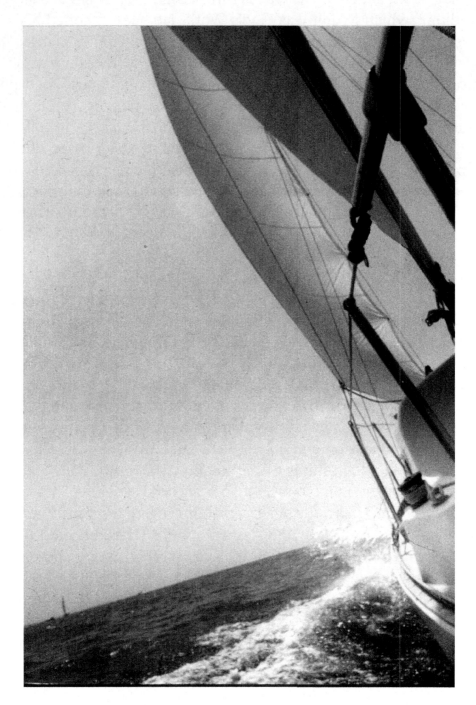

Destination: Virginia Beach.

Chapter 5

The Work

As an Atlantic University graduate student, I had chosen for my master's thesis a case study comparison of selected *normal* biblical personalities (i.e. those not seen as deities), detailing lifestyle links suggesting reincarnation.

Since a major problem in my approach was choosing which characters to study, I was excited when I ran across Cayce's reading pointing to John the Baptist. It indicated a substantiation of John's past incarnation as Elijah. In establishing such a linkage, a key could be produced which unlocks the evidence of reincarnation within the Scriptures (some 31,173 verses, including the born again statements of Jesus). This would prepare the way for new theological information and discussion.

Being eager to get started, I figured the Cayce *one-liner,* would lead to a swift and straightforward project. Setting sail (I lived on my sailboat), I moved to a marina near Lynnhaven Bay, an estuary whose waters edged closer to the school than did my domain on the Chesapeake. Though gasoline cost fourteen cents a pound and a pound of protein a dollar, I still found it cheaper to fuel my body, rather than the multi-toned Detroit iron chariot which normally provided my transportation. So, to reduce expenses further, I stored the ancient antique of Ahab's army on blocks, and rode a bicycle. I muscled this, on a journey totaling about a hundred miles a week, back and forth to the Association for Research and Enlightenment's library and the Atlantic University campus.

Though the pirate Blackbeard had once caroused near my new location, another assertive waterman, as you'll soon see was to head up the region (At the time of my move, I was unaware of these passages):

"(Q) Is Virginia Beach to be safe?
 (A) It is the center - and the only seaport and center - for the White Brotherhood." [1]

"(Q) What relation of John the Baptist to the White Brotherhood?

(A) As then, the leader; now among the head of the brotherhood." [2]

Whether *in spirit* or flesh, neighbors had not been a consideration. My move was made to reduce living costs. This would allow a full time effort, which I anticipated would take only a few months. But my time estimate was off by a bit.

The whole process took two years of cheers, fears, beers, jeers, schlock jobs, near-hurricanes, ninety mile an hour *nor'easters*, tested love relationships, meditation, prayer, patience, inspiration, satisfaction, serenity, and a lot of scholarly *business as usual* at the word processor. When the day came that the haggard committee assigned me of three fully accredited Ph.D.s finally endorsed my *Work*, I was delighted!

Fit at fifty-two with sheepskin in hand - not bad, I thought, for a Kentucky Appalachian, raised in a tough Baltimore city neighborhood - I still yearned for new ventures! Visions danced before me: a Ph.D.; Caribbean cruises; California surf; Europe; a circumnavigation.

Then I read the fine print on my diploma (the school imprints the words in gold lettered Greek, and you have to look them up)! Revealed was an affirmation, in the tradition of Plato's ancient academy, stating:

"Those who have the light should declare it unto others."

So it was back to *business as usual* making sure the testimony concerning the light entitled *Biblical Cases of the Reincarnation Type* (as my thesis was named) got declared unto others.

I attempt this, through writing, lecturing and photography. When wit, and the whimsical *spirit of Elijah* show themselves, I like to attribute their presence to the neighbors: Virginia Beach's illustrious, but unseen Admiral and the Brother/Sisterhood of many colors and genders - who so tickle my creative sensitivities. Hopefully, "The Word of the Lord" gets told - like it is; and, if humor presents itself, then so much the better. While some see humor as making light of death or demeaning to the Scriptures I find it stands as a way-mark pointing to the joy and laughter I have found so permeating *my God's* universe. *My God's* universe is the place where:

"The Lord shall laugh." As we're all going to wind up there one day, we might as well get used to Spirit and laughter in the same breath because:

"He [she] that dwells in heaven shall laugh."

I have also found that humor often defuses tensions long enough so that the new understandings about biblical reincarnation, which might seem alien or threatening to Western minds, may be better presented and understood.

My purpose in creating this book is to re-awaken theology's long neglected discussion on reincarnation in the Bible. I hope to accomplish this by reviewing a distinguished selection of supportive metaphysical, historical and scientific sources, leading to a unique method of biblical inquiry that was developed through Atlantic University scholarship. Hopefully, a better world will be the result, as more understand, through this most influential book - the Bible - their human interconnectedness with each other and God.

I would like to see everyone accept my findings. Such will not happen - at least in this incarnation. However, most will be comfortable with the mainline methods of research I used in handling science, orthodox history, and long venerated verse. There is no cause for *Jihad;* and even the most metaphysical of metaphysician, the most scientific of scientist, or the most fundamental of fundamentalist, are to see their differences discussed utilizing similar ground rules. At the least, most will understand how a person can believe in both the Bible and reincarnation. Hopefully, future religious issues will be resolved, or differences narrowed, in the same manner. Thus, in the same way that present researchers can dialogue, a Baptist can dialogue with a Lutheran, or a New Age Christian with an Evangelical Christian, or a Sunni Moslem with a Druse Moslem, or a Chassidic Jew with a Reformed Jew. That is, as reasonable people agreeing to disagree on specific points, while respecting each one's faith and search for truth.

Notes
1. (1152-11) 2. Psalm 2:4 3. Psalm 37:13- 4. (587-6)

Nearing a hundred years of service, the always active A.R.E. Headquarters traffic, gives testament to the throngs of visitors daily seeking its treasures.

The Old Cayce Hospital stands in the background to the left.

Seen from sea, the dunes and condo roofs in the forefront mark the location of Atlantic University's first foundations.

Chapter 6

The Research

In preparing the project, I followed the readings recommendation and consulted John 1:6-8. The Saint recorded: "There was a man sent from God, whose name was John. He came as a witness to testify concerning the light, so that every man might believe by means of him. He was not the light, but a witness to testify concerning the light."

Chapters 3 to 5 also mentioned John the Baptist and contain this statement by Jesus:

"Do not be surprised because I have told you that you must all be born again." [1]

Another born again connection caught my attention. It was not from the Bible, but in the readings: "Did not John come as the voice of one crying in the wilderness and in the spirit of Elijah? Yet he was Elijah." [2]

"*Oho*," I thought, Cayce said Elijah came back as John the Baptist and it was tempting to type:

Cayce said it - I believe it - that ends it!

Next Case!

(Off the record)

But, Atlantic University is a creditable college and the Association for Research and Enlightenment is not a cult. Thus, the entry would need to be tested, as Cayce had long insisted be done on his statements, and Saint Paul's admonition to "prove all things" invoked. Besides, additional evidence was indicated ("the rest as a whole") and the conscious Cayce had cautioned many times, "I can read reincarnation in the Bible, but others can read it right out." For this reason, I was reluctant to begin with the *born again* material, lest the tack result in the same deadlock over context that Cayce had encountered. Context is sometimes difficult to establish in biblical subjects. This problem is certainly not unique to reincarnation. The problem may not be in the Bible, but in the old time *proof text* method of settling an issue based on a pious authority figure's personal interpretation of a verse or two.

To illustrate, Revelations 7:1 reveals, "I saw four angels standing on the four corners of the earth," which could be perceived as biblical proof that the earth is flat, despite other entries - such as this wisdom of Solomon seen in Ecclesiastes 1:6. It leads to a conclusion of roundness, "The wind blows toward the south, and turns about the north; it whirls continually, [about a globe?] and returns again according to its circuits."

Today, sea captains and high-tech satellites settle such issues, as should the mainstream theologian who seeks support in determining biblical context, through history and science.

This was the crux of the problem and the reason why the research took so long. For, to avoid being "read right out, I could not establish the context for reincarnation solely on the authority of an Edgar Cayce, no matter how pious he might be shown. Reincarnation would need a biblical based presentation using verbatim verse, whose context could also be substantiated by history and science.

This I concluded, after some sobering research and soul-searching - had never been done before. So, I had to start from scratch!

Notes

1. John 3:7   2. (1158-6)

Chapter 7

The Dialogue

Realizing in the beginning, that great teachers affect action, I felt it was important that their identities were as well known as what they thought. This seemed especially true if the premises behind their thoughts were the same. Such similarities, when present, help in choosing which side's persuasions are the most reasonable.

Grasping this, I studied many teachings about life after death and found about as many basics being taught as there are religions. All were debatable. Yet, despite there being so many opinions, I found only three basic premises being preached in ancient times. As a truth stands upon the correctness of its premise, starting there saves a lot of later long winded explaining, and explaining away, and also avoids *misunderstanding in, misunderstanding out* conclusions similar to those computers make, when they've been erroneously fed. Ideally, in focusing upon the givens first, assessing teachings about the hereafter can be kept clear, quick, and straightforward.

The first basic premise is *Materialism*. We've seen that materialists define human existence as a creation of zoology and environment. At death, all ends - *you only go around once*. The following line drawing symbolizes such a theory. The vertical marks represent life's limits. Nothing of human consciousness precedes or follows:

| Material | [1]

The second assumption also sees humans as new beings, but at death, they move to eternal invisible realms. The belief is termed, *Instant Creationism*. A simple line, as above, represents physical life. The afterlife is represented with a spaced line pointing toward eternity:

| Material | — — — ▶ Eternity

Both postulates have yet to establish themselves beyond a reasonable doubt. This is due to the lack of evidence that today's *normal means* of data collection and evaluation demand. That is, the materialist's tools for evaluating the physical world have not been proven to work in non-physical realms. Teachers of Materialism claiming that nothing exits outside the material because it cannot be detected, need reminding that as nobody knows everything about anything, the only thing they can claim, beyond doubt, is that their detection devices have limitations. That evidence cannot be found, does not necessarily rule out that it is not present, nor deny that it will one day show up. Likewise, the religious/philosophical teachings of *Instant Creationism* have yet, after having waited some 1,500 years since their imposition, in some cases having been imposed at the point of a sword, to physically prove that those - *going around once* - either eternally burn in hell or fly in the sky!

In contrast, the survival question may be answered in the third premise. It is termed *Pre-existence*. Pre-existence, like Instant Creationism, accepts the immortality of the soul. However, as I had surmised as a teen, Pre-existence acknowledges that a soul's creation could have taken place in some past epoch of eternity, previous to Eden, and somewhere in a universe of infinite dimensions. This concept is symbolized here with a spaced line pointing backward toward a preexistent period. The solid line depicts material life as seen in the other two diagrams. Continuation can carry on eternally in either direction. Previous periods can have had material expression, as well as can those in the future.

Eternity ◄— — —▌**Material**▌— — —► **Eternity**

Eternity lasts a long time and infinity covers a lot of territory. Given such a reality, it makes little sense in insisting that souls are continually created as new entities. Nor does it make much sense in thinking that such beings need be limited to an initial creation in a material form as homosapien, or even become attracted to earth at all. That we were first established as eternal spiritual beings, rather than as material ones, would seem more likely. The biblical king, Solomon, seems to have embraced the same understanding.

He was so smart that three books in the Bible have been attributed to him. The first chapter of Ecclesiastes (verse 9) demonstrates this wisest of king's teachings concerning the presumption of pre-existence. Solomon said:

"There is nothing new under the sun."

If we, as souls, are not new and yet we're here - then we must have been around in the past. That everyone is included is seen in the consistent orderliness of the cosmos. Its consistency not only demonstrates God's omnipotence, who else could make light travel 186,600 miles in one precise second, but that He/She is not capricious. Thus, when it comes to universal laws, as not even a photon of light is exempt, none of us are exempt. And as none of us are exempt, none of us are excluded. In this regard, we would have been initially created as equals, as the American founding fathers' and mothers' had insisted.

Who said what, is often as important as what was said. Examples are seen in Christians placing such importance on direct statements of Jesus and Mohammed's devotees deeming his declarations just as significant. Gandhi's followers freed their country in heeding this teaching of patience, printed throughout India: "Believing as I do in the theory of rebirth, I live in the hope that if not in this birth, in some other birth, I shall be able to hug all humanity in friendly embrace." [2]

The reasonable teachings of Einstein's physics have long taught that matter is neither created nor destroyed. This scientifically confirms Solomon's same teaching: *there is nothing new under the sun.* [3] I am sure the two taught similarly, though using different terms that protons, neutrons, electrons, and all the creative wonders of nature are equally included – including even, the birds. Gandhi and his American counterpart, Dr. Martin Luther King, would surely have agreed. I suspect that such a learned scholar of Gandhi, as was Dr. King, though a *mainstream* Christian embraced reincarnation friendly feelings, or at the least was respectful.

As to the essential equality of all beings, in observing nature, Jesus shared a similar sentiment. He added however, that God's equal attention to minute detail and perfection had been applied, with even greater care, to us: "Observe the ravens; for they do not sow or reap, and they have no storerooms and barns; and yet God feeds them; how much more important are you than the birds?" [4]

Still feisty at 79, Benjamin Franklin (remember him?) had long championed equal rights. He also offered wisdom to the *nothing new* question: "When I see nothing annihilated and not a drop of water wasted, I cannot suspect the annihilation of souls, or believe that God will suffer the daily waste of millions of minds ready made that now exist, and, put Himself to the continual trouble of making new ones."

Franklin's faith and belief, a faith grounded in the Bible - he knew it well - and a belief in science, stands revealed in his adding, "Thus, finding myself to exist in the world, I believe I shall, in some shape or other, always exist; and, with all the inconveniences human life is liable to, I shall not object to a new edition of mine, hoping, however, that the errata of the last may be corrected." [5]

Grasping that we are not new, leads us to ask whether our creation was initially in Spirit or flesh. This might be like trying to establish whether the first chicken started as an egg. I can't answer that, as I don't know much about chickens and I doubt if Solomon, Franklin, Einstein, Gandhi, or Dr. King could answer the question either. As for human beings starting out - in Spirit - the voice of God settled the issue in the readings of Jeremiah:

"Before I formed you in the belly, I knew you." [6]

Again, this must include us. As equally created beings, we are neither exempt nor excluded from God's concern! God is spirit and Jeremiah's reading, like the voice of Cayce, also given in a trance and as unerring - is telling us that our creation was in the Divine's spiritual image. I think the high five - Solomon, Franklin, Einstein, Gandhi and King - would have agreed. (Cayce said we were all created at the same time, which may support the *Big Bang* theory, which postulates that such a creation took place many millions, even billions, of years ago!) As for ourselves, for whatever reason, some of us have appeared in forms, which we call human. And having had such an opportunity once, further opportunities would seem just as possible.

Unlike Materialism and Instant Creationism, Pre-existence can be established using the normal means of the material world. The process is forthright. The essential requirement is proof that a person who was once dead, now lives. That is, if a person can be shown to have *gone around* in a previous life - and proof of that existence can be demonstrated - then human immortality, seen in individuals surviving death, presents itself as verifiable.

These are some of the arguments for Pre-existence, the premise upon which most reincarnation theories begin. There are, of course, a variety of theories on reincarnation and we'll later look at these. For now, let's stick with Pre-existence. As used here, it offers that we were initially created in God's image as eternal spirits and *pre-existed* as such beings. We were never newly created in the material.

Like Jesus, we are, "not of blood nor of the will of the flesh nor of the will of man, but born of God." [7]

Spirit is Spirit! Like begets like!

For forty years, Psychiatrist Ian Stevenson[8] at the University of Virginia had been researching reincarnation using a Pre-existence methodology. The university was founded by Thomas Jefferson, and consistently places among the top twenty in the U.S. *Time Magazine* (May 21, 2001) ranked it as the nation's best public institution of higher learning. Stevenson, before his retirement, led reincarnation research through its prestigious Department of Personality Studies.

He investigated very young children claiming to have recently experienced a past-life. The past-life, often having ended within three years of the child's being *born again*, is organized into events, which are placed, along with the testimony of current-life witnesses, into convenient lists, or tables. These are compared with statements of those who knew the deceased. A straightforward determination of linkages and the credibility of all concerned is objectively evaluated. When testimonies show statistically significant agreements, and it is shown that the child's knowledge could not have come from conventional educational experiences, the case is considered suggestive of reincarnation or a case of the reincarnation type. Because the children spontaneously reveal their memories, Stevenson apparently preferred the term *Spontaneous Cases of the Reincarnation Type*. These cases are compared and major recurring features listed.

Often, the studies are compelling and upon reflection offer lessons like Bible stories. A case in Lebanon told of two neighbors, a man and woman, who constantly argued. He died and she later bore him as an argumentative son. They continued to battle. The biblical lesson, *love your neighbor as yourself,* saw a scientific correlation: We should love our neighbor as ourselves - as in a future lifetime - we might become our neighbor!

A case in India revealed an obnoxious angry kid who bragged of being rich in his previous life. He had committed murder and used his wealth to bribe the police. Feeling imprisoned in the miserable circumstances of his new life, his past-life *perfect crime* didn't seem so perfect. In repentance, he became a changed person. These words of Jesus support the evidence, "if a man is not *born again*, he cannot see the kingdom of God." [9] Stevenson offered a case of long-standing interest. It indicated reincarnation influences genetics in a mind over matter fashion! The case was reported by reliable sources in 1927 and Stevenson personally interviewed the subject years later. [10]

As a child, aged three, he claimed to have once been an English army officer, who had been felled by a bullet, which entered his neck and exited out his skull. Reborn into an Indian family, he was of extremely light complexion, his hair being almost white. He had two prominent birthmarks, which resembled entry, and exit gunshot wounds in the neck and the back of the head. His parents spoke no English, avoided those who did, and sought to suppress the tyke's recollections. In India, it had been the correct thing to do. Past-life memories by children are suppressed there, in the belief that such memories shorten present lifetimes. There was no motivation for them to have encouraged such remembrances.

It was also politically correct. Gandhi's movement was in gear to oust the Brits. Yet the child knew their customs and played English games such as leapfrog and hopscotch without instruction. He preferred to eat with cutlery, rather than with his hands, as did most Indians, and ate bread rather than rice. Such data indicates mind may indeed affect matter (Cayce said thoughts are things: 386-2). This wise proverb of Solomon eloquently states the axiom, as translated in the quintessentially British, King James Bible,

"For as he thinketh in his heart, so is he." [11]

Finally, a child in Israel was coached to claim he was King David returned. The fraud was easily exposed. While the boy's innocence was maintained, his father and a *tabloid* journalist were publicly discredited. The moral being, "Thou shalt not lie"!

At the time, I was sure no biblical case of little ones remembering past-lives were in the Scriptures, though Jesus might have referred to such children, when *He* pointed out a specific child, who had, though not specified, some special ability: "Whoever receives [believes?] A child like this in my name, he receives me." [12]

However, I suspected a history of similar recurring features (comparable to Stevenson's scientific findings) could be seen in a comparison of Elijah and John - and hopefully other Bible personalities.

If such cases were present, then reincarnation's scientific establishment would likewise not conflict with biblical truths. (It would be in the same manner that Columbus' returning ships settled the question of the world's shape, which left the Bible's integrity unchallenged by the science of navigation.) In fact, biblical truths would be amplified and humanity might see a new paradigm of world unity based upon spiritual and scientific agreement.

My next step was to see how questions of life after death was considered in the past, and like a mainstream theologian, hours would be spent sifting through many early documents to accurately understand the teachings of biblical times. As I also wanted to be sure that the information would be compatible as data (per Stevenson's model), I looked for possible parallels. I quickly discovered that, some 2,400 years ago, Socrates had made a similar investigation. Startlingly, he drew the same conclusion that reincarnation provided the best explanation for his data!

Presenting a child who exhibited specific knowledge that could not have been learned through normal educational experiences, perhaps not unlike the Indian/British boy seen in Stevenson's research and maybe more like the children so especially blessed by Jesus, Socrates suggested a non-normal, or paranormal, explanation was in order.

Kindly Plato, at his academy in Athens, reported the inquiry. He said Socrates began in offering that people of wisdom supported his premise (note his esteem for *wise women* in this entry, parts of which we have previously seen in Chapter 2): "certain wise men and women...spoke of a glorious truth...they say that the soul...is immortal, and at one time has an end, which is termed dying, and at another time is born again but is never destroyed. And the moral is that humans ought to live always in perfect holiness."

You might have been struck by Socrates' prominent use of *born again,* voiced some four hundred years before Jesus, when you first saw it, either here or in your previous reading. You were probably impressed, even surprised, as was I. It's easy to understand why someone as saintly as Saint Augustine held Plato's Greeks in such high esteem. He said of their teachings: "That which is called the Christian religion existed among the ancients, and never did not exist, from the beginning of the human race until Christ came in the flesh, at which time the true religion which already existed began to be called Christianity." [13]

Plato's people were often termed *Pythagoreans* after the mathematician and proponent of reincarnation, Pythagoras. He was the same Pythagoras, whose mathematics I had found so challenging during those ancient days of my misspent youth.

Though his thought, and that of his colleagues, still challenges today's student, I considered that some might question *the Greeks* relevance.

Like Socrates, I'll establish that wisdom still favors these astute ancients, before the dialogue continues:

"How can an educated person stay away from the Greeks? I have always been far more interested in them than in science."

The author was Albert Einstein.[14] He went on: "I maintain that cosmic religious feeling is the strongest and noblest incitement to scientific research." Einstein was to receive Atlantic University's first honorary Doctorate, long before his name became a household word. Other Pythagoreans such as Origen, Christianity's first major theologian, reported: "I speak according to the opinion of Pythagoras and Plato."[15] This, like Augustine's edict, dramatically reveals the pre-existence thinking of many early Christians! Origen added: "All spirits were created blameless, all must at last return to their original perfection. The education of the soul is continued in successive worlds."

In the world of today, contemporary commentator, A.N. Wilson, acclaimed biographer of Jesus and Saint Paul, acknowledged Plato's Greeks in stating, "Plato and Aristotle come to the modern world, historically speaking, filtered through Christian monasticism; that Christianity itself, as a doctrinal entity with all its esoteric formulations about the nature of the Deity, and of the soul, and of the self (divine and human) of Christ, and the heavens and the earth, derives largely from the late Platonism."[16] I mention these as an assurance, that prominent pre-existence preaching has long existed and as a *wake-up* call to those still laboring under the notion, despite what has been presented, that reincarnation is alien to the West's finest minds, or that all Christians consider the subject a heresy.

In fact, as in denominations of the Bible-based religions of Judaism and Islam, there are, and have always been, Christian sect's supportive. As for fine minds, those like Einstein's have found the subject worthy of their sincerest inquiry. As an example, Einstein expressed a keen fondness for the more modern Pythagorean movement, which flourished during the Nineteenth Century and was known as *Transcendentalism*. It was founded by Immanuel Kant and included others such as Goethe, Liebnitz, Richard Wagner, Hegel, Walt Whitman, Wordsworth, and a long list of the ages' finest, including Arthur Schopenhauer. Einstein described his work as: "the wonderful writings of Schopenhauer."[17]

These centered upon *wonderful writings* regarding reincarnation: "A new born being's...fresh existence is paid for by the worn out existence which has perished, but contained the indestructible seed out of which this existence has arisen: they are one being. To show the bridge between them would certainly be the solution of a great riddle." [18]

Solving this *great riddle* might have inspired Einstein's charting of today's unified and quantum theories, and theory of relativity. (Einstein described energy, which may be undetectable at certain frequencies, and matter as *one being*. The *bridge between them* might have been the formula E=MC.) His theories declare that these *indestructible seeds* (or atoms) are also capable of simultaneously existing at differing energy/matter levels, in whole worlds, which are independent of the other. (This may be in the same manner that radio waves of different frequencies can simultaneously exist without interrupting each other's program.)

This concept might describe the mechanism humans' use in changing form from the invisible (before birth) to the visible (at birth) and back again (at so-called death). If the *indestructible seed* as Schoepenhaur saw the human soul, is seen in the same light as Einstein's *energy/matter*, and Cayce's *thoughts/things,* then it might follow that souls could likewise interchange between both (seen) material forms and (unseen) spiritual forms, and exist in different worlds which are independent from each other.

While this aside may or may not explain the mechanism for reincarnation in its entirety, it certainly demonstrates that the mystical relevance of the Pythagoreans and the transcendentalists is alive and well with some very potent ideas. Today's Pythagoreans and transcendentalists are said to be those embracing concepts of pre-existence, which Aldous Huxley collectively termed the *Perennial Philosophy*. Those exploring this mystical issue are to be ranked among many fine thinkers. This must include the prime perennial philosopher and brightest figure of our era, Albert Einstein. He wrote: "The most beautiful emotion we can experience is the *mystical* [he's often misquoted on this point with the word mysterious, rather than mystical] this knowledge, this feeling is at the center to true religiousness. In this sense, and in this sense only, I belong to the ranks of devoutly religious men."[19]

Simplicity – Beauty

Einstein felt theories should first offer *simplicity* and then *beauty*. These paired words, along with *The Voice*, and even the loaded *Born Again*, should also be the waymarks in our understanding the devoutly religious Socrates. (*Born Again*, as we have seen, was used in the context of both reincarnation and spiritual renewal for centuries. Its narrowed use as a religious maxim, by many evangelical Christian sects who, ironically, vehemently oppose reincarnation, occurred only in recent times. Hopefully, the day will return when *born again* will be understood as the broader and more unifying teaching taught in the *old time religion* of Jesus, and those before him, that perennial philosophers of all eras so honor.)

Socrates stature, like that of King Solomon, Benjamin Franklin, and Albert Einstein stands as the brightest of his era. They're good people - as souls, they're still around! That they once chose to appear as white males shouldn't be held against them. The gender and racial realities of their times allowed them no other options. If you're carefully reading Socrates, you'll soon see his reference to the soul as, *she,* as you have seen his mention of *wise women*. He could have returned as a scientist with the stature of a Madame Curie, or a figure such as Dr. King.

Along with Jesus, Elijah/John, Jung and Edgar Cayce, these minds make up a *dream team* of inspiration. Many embrace them as allies, and even friends. Friends, whose wisdom lives on in print and in the hearts of sincere seekers of enlightenment. If you're such a seeker, read on. If not, read on anyway. Sooner or later, hopefully sooner, the numbers and consistency of their persuasions will hasten the day, when the eyes and ears of you're very soul will reopen and reclaim a prize of great value, called liberation. It's been within you since your creation.

When the waiting child was presented to Socrates, the sage said: "the soul, then, as being immortal, and having seen all things that exist...should be able to call to remembrance all that *she* ever knew...as all nature is akin...and all learning is but recollection." [20]

Upon being asked for proof, Socrates responded with a carefully planned series of questions. These apparently measured abilities, which the boy could only have obtained from memories outside his limited educational experience. Correct answers would establish, as seen in Stevenson's similar scenarios, that some children have knowledge, which cannot be attributable to normal means.

The child would answer successfully. Socrates then responded, as would any good investigator today, by personally cross examining all involved to make sure no one had instructed the lad in his responses.

Socrates, by choice, had few possessions. Living lightly, his mind moved with the speed and precision of a Pentium® processor. Intel® was inside, and so was compassion. In proclaiming: "But if the child did not acquire the knowledge in this life, then clearly he must have learned it at some other time," the heart, mind, and soul of Socrates spoke with a simplicity and beauty still stirring us twenty four centuries later.

He spent the last morning of his life counseling two troubled teens facing doubts about life after death. They were reassured, by a man sentenced to die that very evening, that unexplainable memory: "Implies a previous time in which we have learned that which we now recollect." [21]

Ironically, Socrates had been charged as corrupter of youth. He died, as would Jesus, because tyrannical regimes fail where individuals are reminded, *you are gods*. As the American Masons proved, gods don't need the guidance of the world's *bigwigs*. The world's *bigwigs* need the guidance of gods, through the wisdom of the ballot box.

Regarding the effect of hemlock as a minor inconvenience, Socrates said farewell to his beloved children and family. His final hours were to have been spent with twelve of his disciples. That only eleven were present occurred because Plato's grief was so debilitating, that he could not attend. As would Jesus, Socrates lifted his cup in bidding his friends' farewell. Soon, he knew, a transition would see him soar about the universe, no longer a terrestrial entity living lightly, but an immortal one, an immortal being of living light. Of the many words he imparted that night, these stand among the most memorable: "There comes into my mind an ancient doctrine which affirms that souls go from here into the other world, and returning hither, are *born again* from the dead. Now if it be true that the living come from the dead, then our souls must exist in the other world, for if not, how could they have been *born again?*"[22]

Plato lived to proclaim Socrates convictions of simplicity and beauty. This most devoted of students offered that all should lead lives that: "hold fast ever to the heavenly way and follow after justice and virtue always, considering that the soul is immortal."[23]

Socrates may not have been entirely correct in affirming that, "all learning is but recollection," in setting up his premise of pre-existence. But he didn't have to. He needed only to establish that some learning, *is but recollection*. Any memory, if established as resulting from past life learning, even if only a little, points to pre-existence.

Most of us reveal past life learning in inherent skills or traits. On this point, Socrates would be entirely correct. Of course, in all learning, memory is still a key factor. As to why so few have past life remembrances (about one in five hundred, according to Stevenson) today's thinkers theorize that daily life demands displace the brain's memories of past lives, in the same manner that memories of dreams are displaced. Stevenson[24] sought out verifiable details and finds most memory fades after age eight but notes such loss does not negate having had a past life. An example might be seen in one claiming they weren't alive at the time of their first birthday party because the event wasn't remembered. A birth certificate and the memories of those attending would disprove such a claim.

While Socrates presumably knew of other cases, he presented only one. In contrast, as a scientist, Stevenson had collected thousands and made an exhaustive study of alternative explanations. Some include fraud, unconscious absorption of knowledge about the deceased from outside sources, possession, and extra sensory perception. However, as had Socrates, Stevenson likewise concluded, "But if the children did not acquire the knowledge in this life, then they must have learned it at some other time?"

Well, not exactly.

He generally presented his findings in words typical of these: "There is an impressive body of evidence, and it is getting stronger all the time. I think a rational person...can believe in reincarnation on the basis of evidence." [25]

Simplicity, beauty!

Nothing is New

In evaluating the learned teachers of the past, concerning life after death, it quickly became obvious that, as in today's world, the pre-existence/reincarnation issue was prominent among the major movers and shakers, including those in the Mediterranean community, and the Holy Land, in biblical times. But, just as today, there were disagreements (nothing is new) and it wouldn't be fair to continue without their mention.

Those opposed often justified their beliefs in Plato's very young student, *Aristotle*. He once reasoned that a heavier object would fall to earth more quickly than would a lighter one. His pronouncement went unchallenged, for centuries, until *Galileo* dropped two dissimilar weighted objects off the leaning tower of Pisa. When they reached the ground at the same time, Galileo got locked up by the thought police. He wasn't cleared until the Twentieth Century. Aristotle's reasoning, which he had termed *Pure Thought*, proved not to be so pure!

Through a similar process of not so pure *Pure-Thought* Aristotle's approach also determined, "the soul cannot be without a body."[26] Though, one of history's greatest, his lack of Einstein's empirical insights would have made it difficult for Aristotle to grasp that matter (seen as *bodies*) and energy (seen as *Spirits*) can interchange.

Likewise, many materialist teachers.

Like those of old - many still tend to overlook information with which they disagree, even if obtained from experimentation, and tend to make claims based upon partial facts alone. The late anthropologist, *Margaret Mead*, reminded such teachers to keep in mind that science has historically proven the existence of all manners of things which were not apparent in the past: "The whole history of scientific advance is full of scientists investigating phenomena that the Establishment did not believe was there." [27]

Her insight prompted the prestigious *American Association for the Advancement of Science* to embrace parapsychology within its ranks. Yet there still remain many who insist that unless they can detect a deceased being's presence - it doesn't exist. Such obstinacy, if it were held on a subject other than human survival after death, would find few supporters. But the days of doubt, concerning the subject, are behind us. Parapsychology is a science and its compelling data obtained, *in investigating phenomena that the Establishment did not believe was there*, can no longer go overlooked by the obstinate.

The famous Middle Eastern historian, *Flavius Josephus*, a New Testament contemporary born near the time of Christ's crucifixion (his major works were *Wars of the Jews* and *Antiquities of the Jews*) wrote of materialists. Materialism is *nothing new.* Materialists were known then as *Sadducees* and Josephus reported, "The Sadducees ...take away the belief in the immortal duration of the soul, and the punishments and rewards of Hades." [28]

They probably posed this biblical line from Geneses 3:19 to support their beliefs:

"For dust you are, and to dust shall you return."

The Sadducees were very sad, you see.

Many instant creationists also traced their thinking to Aristotle. Their resistance to reincarnation might be based on another of his notions: "Reflection confirms the observed fact; the actuality of any given thing can only be realized in what is already potentially that thing." [29]

Thus a deceased person might either have to wait for a miraculous return, intact in the same body, or be removed to a spiritual body (its potential). If it were removed to a spiritual body, then earthly returns would seem impossible, since the mechanism for terrestrial existence (the deceased's physical body) had disintegrated. Josephus, seemingly, had these instant creationists in mind,

"The Pharisees say that all souls are incorruptible; but that the souls of good men are only removed into other bodies, but that the souls of bad men are subject to eternal punishment." [30]

As *bad men* cannot be *removed into other bodies*, new souls must be created to fill the bodily beings constantly needed in replenishing the departing population of the many, *subject to eternal punishment*. Saint Paul was born a Pharisee: "I am a Pharisee."[31]

Before his conversion to the teachings of Jesus, like the Pharisees of that era, as well as those of today, Paul might once have found support in this parable of theirs he briefly alluded to in Hebrews 9:27. It has become the *one liner* of choice, for proof context practitioners, in reading reincarnation out of the Bible: "It is appointed for men to die once, and after their death, the judgment." (We'll get back to this.)

Josephus indicated only three religious sects existed in his time. Today's scholars, since the Dead Sea Scroll discoveries, confirm the Cayce readings that had said, for a long time, that John the Baptist (remember him?) belonged to the third sect, called *Essenes*. The plainspoken preacher, in Matthew 3:7), called the Sadducees and Pharisees: "Offspring of scorpions"

This could confirm his Essene membership. He would not likely have condemned his own sect, nor his close cousin, the gentler Jesus. A Jesus, who said of these same adversaries: "Beware of the leaven [teachings] of the Pharisees and of the Sadducees."[32]

Josephus also referred to the Essenes in writing: "These men lead the same kind of lives as those whom the Greeks call *Pythagoreans.*"[33]

This invites one to conclude, with the precision and surety of a mathematical *Ace*, that the Essenes professed pre-existence. Those doubting Josephus often mention he was out to maintain his cushy position with the Romans, as the favorite of Emperor Vespasian. While probably true, Josephus obviously sought to also impress Rome with an accurate history of his people. Many measure his veracity in this brief mention of an especial countryman:

"Now there was about this time Jesus, a wise man, if it be lawful to call him a man, for he was a doer of wonderful works - a teacher of such men as receive the truth with pleasure. He drew over to him both many of the Jews, and many of the Gentiles. He was the Christ; and when Pilate, at the suggestion of the principal men amongst us, had condemned him to the cross, those that loved him at the first did not forsake him, for he appeared to them alive again on the third day as the divine prophets had foretold these and ten thousand other wonderful things concerning him; and the tribe of Christians, so named from him, are not extinct at this day." [34] (The translator inserted the date of the Resurrection as April 5, 33.)

This is one of the few authentic mentions of Jesus outside the Bible. Though questions over minor details of the passage exist, archaeology attests to Josephus' general accuracy. Detractors more often find themselves on the defensive. At his best, he's a witty wordsmith of well written history. At worst, he's not above an editorial exercise, here and there, to keep his behind side secure. He had his prejudices and wrote of scandal with a sensationalism standing head-to-head with that of today's supermarket tabloid. You'll see this in his bias against the Herod's, whom he detested. Their bad biblical press may owe something to him.

Most importantly, as he had lived among the Essenes during his teenage years, his Pythagorean mention would seem among his more accurate observations. This is important because such a connection, in determining reincarnation in the Scriptures, while subtle at first glance, is about as subtle to any attentive theologian as an atomic bomb! Pythagoras's name, like *Plato*, *Neoplatonism*, and *Hellenism*, is virtually synonymous with reincarnation.

The theological equivalent of a hydrogen bomb is history's suggestion (which Cayce backs) that Jesus, and many close to *Him,* were also Essenes! Remember, that like John, the sects, who upset Jesus, were the Sadducees and the Pharisees. If Jesus and John were averse to Essene beliefs, they would have made similar broadsides of simple, but not so beautiful shots, such as this Jesus, in a less gentle mood, let loose all over them in Matthew 23: "Offspring of scorpions...those who strain at gnats and swallow camel [?] Blind fools...blind guides...woe unto you!"

From what's been seen, the *woes* of the Sadducees and Pharisees, like the *woes* of today's materialist and instant creationist (at least when it comes to reincarnation) were based upon their use of Aristotle's not so pure, *pure thought.* The method looks good on paper, especially in proving, without a telescope that the sun and planets revolve around the earth - misunderstanding in, misunderstanding out. Obviously, history has shown *pure thought*, unless backed by data upheld through continuing experimentation, often leads to error.

A look at Aristotle's personal life, and the conversion experience which led him back to Plato, reveals more problems for the obstinate. Like Socrates, Aristotle was a family man with several children. A regular guy, he came from a fine family, his father had been a doctor. Aristotle's career began well enough in his acceptance of pre-existence and reincarnation. But during his middle period, he reportedly rejected them, over Socrates' issue of soul memory.

Aristotle felt that learning, as Skinner would postulate, is purely a psychophysical phenomenon. This, of course, was before Stevenson's scientific work that demonstrates Socrates was on the right track.

The split among the Pythagoreans saw Aristotle embraced as the father of Western materialism. A lot of short-sighted teachers, in overlooking that the thoughts of his middle period had changed, decimated Greco/Roman faith in its gods. A similar spiritual havoc was wreaked in our era, through the thoughts of a later father of materialism, *Karl Marx*.

Of course Aristotle and Marx were not personally at blame for the horrors committed in their names (Marx was so appalled that he once cried, "I am not a Marxist"). Like Aristotle, he called the shots as he best saw them. Right or wrong, that's the thinker's job. Resulting actions are the responsibility of those who undertake them.

Aristotle and Marx, had they been able, would have rolled over in their graves at the sins of their followers. Of course they couldn't have done so, as souls aren't to be found in such places. The Bible reminds us in Luke 24:5: "Why do you seek the living among the dead?" It is biblical to remind ourselves that, as immortal souls in a material world, we have nothing to lose but the chains that keep us here. *Spirits arise!*

As for Aristotle on materialism, he changed his mind. The change resulted in a new movement known as *Neoplatonism*. The obstinate have, for far too long, overlooked Aristotle's reconciliation with his teachers and the contributions of neoplatonic thought. It sought to meld the practicality of Aristotle with the spiritual sweetness of Plato and Socrates.

Like Plato and Socrates, Intel® sparked Aristotle. Though a man, he was a walking talking Pentium® processor. But he was a human being *like ourselves*. Having a heart, he would not have found salvation in logic alone. My guess is that a return to his senses resulted from the misdeeds of his most famous pupil, Alexander *the Great*. Aristotle had been his tutor.

Alexander was a man of vision and possessed an unparalleled faculty for leadership. But, *The Great* also demonstrated an appalling capacity for fermenting bloodshed. The worst example was his destruction of Tyre. Three hundred years previously, the seaport had been Jezebel's hometown. Massacring its defenders, they died to a man. Alexander, in his mid-twenties, then sold each individual woman and child into slavery.

A caring Aristotle now at an age when spirituality, as Jung had noted, was so critical, would have lost more than a little sleep in wondering if such atrocities had resulted from what he had imparted. The ever observant Josephus noted similar behavioral flaws, like Alexander's, ran rampant - as an inherent dysfunction - among so many materialists: "Sadducees suppose God is not concerned in our doing or not doing what is evil; and they say, that to act what is good, or what is evil, is at men's own choice...The behavior of the Sadducees one towards another is in some degree wild."[35]

Teachers, like parents, who see those under their tutelage go astray, experience the same sleepless nights that Aristotle surely endured. I once had a Norfolk Marine student who shot at another and one who held up a restaurant with a loaded shotgun. Trust me, you lose sleep in wondering where your teaching technique might have gone wrong. Alexander surely foisted upon Aristotle the same uncertainties that the teachers and parents of troubled souls everywhere, and of every age, have and still, endure. Karl Marx was another such teacher.

History honors him as an honest and gentle human being, though he taught that religion was the "opiate of the people." A revolutionary worldview ensued. But this worldview, like that of the Sadducees, was based upon a failed assumption. The assumption's failure can be measured in the cultural *hemlock*, that the blocking of religious freedoms has seen resulting in Marxists' regimes wherever they have appeared. As an example, Cuba's literacy rate undoubtedly rose (about 5%) after the imposition of communism. However, it's doubtful if happiness increased when the island's five-hundred year old tradition of Christmas was banned!

Marxists might have faired better in promoting the separation of church and state, thus keeping each from being exploited by the other (*absolute power corrupts absolutely*) rather than eliminating religion.

While today, we might rightly fear the excesses of unbridled fanaticism, as religious meanness has erupted in the movements of bigots everywhere. However, we make a critical error in overlooking that such meanness runs counter to true religious *endeavor*. The evils attributed to religion do not come about because of sentiments in the *Bible*, the *Koran* or the major Holy Book of the East, the *Bhagvad Ghita*. Evil derives primarily from zealous desires for quick cash, zealous acts of madmen, and the zealousness of envy, all disguised as religious and exploited by those who are not.

Marx did not live long enough to see, first hand, that even if materialism were true, its premise was not new, let alone revolutionary, and would offer few benefits. Without exception, throughout the twentieth century, Marxist regimes would exact upon their citizens a terrible price in bloodshed and diminished human happiness. Though living standards were occasionally raised, surely similar gains could have been achieved through less radical means, such as the establishment of a constitutional monarchy, like that of England, in Russia.

In all, Marxism would prove to be a losing proposition. It never adequately defined the nature of human beings nor developed a successful formula for government. Though materialism has been discredited by history and proven to be obsolete, tired, and an out-and-out loser as a premise upon which to build any rational theories of human existence, materialism still remains the focus of so many academics in the social sciences and history. Unfortunately, a majority holding these views head up most of the departments teaching these disciplines on our campuses. A major result would seem the growing neo-Marxist movement in our nation and the resulting turmoil of the growing "culture war," which seems to so confound our politics, and even our daily lives.

I'll bet my advance that not one in ten teachers of anthropology, history, or sociology are aware of the Masonic beliefs of Benjamin Franklin, George Washington, or the many like-minded signers of the *Declaration of Independence*, let alone introduce anything on how their esoteric thought contributed to American history.

Since the manifestation of the *New Order of the Ages* in 1945, as Benjamin Franklin had named it and seems to have so ably predicted (he was an uncannily accurate astrologer) it should be apparent that a great gift was given, not only to the United States but to the world. The gift is in the wisdom of the perennial philosophy, which so subtly under-girds the secular face of the American Constitution. Nations observing its winning formula, though like most in America itself, are probably not aware of its Spiritual foundation. Nevertheless, they experience similar blessings of unparalleled growth in civil rights, medicine, technology, the arts, environmental progress, and genuine human happiness.

But a lot still remains to be accomplished if this *New Order* is to sustain itself. The task at hand is that a lot of academia must *wake up and smell the coffee* and begin siding with the winners in understanding what, despite their still unsolved problems, makes the world's winninges't nations *tick!* Schools like Atlantic University can be of great help in *declaring the light unto others*. When understood, the Constitution's now subtle principles must then become front-burner issues.

The danger in not doing so is that pre-existence risks getting disastrously *read right out*. Such a risk stems from the incessant headlines heralding the constant infighting between the more often materialist *left* of today's Sadducees and the predominant *right* of the Pharisee - the present heirs of those Jesus and John condemned so long ago (nothing is new). *Left* and *right* hysteria threatens a drowning out of the wiser, though quiet, voice of the perennial philosopher. At stake, is the loss of winning formulas for the world's nations.

As to what had motivated Aristotle's move from materialism, unlike Marx, Aristotle lived long enough to see that, like the Sadducees of Josephus and the future dictators of the twentieth century, dismissing the soul's immortality doesn't lead to good ends. Alexander's court hardly exemplified the virtuous life of Plato's teachings: *hold fast ever to the heavenly way and follow after justice and virtue always, considering that the soul is immortal.*

Guilt and a yearning for the happier times as a proponent of the Pythagoreans might have brought Aristotle around. Ultimately, Spirit moved, for few, as will be seen in Saint Paul, make such radical turnarounds in thought, through logic alone.

Cayce considered heartfelt experience was the most convincing persuasion. Aristotle, in his faith-based searching (I don't believe it was intellectually motivated) might have asked someone like the gentleman from Kentucky:

"(Q): What will convince me of reincarnation?
(A): An experience." [36]

As do many, in grasping reincarnation's realities, Aristotle might then have asked:

"(Q) Will it be necessary to re-enter the earth plane?"

Aristotle would have gotten a similar reply:

(A) So live, so act, in the present, that it will not be necessary." [37]

Ignoring Aristotle's personal spiritual growth leaves those doing so at the mercy of strictly second-stringer sources. None of us belong in the minor leagues and the majors are calling through the *voices* of their heaviest hitters, which include Aristotle:

"It remains that the rational or intellectual soul only enters the body from without, as [the soul] is only of a nature purely divine."[38]

Simplicity. Beauty.

The School of Athens

Standing as a masterpiece in the Vatican, this work by Raphael reflects the spirit of the High Renaissance. The two central figures are Plato, to the left (he gestures to the heavens), and Aristotle, to the right (he points to earth). They walk among the Pythagoreans, including Socrates and Pythagoras himself.

Raphael rendered himself peering inward near the lower right hand side. He painted Plato's likeness after that of Leonardo Da Vinci.

Da Vinci's written works covered some four thousand pages. Like many masters of his time, he shared an interest in reincarnation. This closing passage was composed in the Madrid Ms Manuscript, folio 6 Recto. Dated between 1497 and 1503, it reveals not only his personal self-esteem, but the thinking of one of history's most advanced minds. I'd like to believe he'd been Socrates, who Raphael prominently displayed reclining in the forefront:

"Read me O reader, if you delight in me, because very seldom shall I come back into this world."

Notes

1. See Puryear (1982) p. 28
2. See Head & Cranston p. 561
3. Ecclesiastes 1:9
4. Luke 12:24
5. Franklin p.174
6. Jeremiah 1:5
7. John 1:13
8. Stevenson (1966)
9. John 3:3
10. Stevenson (1997) p. 33
11. Proverbs 23:7
12. Matthew 18:4
13. Head & Cranston p. 134
14. Albert Einstein (1950)
15. Head & Cranston
16. Wilson (1997) p. 156
17. Albert Einstein (1954) p. 38
18. Head & Cranston p. 281
19. Wilbur (1981) p. 4
20. Meno
21. Head & Cranston p. 21
22. Ibid
23. The Republic Book X
24. Stevenson (1997) p. 61
25. Head & Cranston p.
26. On the Soul Book II ch.2
27. Stevenson (1997) p. 66
28. *Time* 3/4/1974 p. 66
29. On the Soul Book II ch.2
30. Wars II 8:11
31. Acts 23:6
32. Matthew 16:6
33. Antiquities XIV 10:4
34. Antiquities XVIII 3:3
35. Wars II 8:4
36. (956-1)
37. (295-2)
38. De Generatione Animae

The Dialogue

(Photo by Karen Richards)

On souls, Jesus said: "You are gods." John joyfully enjoined: "I am the voice." Solomon said: "There is nothing new." Jeremiah joined in, quoting God: "I knew you." Saint Paul preached: "You reap what you sow." Socrates stated we are: "Born again." Plato proclaimed: "The soul is immortal," and Aristotle added: "The soul is only of a nature purely divine." Gandhi gladly wrote about: "The theory of rebirth." Einstein soulfully sided with Schopenhauer: "The indestructible seed." Stevenson scientifically stated: "Believe in reincarnation on the basis of evidence." Ben Franklin (frankly) put it this way: "I shall not object to a new edition of mine."

**They said it. I believe it.
That ends it!
Simplicity. Beauty.**

Cape Henry Light House

Cape Henry Light stands serving Atlantic Ocean and Chesapeake Bay mariners. It was here in 1607 that the British expedition leading to the Jamestown colony landed, under the auspices of King James - of the King James Bible. A Freemason, he counseled that the spiritual lives of, "those in need," – whether Brit or Native - should be attended to and sent his personal vicar, Robert Hunt, to serve as Chaplain. Rev. Hunt mentored the spiritual life of Princess Pocahontas and attended to the many facing death. He died in that endeavor.

Such beacons and mentions from saintly lives are not final destinations of course, they serve only as guides to the seeking sailor's home port. The same can be said about the purposes of the Bible and religion as beacons in the seekers search for God, that Jesus said lives within us.

The home port of our Divinity is sometimes experienced as the "Word" or "still small voice" that Elijah had heard. Such seeking - though Bible and spiritual endeavor helps – is a calling for an inner voyage which no one, but ourselves, can accomplish.

Mr. Cayce's most made biblical quote was from the King James version of Deuteronomy 30, that had put it this way: "Neither is it beyond the sea, that thou shouldest say, Who shall go over the sea for us, and bring it unto us, that we may hear it, and do it? But the word is very nigh unto thee, in thy mouth, and in thy heart, that thou mayest do it."

Chapter 8

Saint Paul

Saint Paul appeared after the life of Jesus and the Gospel events. He was neither a direct disciple nor an eyewitness. Of the twenty-seven books in the New Testament, only the first four directly describe Jesus. Yet fifteen, including Saint Luke's account in Acts, are devoted to Paul's ministry.

His calling concerned the dissemination of the deeply held insight he found, through intense intellectual and paranormal processes, in the *Good News* Jesus taught. Paul wrote: "I did not receive it nor learn it from man, but through the revelation of Jesus Christ."[1]

Spreading this *Good News* was to be accomplished as a personal initiative and that of his small flock called, *The Way*. The expectancy that Jesus would shortly return, during Paul's own lifetime, was strongly conveyed, as this brief byte in a letter to his congregation in Judea contends. Titled, *The Epistle of Paul the Apostle to the Hebrews*, verse 9:26 reads: "But now at the end of the world." Statements like this make it doubtful he envisioned *The Way* would be around long enough to have formed the foundation for the Roman church.

At best, the *Apostle's* interpretation can be challenging. Of all the books in the Bible, those attributed to him are usually the most quoted in *reading right in* the views of those upholding strict sectarian religious beliefs and in *reading right out* the strict sectarian religious beliefs of those with whom they - those upholding strict sectarian religious beliefs - disagree. The result has been that there are probably as many opinions on Paulist thought, as there are individual members among the thousands of sects labeling themselves as Christians.

One example of the considerable impact of Paul's one hundred or so biblical pages can be seen in comparing their numbers, with the sheer length of the two thousand one hundred eighty paged (no pictures) commentary concerning them, to be found in the very mainline multi-volume *Interpreter's Bible*.

Incredibly, such staggering numbers of pages represent but one Protestant perspective! Typically, other Protestant volumes, Roman Catholic, Greek Orthodox and many other Christian texts are just as prolific.

This must force many a theologian, when pressed, to question whether Christianity rests upon the teachings of Jesus, or upon those of Paul! This is not an important issue, so long as the two appear to be in agreement. But as most Christians, especially Roman Catholics, revere both, a hint of disagreement can present problems in defending the cohesiveness of the Scriptures. And as many believers base their faith upon such cohesiveness, magnifying where Jesus and Paul agreed can become an imperative. And as just such an imperative (the maximizing of faith) stands among the foremost purposes of this book, pointing out the two's shared understanding on, at the least, the principle of pre-existence is important.

In establishing such a shared stance, it won't be necessary to cover Jesus and Paul's entire range of subject matter. Where the two essentially stood can readily be determined in seeking their positions on pre-existence and examining a sharing of similar ideas with the perennial philosophers. This, hopefully, will avoid the controversy that any interjection of Paulian thought traditionally invites which includes accusations that his *Voice* was later adulterated by sectarian and secular authorities unwilling or unable to grasp the multiple meanings Paul placed as stepping stones, toward enlightenment, in his dutiful development of a ministry devoted to a large spectrum.

Paul and Pre-existence

Determining where Paul stood on most any issue, let alone reincarnation, requires real effort. As for reincarnation in particular, because he apparently understood that the world was soon to end with the *Master's* return, for Paul, the subject might have been irrelevant.

Pre-existence, however, was another issue. The teachings of Jesus and the Essenes, as we have seen, were ample. And while Paul had been raised outside their tradition, he was a strict Pharisee, his Greek education would nevertheless have introduced him to the subject.

At some point, perhaps during his studies in preparation for his ministry, he would also have read a transcript (the New Testament had yet to be completed) or heard the following prayer by Jesus. It expressed, in John 17:5, the *Christed* One's personal persuasion concerning pre-existence. Like the similar circumstance of Socrates, it was rendered after a parallel

Last Supper scenario and would be among the final words heard by the disciples: "O my father, glorify me with thee, with the same glory which I had with thee *before* the world was made."

Paul's agreement is revealed in Ephesians 1:4: "From the beginning God has chosen us through Christ *before* the foundation of the world." Though this might seem overly simplified in view of the Apostle's complexities, the simplicity and beauty of his position on pre-existence is direct and clear in the use of the word *before!*

Before (like *up*, *down*, and *after*) is an unassailable determiner of position! Such a word is not open to nuances of translation or easily *read right out*. It also *reads right* in accordance with the same pre-existence position we saw in Jeremiah: "*Before* I formed you in the belly, I knew you." Likewise, *before* fits in nicely with another of Solomon's insights on the spiritual nature of human beings: "Then the dust shall return to the earth as it was: and the spirit *shall return* to God who gave it."[2] (Would not such a spirit had to have existed *before* its entry into a body of earthly *dust*? If it had not pre-existed in a spiritual state, how could it have been described as a *spirit* that *shall return?*)

Simplicity, Beauty.

Paul personally used the word *before*, close to fifty times. Granted, each use did not refer to pre-existence, he and/or his disciples were too creative as writers to belabor their readership in the word's overuse. However, as a world class master of both spoken and written words, he/they creatively used a variety of expressions such as *foreknew* and *knew* to keep the point of pre-existence sharp and clear: "God has not rejected his people whom he *foreknew*."[3]

"[God] *knew* them in advance and he marked them with the likeness of the image of his Son."[4]

Also sharp and clear, is the value in seeking out the basic premise of a diverse figure like Paul first, before delving too deeply into his material. It saves a lot of time and avoids confusion in navigating the, often circuitous course, his reading demands. The process also unlocks the door to further evidence.

Die Once

Starting with the *die once* passage in Hebrews 9:27, as promised in the previous chapter, a look at Paul's brief mention reveals the phrase does not focus on an in-depth explanation of life after death, but concerns Christ's role as a mediator between the teachings of the Old and New Testaments. This is seen in 9:15: "For this cause Christ became the mediator of the new covenant and by his death he became salvation for those who transgressed the old covenant [a reference to karma?], that those who are called may receive the promise of eternal inheritance [meaning forgiveness?]"

The chapter's closing three verses (9:26-28) concern Paul's point, that Jesus needed to accomplish this only once: "but now, *at the end of the world*, only once by his sacrifice did he offer himself to abolish sin. And as it is appointed for men to *die once*, and after their death, the judgment; So Christ was once offered to bear the sins of many; so that at his second coming he shall appear without our sins for the salvation of those who look for him."

Obviously, *at the end of the world,* all of us would be appointed to *die once*. But as the event never took place, can such a passage be taken literally? A more metaphorical interpretation would seem appropriate. And in view of Paul's pre-existence sentiment, shared with the *Christed* Jesus and the perennial philosophers, a more rational understanding offers that, after death, judgment takes place and is a continual process, which occurs after the completion of each lifetime! When the soul reaches the point of purification, when reincarnation no longer is necessary, it will be appointed to die one last time and receive the judgment, which sets it free.

As to, *die once*, it is presented as an aside and corroborating verses appear to be nowhere else (in such cases, I doubly search for more material with both electronic and traditional concordances, and seek out scholarly opinion). That only one such entry was made is important. Traditional biblical interpretation doesn't normally take such short mentions to heart, unless they, or something similar, appear at least twice: "For wherever *two* or *three* or more are gathered in my name, I am there among them."[5]

The *Interpreters Bible* contains comments along a similar vein by theologian, Alexander C. Purdy: "The words 'It is given to die once,' suggest that judgment for each individual follows death immediately, and this interpretation would be consonant with his thought throughout; but the rapid movement of ideas directed to another end makes it dangerous to draw a final conclusion about this."

With Paul, it's always a good idea to read at least one of the verses preceding the verse one wants to present, and at least one, which follows. This helps to assure that the context of what is being expounded upon is appropriate.

As to the seeming misunderstanding on the nature and timing of Jesus' return, those of both Paul's proponents and detractors - who must insist he avoided the use of *simile, metaphor, meaningful myth*, and *allegory* and spoke only in literal terms - must ultimately conclude that Paul was not a prophet and, as such, was not the only Holy Man to have made a miscalculation on a significant issue.

But even if so, he would have been in good company. Another such person was the prominent Protestant reformer, *Martin Luther*. He once noted: "Of course the world is flat. Any fool can see that!" This was said after Columbus' return! The lesson is that ecclesiastical titles are no-guarantee that what was said by those holding them hold an especial merit. Saints and Sages are not awarded their vaunted positions for good creeds, but for their faith and good deeds!

Luther and Paul were men of faith and their efforts were for the good! Likewise, so were both the faith and works of others. Though not addressed as *Saints*, they were bestowed other honorable titles. Solomon was honored as a wise *King;* Franklin, Einstein, and Jung were, as was Ian Stevenson: *Doctors!*

Columbus was an *Admiral!*

Every American president since George Washington has been hailed: *Mr. President!* When the first woman becomes elected to that August rank, I am sure she will become: *Madam President!*

Whether one is addressed as Saint, King, Doctor, Admiral, President, Madam President, Ms, Mr., Captain, or just plain, *Hey You*, their works should be gauged upon accuracy. The title or how *holier than thou* those holding them in esteem might wish to place them doesn't count, if such an *Esteemed* proposes two plus two equals five! In such cases, the *esteemed* then becomes an esteemed Saint, King, Doctor, Admiral, President, Madam President, Mzzz, Captain, or just plain *Hey You*, holding a divergent opinion on a single subject open to serious scrutiny. This does not necessarily invalidate whatever else they might have proposed but stands as a reminder that, as was Elijah and other human beings - *like ourselves* - our passages through the Scriptures require a careful navigation. And in this navigation, some *serious scrutiny* is going to be necessary in grasping how reincarnation got *read right out*, by some mistaken, but otherwise, great minds of faith.

As to the quality of their faith or that of anyone's, that's for God to judge. It bears repeating that all we, as individuals, can see in others is determined by our own personal perception. Thus what we would judge in them, is only a judgment of that perception. So in judging, we only judge ourselves. Saint James offered that: "faith without works is dead."[6] He went on that attempts to gauge faith in others reveals but one fact: "You can see how his faith helped his works, and how by works his faith was made perfect."[7]

Paul's faith and works profoundly altered the course of Western civilization. The West would hardly be the same without the influence of its many houses of worship. While religious strife presented problems, Roman excesses were curbed and the wild tribes of the desert regions to the south and those of northern Europe were tamed.

Even *Vikings* learned kindness. If you doubt this, vacation on a Norwegian cruise ship or examine the conscientious attention to passenger safety found in Scandinavian automobiles.

Paul's ministry ended most likely in Rome. Along with Saint Peter and his wife, and much of the early Christian leadership, Emperor Nero and the Roman mob saw to his either being beheaded, crucified, or devoured by beasts. Yet Paul's promised Messiah had not appeared. But Paul preached an additional promise. His mission must go on. The Christ could not appear until the hearts and minds of all God's children had been made ready. To that end Paul promised to return if needed. *The Way* would continue:

"My little children, of whom I travail in birth *again* until Christ be formed in you."[8]

Paul's faith and Work left the world a better place than *before.*

Notes

1. Galatians 1:12
2. Ecclesiastes 3:20
3. Romans 11:2
4. Romans 8:29
5. Matthew 18:20
6. James 2:17
7. James 2:22
8. Galatians 4:19 (New English Bible)

Chapter 9

Saint Peter

Tough as nails, Jesus had named Simon Peter, the *Rock* of the disciples. When Saint Peter spoke, you paid attention. A realist and plain spoken, he pointed out the difficulties in grasping "beloved brother Paul's" complexities: "There are certain things so hard to be understood that those who are ignorant and unstable pervert their meaning."[1]

A direct eyewitness to many New Testament events, though Peter probably never met the Baptist in the flesh, this reminder from his two short epistles sum up the truths which molded his faith: "For we have not followed cunningly devised fables."[2]

Pay Attention!!!

A small business owner, he worked alongside his men fishing. Forced to deal with markets, employees, equipment, environmental concerns, taxes, payrolls, and all the similar issues of today's typical *stiff* trying to better themselves and their families (nothing is new) makes Peter, of all the disciples, the easiest for us working people to make a connection.

His story also makes for an interesting connection with an earlier biblical figure. One who also dealt with fish - but in reverse. A connecting clue might be seen in Jesus identifying Peter three consecutive times as *son of Jonah*.

It happened on Jesus' third encounter with the disciples, after the Resurrection:

"Simon Peter *son* of Jonah."[3]

Again: Three is often significant in biblical literature.

On *first* thought, the mention might merely refer to Peter's father. But on *second* thought, as men back then often had more than one wife, sometimes their kids were just as often identified in mentioning the name of the mother, as in "son of Mary"[4] or "Joseph the husband of Mary, of whom was born Jesus."[5]

Dr. Lamsa notes "the reference to Mary is to show that Jesus was born of her and not one of the other wives of Joseph." In this case

Christians would assert the passages purpose is to point out God, rather than Joseph, was Jesus' father. Peter's dad was different of course and in this context the good doctor continues: "Even today in many eastern countries, where polygamy is still practiced, whenever a son is mentioned, reference is made to his mother as the one who gave birth to him."

It seems an easier way of keeping track if there were a lot of kids. If this were the case here, and Peter's dad as was the norm, had more than one wife and child, then on *third* thought; it might be that Jesus using "son of Jonah" rather than inserting his mother's name, as was the common custom, might indeed be identifying Peter as having been Jonah in a previous life. It's a fifty-fifty chance. He was or he wasn't.

It's not too much of a stretch. Consider that if each of us is the *creation* of our past-life thoughts and deeds, and that the word *child* or *son* or *daughter* is easily substituted in place of *creation*, then the idea that Jesus, in using *son of* in referring to Peter as having been Jonah's *creation* - <u>as in Jonah's *Karmic creation*</u> – makes the whole thing not so far fetched at all. If this was the case, then Jonah and Peter's similarities may indicate actual karmic connections.

Jonah was reluctant to serve God's call and was swallowed whole, as food for seafood. Actually, according to Dr. Lamsa,[7] it didn't quite happen that way. In those times, being swallowed by a fish meant you're into something pretty deep. Today, the same thing is meant when we're being pointed out as someone being "in the hole." In ignoring Gods call, Jonah wound up "in the hole," "down the tubes," and "over his head."

He paid attention.

In realizing he'd better listen, Jonah was released and called a whole city to repentance. Many heeded his message and the city was saved.[8]

The Fisherman

Returned as Peter, it seems fitting that he's the one who gets to swallow the fish. Though reluctant to get involved, as was Jonah, Jonah/Peter again heeded the call. His words called the whole city of Rome to repentance. Many heeded his message, and to this day, the metropolis still stands as the *eternal city*. Like Jonah, Peter had a comical side. Jonah stubbornly sat in a shed expecting the demise of the town God was to spare. Peter puts on his clothes, before jumping into the water to greet Jesus.[9]

But regardless of his past-life, Peter's present-life leadership abilities were put to the test. He headed the disciples after Jesus departed and became Rome's first Bishop. This makes it important to point out where *the Rock* stood on both Paul's *before* word, denoting pre-existence, and on Paul's *again* word, as *in born again*, *birth again*, and *again*, and *again*, and so on - as in reincarnation - until you get it.

Regular Folks

Regular folks, like Peter, probably shared in a mixture of beliefs, each stemming from the inputs of Pharisees, Sadducees, and the Essenes. But I suspect most embraced reincarnation, as can be seen in Josephus. He was once a general and would well have understood the creeds of his troops. Their beliefs would have reflected those of the civilian population.

When his army was defeated and faced enslavement, he made this eloquent appeal in an effort to keep those under his command from taking their own lives: "The bodies of all men are indeed mortal, and are created out of corruptible matter; but the soul is ever immortal, and is a portion of the Divinity that inhabits our bodies... Do not you know that those who depart out of this life, according to the law of nature...obtain a most holy place in heaven, from whence *in the revolution of ages, they are again sent* into pure bodies; while the souls of those whose hands have acted madly against themselves, [as in suicide] are received by the darkest place in Hades."[10]

As you recall, he was a Pharisee and eternal consignments to *heaven*, *Hades*, and celestial bodies reflected notions of his sect. However, *in the revolution of ages, they are again sent,* reveals his outreach to the faith of the rank and file.

Jesus revealed a similar outreach in John 16:28. Like the rank and file of Josephus, the plainspoken Peter and the disciples reveal, in their response, the same commonly held understanding. Jesus said:

"I came forth from the Father and I came into the world: *again,* I am leaving the world and I am going to the father.

His disciples said to him, 'Behold, now you speak plainly."

Plainly speaking, in hearing "*again,*" the disciples *got it!*

Though often missing their teacher's meaning upon first exposure, the disciples (like ourselves) were hardly simpletons. Jesus observed in them, as in us: "For they are not of the world, just as I am not of the world."[11]

Got it?

Got It?

Notes

1. 2nd Peter 3:15-16
2. 2nd Peter 1:16
3. John 21:14-17
4. Mark 6:3
5. Matthew 1:16
6. Lamsa (1936) p. 5-6.
7. Lamsa (1936)
8. See Book of Jonah ch. 1-4
9. John 21:7
10. Wars III 8:5
11. John 17:1

Chapter 10

Voices: Hear O Israel, The Lord Thy God is One

The Gospel's authors, as you recall were Matthew, Mark, Luke, and John. What you might not recall is that Luke (often referred to as Doctor Luke) and John wrote additional biblical works. Dr. Luke, he was probably the equivalent of today's PhD, is credited with The Acts of the Apostle's and Saint John is traditionally identified as authoring the First and Second Epistles of John and the Revelation. These, along with Paul, Peter, Jesus' brother - James the Just - and yet another brother named Jude, make up the New Testament.

A fine collection, but: there were additional voices. As to why some were chosen and others deleted from the Canon, can be perplexing, particularly to proponents of reincarnation. Benign politics, as may have been the case at Nicea, might be one reason. Not so benign politics, which we'll see later, could be another. Certainly the interpretation of both the Hebrew and Christian Canon has long been subject to political pressure. Politics are not inherently evil and neither are politicians. Nothing under the sun gets done without the cooperative, as in political, interactions of all involved. Trouble usually results when there are those who, in not being heard, get left out.

The problem of mixing politics and religion wasn't resolved until after the American Constitution, though even now, issues remain.

For this *voice* or author of *non-fictional narration* (yesterday I couldn't spell it, today I are it) the subject doesn't seem so sinister at first glance. That is, the question of inclusion. In books, only so much can be included. Politics is another issue, of course.

The biblical issue, though many might disagree, is simply one of practicality in the wise and prudent application of good literary technique. Jess Stearn was one among many who felt the Bible stands among the pillars of the world's greatest literature. He loved to pontificate. He was not alone in encouraging his students, whether religious or not, to read it for examples of masterful writing along with Shakespeare, Mark Twain, Melville, the short stories of Somerset Maugham and even the *English*

Book of Common Prayer. Gospel means *good news*, and as a newspaperman, he had long preached that for words to be effective, they needed to not only be well chosen, but presented with discretion and economy.

More is not better.

I'd often heard him voice, "It doesn't get any better than the Bible!" A good example is this poetic description of Elijah's wilderness experience. The lesson: the *Voice* of God is experienced as a *still small Voice*. It's heard from within:

"And, behold, the Lord past by, and a great and strong wind rent the mountains and broke in pieces the rocks before the Lord; but the Lord was not in the wind; and after the wind an earthquake; but the Lord was not in the earthquake:

And after the earthquake a fire; but the Lord was not in the fire; and after the fire a *still small voice.*

And when Elijah heard it, he wrapped his face in his mantle and went out and stood at the entrance of the cave. And behold, there came a *voice."* (1st Kings 19: 11-13)

A Sermon

There is already enough written within the Scriptures to trigger a metaphorical wrapping of our faces in our mantels and standing at the entrance of our earthly caves and beginning to listen! Not only about reincarnation, but to hear that, as life is eternal, it's composed of many opportunities. We've been given free-will and it is up to us to make the right choices. Just as there is no free-lunch, there are no shortcuts in navigating this earthly realm. Fortunately, forgiveness, as demonstrated through the indwelling thought, or consciousness of Jesus (The Mind of the Christ, or Christ Consciousness, as Cayce voiced it) will get us through whether we're Christians in name or not. Doing, "Unto others as you would have them do unto you," is found in the wisdom traditions of all truly spiritual beliefs.

For this voice, deeds, <u>not creeds,</u> matter the most.

(Captain *L.*)

Back to the Bible

The voices that were left out of the Bible, though inspirational, it's argued, were deleted because there wasn't enough room and they offered little more in creating a sound Spiritual lesson. Seeking them now should be like looking for more information to supplement a newspaper headline or a mention in a broadcast. Interesting, but not all that necessary. It's done all the time as an editorial norm in nonfictional narration. Thus there is the understanding, that only so much could have been presented.

It makes a good *pure thought* type theory until you begin looking. Recent archaeology has discovered such a quantity and quality of new information that even the most traditional believer's must ask: how could such *Godsends* have been left out?

One such *Godsend* is the *Gospel of Thomas*. Found buried in a cave in 1945 C. E., along with over fifty other works, whose originals may date from as early as 50! (*Fifty* is not a misprint) to no later than 350 to 400, which is where scholars date their copy.[1] In comparison, the oldest extant copy of both the Old and New Testaments is the *Codex Ambrosius*. Written in the Aramaic, it dates from the sixth century.[2]

Thomas records over a hundred direct statements of Jesus, including this masterful mirroring in verse three of Elijah's insight, that as the *Voice* of God comes from within, discretion is wise in accepting what ecclesiastical hierarchies might present as *Gospel:*

> "Jesus said, "If those who lead you say to you, 'See the kingdom is in the sky,' then the birds of the sky will precede you. If they say to you, 'It is in the sea,' then the fish will precede you."

Another book, found bound within the Gospel of *Phillip* reveals the intimate sweetness between Jesus and the disciple he loved. It helps in answering an age-old question: If something is natural, how can it be sinful? Knowledge of such a verse could have prevented centuries of needless anguish for many:

> "The companion of the Savior is Mary Magdalene. Christ loved her more than all the disciples and used to kiss her often on her mouth."

(Gospel of Philip 63:32) (See Hoeller 1989 p. 65)

Similar questions might be asked about information being omitted in the Hebrew Bible. A good example is Ahab's preemptive strike against the Assyrians (roughly today's Iraq.) Though evidence of the battle abounds, his heroism, like the love between Jesus and Mary Magdalene, is not mentioned.

As for the Hebrew Scriptures, a ready answer is in looking at ancient Judaic history. First: It's very long and had a lot of time for things to simply wear out or to be forgotten. Second: because of Palestine's critical geographic location between the Orient, Africa, and the sea-lanes to Europe and Asia, ancient super *powers,* such as Egypt in seeking their own interests, made numerous incursions. Nothing is new. Assyria, Babylon, and Rome each, when at their heights, leveled the *Holy Land's* capitals and exiled its people. That even their Bible survived is a miracle.

It was translated into the *Coptic* Greek, of the city Alexander founded in Egypt. Its purpose was to serve the many *Sons and Daughters of Abraham,* living throughout the Mediterranean community, who spoke no Hebrew or Aramaic. They respected education and, as a consequence, tended toward the professions and positions of prestige and income, as is often the case today. Josephus would boast these well-assimilated ancestors of his had educated the Greeks. By the time of the Christian era's first century, about ten percent of the Roman Empire embraced Judaism and Alexandria boasted a Jewish population of about thirty percent. Mostly Essenes, they were known there as the *Therapeutae.*

Though there had been the usual religious riots in the *City of David* over nuances in the wording, despite the translation being unanimously agreed upon by seventy two-separate scholars - working independently - it was officially canonized and has survived virtually intact. Since some two hundred and fifty years before the birth of Jesus, it's been praised as the *Septuagint* (meaning seventy), which is often abbreviated to LXX. The closing chapter, which didn't go unnoticed by the Essenes/Therapeutae, still profoundly proclaims:

"Behold, I will send you Elijah the prophet."

Israel's glory days roughly ran throughout the Eighth Century B.C.E. They began with the reigns of David and Solomon and continued through the remarkable northern kingdom ruled by the dynasty of King *Omri.* Often the region was known as Omriland. Ahab, Jezebel, Ahaziah (who died early), Joram ("and Jehu smote Joram") and his sister Athalia, presided. She married the king of Judah of the same name as her departed brother: Ahaziah. Among them, one essential foreign policy prevailed. They understood that their independence, as today, depended upon keeping closely allied with strong nations to the west. In their day, it was the

Phoenician empire. The alliance was undone with the fall of the *Omrid's* at the hands of Jehu.

Elijah may have had a part as well, which Athalia wouldn't forget.

With few allies, the nation in becoming easy pickings, floundered. Though there was a brief respite under the *Hasmoneans,* or *Maccabees,* in whose dynasty Josephus had been born as a prince, the return to the tried and true foreign policies of the past came with the Herod's. Like the Omrid's, they were able administrators and as adversaries, if provoked, played *hardball.*

They understood geopolitical leverage and Rome's need to counterbalance their vulnerability to the rival Persian Empire to the east. It made up what is today's Iraq and Iran. Nothing is new.

An Arab by birth, the Roman's mentioned him as Herod *the Jew.* Historians list him as Herod *the Great.* By the end of his long rule he had outwitted, outlived, and in having ten wives, probably "out-wedded" the likes of Julius Caesar, Mark Antony, and I wouldn't be surprised, if he hadn't made moves on the Queen of the Nile herself. Though a woman, she was Egypt's last Pharaoh. Cleopatra was a beauty.

Even Augustus, who was to rise bodily to heaven according to the Roman senate (if you can't trust you're senator's word, whose can, you trust) must have become befuddled. Though history doesn't list a Herod *the Good* and a sometimes crotchety Jess Stearn, who didn't always approve of humorous approaches to the Bible and once made me back down with the challenge, "Say something funny about Herod the Great," the old tyrant's policies were seen by many as a *Godsend.*

Herod not only rebuilt the *Temple* and refortified Jerusalem's defenses, but instituted a relative regional autonomy, negotiated the lowest tax rate in the empire (Rome never making a dime on the deal[3]) and even got his subjects exempt from its military. In all this, the economy boomed. A lot had been gained and most wanted the status quo maintained. There were many among these who saw the small sect of Judaism, later to be called Christianity, as a threat. This was a key factor in their demand that Jesus die.

Still, Christian history was to be very different than that of Judaism.

Though tough going at first, since the time of Constantine's conversion, Christians, seldom suffered the destruction experienced by their brother and sister Jews. Though inevitable friction developed between the geographic borders of Christianity's other Bible believing brother and sister *Muslims,* along with the challenges of short-lived communist dictatorships in the twentieth century, and the present well-financed *Saudi Wahabbism* or *Petro-Islam* of today's headlines (other than from within itself and from within the gates of Hell) Orthodox Christendom's many sects have long fended for their collective selves and, as a group, remain the world's predominate and fastest growing religion.

For Jerusalem's Jews, a tragic breakdown between fanatical forces of zealots inflamed - as are today's Muslims - by outside interests eager for gains through political de stabilization, and a demoralized middle class unwilling or unable to curb the blind patriotic passions of their offspring, along with an incompetent diplomacy of ham-fisted bureaucrats on all sides, brought about the city's destruction during the final quarter of the first century. This is in contrast to Roman administration of its vast territory and religiously diverse population, which more often saw success. This is measurable in the empire's long historic length and in the many cases of its subjects being better off than under their previous homegrown governments

. Often these had been inept, ineffective, brutal, and corrupt. Civilians didn't complain in seeing their former official's step aside and accept bribes of citizenship, cash, and cushy villas in the far off city. Patriotism was a small price to pay for the relative peace and prosperity, called the *Pax Romana* or Roman Peace, which followed. In fact, it was a bargain. While the bloodcurdling sight and sound of her soldiers on the march, made up of sons from throughout the empire, beating the flat sides of well-sharpened swords against their shields ready for battle played a part, the average citizen living in the provinces more often saw such swords directed between imperial armies in civil strife, rather than in wars against themselves. There being no elections, an emperor could be expected to last from between two to ten years before assassination or open combat, rather than the ballot box, brought about a new *first family.*

When Paul's career began, Jerusalem was yet to fall. Yet within its walls, and those of the provinces, and even Rome itself, all understood they had a stake in the central government's stability.

Memories of Emperor Caligula lingered. His insanity was a reminder of just how fine was the line between *the good life* and catastrophe. He had directed his statue be placed in Jerusalem's temple. Fortunately, Herod Agrippa, whom you remember as, *the man of the grape,* was somehow able to get his old drinking buddy to change his mind. An assassin added to the persuasion's permanence.

Had Agrippa failed, not even he could have stopped the pandemonium and the Roman garrison's response. They could see on a daily basis that most lived better than their families back home. As there were few, if any, Jewish barracks buddies among them to insure restraint, resentment would have prevailed.

Rome's record towards spiritual seekers had normally been without blemish, though she maintained minimums of respect. Generally all that was required was an acknowledgment of the emperor's divinity, that the city had gods of its own (thank you) and that trouble makers mind their manners and keep their opinions on religion and politics to themselves.

Nobody needed to make waves.

Then came Paul.

Unlike the pictures of godlike beings Jesus and John presented, Paul was a little guy and short in stature. But when called to preach, his *voice* was second to none. The difficulties of his life might have accounted for the psychological liabilities Doctor Luke would record. It's important in understanding Paul's pluses and minuses, and especially his relationship with those commonly called Greeks: Pythagoreans, Essenes / Therapeutae, Gnostics, and the always important Perennial Philosophers. It's critical. Paul has traditionally been presented as being miles apart from the Greeks, *et al*. Present scholarship, such as *The Gnostic Paul,* by Dr. Elaine Pagels,[4] has, since its publication in 1975, long made straight the highway in correcting the miss-perception.

Paul and the Athenians

When the Apostle preached in Athens, cir. 50 C.E., he made few converts. It's unlikely that his audience had ever read Deuteronomy (30:12 - 14) and its admonition that all should think for themselves when it comes to religion because the Word of God:

"Is not in heaven, that you should say, who shall go up for us to heaven and bring it to us, that we may hear it and do it? Neither is it beyond the sea that you should say, "Who shall go over the sea for us and bring it to us, that we may hear it and do it?" But the *word* is very near you, in your mouth and in your heart, that you may do it."

Nor would they likely have read Jesus' similar sentiment:

"If they say the kingdom is in the sky."

The Athenian's were hardly birdbrains, and as such, already had the same understanding. Being an independent lot, the Apostle's apocalyptic vision that the world was soon to end, followed by an unknown god named

Jesus, who was to return and send those questioning Paul's teachings to Hell, wasn't being bought by the city's doctors of philosophy. Luke, himself a doctor of similar rank, confided as an eyewitness in Acts 17:16-34, that Paul's bizarre behavior and speech were so incredulous, that the police had to be called. Many asked in dismay: "What does this babbler want?"

But Paul hadn't been entirely dismissed. His keen intellect, formidable debating skills, and sheer doggedness would not allow for such. Luke described the Athenian good doctors, in terms typifying academics everywhere: "uninterested in anything except something new to tell or to hear." But unexpectedly, and surely to Luke's embarrassment, Paul insulted them: "Men of Athens, I see that above all things you are extravagant in the worship of idols."

Insulting their beliefs hardly opened the hearts and minds of the ancient world's ivied hall of learning. Its men and women no more worshiped idols than do New Yorkers worship the Statue of Liberty, the redoubtable baseball stars of the *Mets*, and in a similar vein, no Baltimorean ever worshiped the old *Colts* (well, maybe the old *Colts)!* Baseball and football aside, the same can be said for worshipers, wherever two or three or more are gathered, worshiping in today's typical church, mosque, ashram, mountain top, teepee, home, or synagogue!

Sincere believers don't worship idols! Sincere believers don't *voice* hurtful words like infidel, heathen, or pagan! Nor do they *voice* the hurtful words: honky, nigger, kike, gook, or rag head!

Such words, and the sentiments they represent, have no place among the faithful.

The dignity the *Men of Athens* hard earned positions deserved, even if Paul disagreed with them, should still have garnered his respect. He was, after all, a man of the cloth. But as so many of the truly important issues among the Greeks and the Hebrews were similar (as are so many of the truly important issues among most religions of today), and as most persons of the cloth don't characteristically exhibit rudeness, Paul's outburst may pinpoint psychological problems that had little to do with a theology.

Understanding this is important. The simplicity and beauty, which lay at the heart of his message, that a caring God defined as *love incarnate*, had offered a way for the soul's salvation through forgiveness should not become lost among a wrangling of issues.

As to the wrangling of issues between Paul and the Athenians, though Jewish, Paul's schooling included the fine Greek, which had normally stood him so well. He might not have read Pythagoras, Plato and

Aristotle directly, but he would have been well exposed to their beliefs through such sources as Cicero and others, which were then in vogue.

During a later time, 1871 c. e., an old time Master Mason, Albert Pike (the same Albert Pike whose famous *Peak* still bears his name) wrote in his 861page volume, *Morals and Dogma*,[5] which concerns Freemasonry, about one such treatise by Cicero.

Paul would have heard this *Voice* of Pythagoras:

"God is the Universal Soul, resident everywhere in nature, and of which our souls are but emanations."[6]

With the same enthusiasm, as had Alexander's and would Paul's trigonometry teachers, along with those of the founding mothers and fathers - especially the astute scholar of the Greeks, Thomas Jefferson - Pythagoras' equally as accurate theorem would have likewise been imparted: "In right angled triangles, the square of the hypotenuse equals the sum of the squares on the other sides."

Pythagoras knew what he was about!

He also knew that two plus two always equals four.

Pike further noted the respected scholar, Justin Martyr, though some centuries after Paul, also quoted Pythagoras. *The Voice*, and the wisdom which had derived the Pythagorean Theorem, spoke with the same persuasion. It remains unchanged from that of Alexander, Paul, and Jefferson, to our own time:

"God is *One* ...the Light of Heaven, the Father, the Intelligence, the Soul of all beings, the Mover of all spheres!"[7]

The Great Seal of the United States.

Magnificent eagles have long been featured on national emblems. The U.S. version is unique. The olive branch of peace is extended in the bird's right talon. In contrast, most nations depict such talons holding swords or lightning bolts. Note that the eagle's eye looks toward the direction of peace, though potential enemies are forewarned in the arrows held to the left.

Overhead is a six-sided constellation composed of thirteen five pointed stars. (Shown here with connecting dots for greater clarity.)

To Masons, six refers to the Divine and five symbolizes humanity. While the configuration resembles the Star of *David*, dictionaries define two such equally intersecting equilateral triangles as the older *Pythagorean* star - the symbol of *Pythagoras!* Benjamin Franklin, John Adams and Thomas Jefferson submitted the design for congressional approval. Since 1782, it has authenticated the signature of our nation's every president.

Paul, like any good student studying Pythagoras, grasped that the twelve gods of Olympus were perceived, by the knowledgeable, as a single collective entity. The highly monotheistic Plato addressed them as *Heaven*. Today, many good Catholics of Paulist persuasion, as well as the faithful of other religions, likewise believe in God's multifaceted presence. As a way of grasping an enlightened appreciation of His/Her ever-present nature, today's believers, rather than looking to Olympus, look to the behavioral functions of the twelve sainted disciples of Jesus, and a myriad of other saints. As an individual aspect of God's goodness, Peter kindly opens the *pearly gates*, Mary tends to the feminine side of things, and Saint Christopher protects the weary traveler. Certainly, few represent aspects of the good better than Saint Valentine and Santa Clause.

Collectively, as Plato had discerned in his gods, such sainted beings embody *Heaven*. Cayce, like Pythagoras, spoke of this *Heaven* as *Oneness*. He addressed it as: "The creative forces which you call God." His prayers often began in revering this collective *Oneness* as "Father/Mother God."

Oneness would have been a good place for Paul to start. Even in his time, as debating religion usually ended in all sides losing, there would have been a need for a constructive dialogue, rather than a debate. Another area where he could have begun was in the shared Hebrew and Greek understanding that human souls were created in the image of their creator: "In the image of God… male and female he created them."[8]

Both believers shared a mutual problem. The problem resulted from returning the compliment. That is, in assigning human qualities to their gods, capricious behaviors were depicted in the Greco/Roman deities and seen in the vacillating and sometimes wrathful qualities, and gender bias, projected upon the Hebrew god itself. Such personifications were distracting in that so-called mortals weren't always sure how gods should act. This made it more difficult for the Pythagoreans, Paul himself, and even Jesus, in calling upon the created to behave as their Creator.

Remember, Jesus' reminder, *you are gods*. Paul put it this way, "And this Spirit bears witness to our spirit, that we are the children of God; and if children, then heirs, heirs of God and joint heirs with Jesus Christ."[9]

In the twentieth century, Cayce made the same call to remembrance. Always the practical prophet, he went on that a mere intellectual realization wasn't enough. For when the soul's divinity is realized as being an aspect of God, and was, in being a part of the whole, a God itself, then such a *God* should do something about it: "What are ye going to do about it"?[10] For Cayce, the correct pattern was to be found in Jesus: "For indeed in him, the Father God, ye move and have thy being. Act like it! Don't act like ye think ye are a God! Ye may become such, but when ye do ye think not of thyself. For what is the pattern? Jesus thought it not robbery to make himself equal with God, but He acted like it in the earth."

Cayce, like Paul and Jesus, offered this as the path to salvation: "Jesus life is offered rather that ye may apply the principles of truth, patience, longsuffering, brotherly [sisterly] love, kindness, gentleness. For if ye would be forgiven, ye must forgive."

And Forgive would have been the *something new to tell and new to hear* that the Greeks had sought. The best that Plato had been able to come up with, in dealing with the pain and unhappiness, which seemed so axiomatic to the human condition, was that *Heaven* was blameless. He could offer little on how these might be overcome, other than through the difficult route of karma.

That the Divine offered a *Way*, motivated through love, "For God so loved the world,"[11] led the Greeks to create the enlightened Christianity of *Gnostism*.

Paul and the Greeks had their differences, but because they had so many areas upon which they agreed his rudeness toward the Athenians might have been attributable to stress. He endured quite a lot throughout his turbulent life and ministry and evidence of psychological problems occurred at other times and in other places. He once let loose an outburst so intense that Porcius Festus, Judea's governor - while in the open court of King Agrippa himself - compassionately counseled the Apostle: "Paul, you are overwrought. Much study has made you mad."[12]

Paul and the Perennial Philosophers

Among the perennial philosophers, no less a figure than Thomas Jefferson had found the many interpretations of Paul a pain. None of the words attributed to the saint were included in the president's personal book of devotions, which he titled, The Philosophy of Jesus. Compiled over a sixteen-year period, being completed when Jefferson was seventy-seven, it was published by order of Congress in 1904, nearly 100 years after its inception. Known today as the Jefferson Bible,[13] essentially, only the direct descriptions and words of Jesus are quoted. This may reflect Jefferson's desires to minimize sectarian issues in his seeking universal spiritual truths, rather than any wholesale dismissal of Paul – though he generally detested the doctrines of Paulians.

As to the principles found in the Master's message, Jefferson's approach identified three main points in declaring, "the doctrines of Jesus are simple, and tend all to the happiness of man." (1) God is one (2) there is a future state of rewards and punishments and (3) all should "love God with all thy heart and thy neighbor as thyself."[14]

Jefferson called these *pure principles*, which, for him, embodied the teachings of all true religion and spiritual endeavor.

Those leading their lives with such conviction may disembark. There is little else that can top these three. *Nothing is new*, whether *under the sun* or in these pages. But as there are no refunds for their purchase, whether your faith is up to that of a Jefferson, or you still suffer sleepless nights and free flowing anxiety, attributable to fears of death (which Jungian analysis will reveal at mega-dollars per hour) your biggest bang for the buck, in terms of pages to be read per unit of cost, will be found in continuing.

Jefferson was a man so down to earth, and of such common sense, that the invention of a plow and the wheelbarrow have been attributed to him. This shouldn't go unnoticed. Nor should his direct dealing in getting to the heart of the Gospels. Like Saint Mark, Jefferson did not waste words. Nor was he one to leave out the essential key to understanding biblical reincarnation, seen in the *Saga of a Certain Three*:

"And the same John had his raiment of *camels' hair*, and a leathern *girdle* about his loins . . . Herod on his birthday made a supper to his lords, high *captains*, and chief estates . . . And *she* said, 'the head of John the Baptist!'"[15]

That many lifetimes of spiritual expression are needed, because there are so many expressions of God's goodness that need learning, might have been a factor in Jefferson's creating Virginia's law of religious freedom:

"We the General Assembly of Virginia do enact that no man [woman] shall be compelled to frequent or support any religious worship . . . but that all shall be free to profess, and by argument to maintain, their opinions in matters of religion."

It was the first such statute of its type in the country. The considerable political infighting, required in its passage, had earned Jefferson many enemies among the bigoted. Attacked by them as an atheist, his defense rests in this description left in his little Bible: "It is a document in proof that I am a *real* Christian, that is to say, a disciple of the doctrines of Jesus."[16]

Understanding Jefferson is important, as his *Greek*-like mind mirrors the many whose thoughts and actions undergird the freedom of today's seeker.

While its clear Jefferson considered himself a *real* Christian, it takes a little more doing in determining where he stood as a *real* Christian, in embracing reincarnation. If he had been a Freemason, the issue would be easier. Masonic membership is usually a good litmus test, though entry level members and most of the general public perceive the craft as a philanthropic social club. In contrast, the order's eschatological foundations are well known to old time Master Masons. Ranked among them are at least seventeen American past presidents.

These include not only Washington and Franklin Roosevelt, as we've seen, but also *Teddy* Roosevelt and Woodrow Wilson. Both received Nobel peace prizes. Other members were Truman, Ford, and Jefferson's young law student and protégé, James Monroe.

Yet Jefferson made no claims to membership and modern Mason's are reluctant to claim him as having been a card-carrying brother. This is due, in some part, to insufficient evidence. One problem is that Jefferson was a somewhat secretive sort. He was not only the father of modern *cryptology* (the science of code making) but also kept quiet about his religious beliefs, "I not only write nothing on religion, but rarely permit myself to speak on it." Curiously, that the similarity stands so close to sentiments printed in *Sacred Laws,* which is a guidebook placed prominently in Masonic lodges, hints at his membership. *Sacred Laws* encourages a good Mason: "In refraining from discussion on religious topics."

Many of Jefferson's personal thoughts were recorded in his letters. At present, large numbers can be seen on the University of Virginia's website: *Thomas Jefferson Digital Archive.* Upon his death, twenty six *thousand* were found, along with sixteen thousand responses! But even among his most intimate associates, he kept his spiritual views candid. His fear was that they might fall into the hands of his opponents. His rather mild statement, at least by today's standards: "It does me no injury for my neighbor to say there are twenty gods, or no god. It neither picks my pocket nor breaks my leg,"[17] was attacked with such vehemence that Jefferson was labeled the "Infidel from Virginia."

As a consequence, his works were banned from the Philadelphia library for thirty years! Religion was such a part of the time's electoral realities, that even a hint of something as volatile as reincarnation, would have cost him his political fortune. It could also have cost him his physical life. Memories of Massachusetts witch trials lingered and in tidewater Virginia, now called Hampton Roads, persecutions continued. *Witchduck Road* still exists in Virginia Beach. So named because, those accused of witchcraft (all *Levites* of course) were dragged down that very road and sat in a ducking stool. Weighted with Bibles, when ducked, if they drowned, their innocence was rewarded in heaven. If they floated, hanging or worse, could come next.

Jefferson's election, like that of president Bush (*the younger*) became too close to call. The House of Representatives had to settle the issue, and even then, it took *thirty-six* separate balloting attempts to break the deadlock.

The necessity of his public avoidance of personal religious issues, makes for a challenging search in locating evidence, even hinting at reincarnation, that sometimes stand out so conspicuously in Paul: *whatever a man sows, that shall he also reap.*

Additionally, 18th century Masonic memberships were customarily kept secret and many of the order's records were destroyed during the revolutionary war. Along with these went many a good Mason. Many died. Among them might have been some who could have provided more information. This may account for the mystery, though right after his death, at least twenty-nine Masonic references mentioned him as having been a devotee.[18] That, the *Declaration of Independence*, his major work, was signed by many of like mind may also be significant.[19] As to other evidence, Jefferson's closeness to similar thinking persons, suggests a sharing of beliefs.

He also corresponded with major *Unitarian* thinkers. A *smoking gun* was his mention: "there is not a young man now living in the U.S. who will not die a *Unitarian.*"[20] An examination of Unitarian thinking of that time reveals yet another *smoking gun*. Unitarian ideas had found their roots in the growing transcendentalism, as we have seen, which was established in 1781, by Emanuel Kant: "If we could see ourselves and other objects as they really are, we should see ourselves in a world of spiritual natures, our community with which neither began at our birth nor will end with the death of the body."[21] Later, in the New England of the 1830s, the embracement of pre-existence stood out in the *smoking gun* of the foremost mind of the Unitarian ministry, Frederic Hedge: "The *supposition of pre-existence…* seems best to match the supposed continued existence of the soul hereafter. The eternal destination which faith ascribes to the soul *presupposes an eternal origin.*"[22] Many Unitarians' claim Jefferson's discipleship, as do many Masons, and the Episcopal parish in Williamsburg, Virginia. His name is still emblazoned on the front pew where he publicly prayed. He apparently attended during those periods when he was a legislator and on becoming the state's governor.

Unitarianism, as an organization, would experience periods of upheaval. Today it is known as the *Universalist-Unitarian* church and accepts a broader range of belief. This may allow pre-existence its detractors. Universalist-Unitarian's claiming Jefferson's support, has merit. But such claims must acknowledge that the teachings of its founders were what had attracted him, including this primary teaching of his beloved Jesus: *You are gods.*

It may be that Jefferson sided with all three. Masonic, and Transcendental/Unitarian thought was lively, his buddies thought the same way, and though he often avoided church, there might have been times, especially if the sermon were short, when he found solace in the beauty of its traditional ritual. Cayce and Jung placed a great value in such traditions. But Jefferson might have belonged to yet another organization.

It paralleled Masonic thought and was known as *Rosicrucianism*. Rosicrucians claim an order known as the *Knights Templar* were among their predecessors. That their cross, rather than Spain's Maltese cross was displayed on Columbus' sails, indicates yet another reminder of the

Perrinial philosophy's participation in American history. (Freemasons also list the Templars among their ancestors. They protected pilgrims traveling to the Holy land.) Some of these organizations trace their origins back to the times of Solomon's temple and the Pyramid builders of earliest Egypt. A hint as to why America's founders, seemingly so far removed from the Nile, would utilize such a structure might be seen in the meaning of the *Egyptian* word *Ka.* It means Soul! *A - Meri* are the English equivalent of *Place Of The or Great Land.* Putting them together sees *AMerIKa* translate as *Place of the Soul* and sometimes *Great Beloved Land.* Check out Krajenke (1976), Dr. Quest (1969) and Dr. Hironimus (1989) in the Bibliography. They're more believable than the far-fetched theory that our nation's name was from the geographer, *Amerigo Vespucci.*

Geography honors an explorer with their last names. Not the first. *Vespucciland?*

With all due respect to Italian Americans everywhere: I don't think so!

Be that as it may, further evidence of reincarnation friendly feelings stand out, as we've seen in Einstein and Jefferson's similar advocacy of the Greeks. Though he criticized some as *Platonists,* he generally supported Plato. But in politics, he leaned more toward Aristotle's practicality. Those advocating approaches seen in Plato's *Republic*, would have been dismissed as pie in the sky amateurs, by a hard nosed political pro like Jefferson. He well knew the ins and outs of Platonic/Aristotelian dialogue, having long read the *Greek* in the original.

Not bad for a guy who, in his late teens, flunked out of the College of William and Mary. Its *Greek* alumnae insist this was the case (especially whenever a case of beer or two or three or more are gathered - and sometimes a *fifth*) and mention is made of their alma mater's arch rival, the University of Virginia. Its *Greeks*, of course, disagree. While agreeing that Jefferson never graduated, they make the case, after consuming a few or more themselves, that their founding father left because he was so smart, that he very quickly absorbed all that the little college could teach in the two short years he attended.

Both sides agree on two points: (1) by age twenty four, despite his considerable wealth which precluded his having to work, he had become a highly successful lawyer on his own merits and (2) at the same age when Alexander was abusing human rights, the only *highs* Jefferson's cases contained resulted from the heady fervor of a fighter dedicated to the defense of those rights: "I have sworn upon the altar of god, eternal hostility against every form of tyranny over the mind of man."[24]

As for Aristotelian and Platonic politics, I recall such debates in my college classes. I also recall that, like Alexander, Jefferson was a man of vision and possessed an unparalleled faculty for leadership. Unlike Alexander, Jefferson demonstrated an admirable level of higher spirituality. This higher level would have evolved from lessons learned in past lives. Such lessons could account for his mastery of classical Greek and his successful statesmanship. Aristotle stands redeemed in this revelation concerning Jefferson: "The entity then, as *Thomas Jefferson*, made contributions to the... people - that are well known... Before that we find the entity... made for the rise and fall of many lands... when that entity... *Alexander the Great* made for the conquering forces of the earth."[25]

Jefferson's advocacy of Jesus suggests an insight that real Christians can base their faith in the simplicity and beauty of His teachings alone. *Reading in and reading out* their wisdom, based upon the secondary sources of preachers pushing their individual brands of Paulian interpretation, and the resulting strife, would not have been something advocated by Jefferson. I suspect he felt that God's universal and many faceted nature allowed for a variety of universal and many faceted approaches.

Unitarian/Rosicrucian/Masonic membership, or the influence of its members, could have sparked his searching the Bible for reincarnation. He would have read the Elijah, Ahab, and Jezebel saga. That he was aware of a connection is seen in the unusual inclusion of John, Herod, and Herodias in a Bible otherwise exclusively devoted to Jes

About now, if you're a meat and potato type, you're chomping at the bit to get to the meat and potatoes of these and other cases. If you can't wait, go ahead and jump to Chapter Fifteen, which is titled *The Grand Slam*. It's your book! You can *dog ear* this page and get back. Be sure to check Chapter Twelve. It addresses *Shore Leave.*

However, I think you'll do better in exercising patience and reading on. The reason is that the impact of the evidence, for many, will be determined by how well the *voices* read here, demonstrate that the Scriptural verses supportive of reincarnation have been presented in the same context as had their authors intended. This is why it's so important that you keep in mind that reincarnation was historically mainstream among the learned throughout the ages, which included biblical times. Keep in mind, as you will soon see, that this was always the case until reincarnation was surreptitiously side tracked in the sixth century.

A convincing case for reincarnation, as Jefferson would have determined, could have been made easier, without the ambiguity of the Paulian's input. But such a case would still have had to rely upon philosophical proofs, as today's scientific data was not available. Now that such data is at hand, obtained through modern research at Jefferson's own school, and is bolstered with biblical history, the teachings of Jesus, and the knowledge of Paul's personal pre-existence persuasion, an unprecedented combination of biblical cohesion and scientific agreement can be established. The measure of such a blessing might one day move the world's people toward a new level of faith and resulting good *Works*.

Another Sermon

As for Jefferson's good Works, his purchase of the Louisiana Territory effectively ended the Old World's expansion into North America. Among his intentions for the new land, was the creation of a slave-free area where African, European, and Native Americans could learn to live together. He would have been encouraged in seeing the educational opportunities offered to Virginia Indians during his college days at William and Mary. Still, he expected the overall process to take a thousand years.

That he owned a hundred and fifty slaves was a reality, which he had inherited. (You've read of his defense in Chapter 3) He abhorred the situation and made numerous legislative attempts to end the nightmare. Unfortunately, the political, social, and economic realities during his lifetime prevented its abolition. Critics fail to consider that the revolutionary war had a heavy toll. The Constitution was barely in place and a second war for independence (the War of 1812) was in the making. Brits don't like losing. A divided nation couldn't have survived.

Emancipation, on such a large scale had never been attempted and it's doubtful anyone had the necessary expertise to make it a success. That such expertise was lacking is seen in the many freed African-Americans who died of starvation and deprivation after the War Between the States, as well as their *rank-and-file* brother and sister southerners of European descent. Dirt poor, they had fought for their homes, not for slavery. Few, if any, owned slaves, including their General, Robert E. Lee.

Jefferson couldn't easily follow President Washington, as had many, in freeing family slaves in their wills. Virginia law, at that time, often forced freed persons to leave the state and the kind treatment characteristic of places like Monticello. Additionally, our third president died broke. He served for many years with little pay. By gentleman's agreement, foreclosures were suspended until after his passing. Owing all, and owning nothing, most of his assets had long been frozen; he met his *Maker* on the Fourth of July!

Through Jefferson's efforts, religion remains free, popular, and prolific. In America, and in nations where his *Work* has been heeded, individuals may freely *voice* their beliefs. Like *Saint* Paul, *President* Jefferson was a *Real* Christian.   (Captain *L*)

Paul's Life and Ministry

Doctor Luke recorded (Acts 9:3-30) that Jesus confronted Paul in a vision. He was ordered (his name, at that time, was Saul) to cease and desist his persecution of the Christian community: "Saul, Saul, why do you persecute me?"

The Apostle fell to the ground and remained blind for three days. The result was his conversion. *Born again*, he dropped the name Saul, and became Paul. But his new life was one of turmoil and danger. Past enemies sought revenge and those opposing his new-found faith hounded him. He was to anguish over many issues as dissension ran rampant throughout his little flock.

Its members quarreled continuously over whether Gentile converts could eat at the same table with Jewish converts. Questions over circumcision and dietary laws were also of concern. A profound personal issue can be seen in this epistle.

Romans 6:19 sweetly proclaim that spirituality and sexual expression are compatible:

"For as you have yielded your *members* to the servitude of uncleanliness and iniquity, so now yield your *members* to the servitude of righteousness and holiness."

Whether or not such *members* were sexual wouldn't seem an issue. Here, as many preachers point out, they might have been. But probably most agree that all human bodily *members*, regardless of their function, should be used with the best of intent. Thus a spiritually-evolved being would express such use in a more conscientious manner, than they might have expressed in some past period of lesser enlightenment. It wouldn't seem to matter whether the activity had been sexual or otherwise.

On this point, I don't think that Jung, Skinner, Dr. Ruth Westheimer or even Freud would have disagreed, let alone Mr. and Mrs. Martin Luther (who together conceived seven children) nor the highly spiritual Solomon and his entourage of 700 wives and 300 concubines! (He took some bad press over the issue, not for their numbers, but because some had been foreigners.)

But unfortunately, in other passages, Paul's pundits push that he condemned sexuality for himself:

"For we know that the law is spiritual; but I am of the flesh enslaved to sin ... For it is not the good that I wish to do; but it is the evil that I do not wish to do, [his sexuality?] That I do ... O wretched man that I am."[26]

Such a statement, if actually addressing sexuality, forces the spiritually-minded free thinker to ponder which, if any, of these revelations reveal the word of a compassionate God, or simply reveal the word of a compassionate, but very troubled, guy - and even more troubled followers. Guys and gals, and genders in between, pushing that Paul's perceived personal sexual issues apply personally to them, as well as to the rest of us, might do well in rethinking a quick point or two or more and rereading his statements seen in chapter three.

And Yet Another...

1.   Oftentimes, the interpretations given to such passages reveal more about the *hang-ups* of those expressing them, than they do about their author. Libido levels and their natural expression among consenting adults, while they may reflect genetics and social conditioning, often have little to do with one's level of spirituality.

2.   While the Bible reveals the *Word,* it also reveals the words of human beings. Like Elijah/John and Paul, who lived in a world and time far different that our own, they were *like ourselves*. And in being like us, they were unique individuals; in the same manner that each of us is unique. Thus what might have been appropriate for them, in their particular circumstance, would not necessarily be appropriate in our own. Never forget Paul's disclaimers that many of his concerns were his personally – and not necessarily God's.

3.   Appreciating Paul, I've learned, requires a similar effort in appreciating the work of any great artist, whether with words - as was the *Apostle*, or with other media, like the painter Van Gogh. Like Paul, Van Gogh had

> deep psychological challenges. He cut off his ear. Nevertheless, nearly everyone loves his paintings. Would such love be enhanced in devotees cutting off their own ears? The same consideration must be made for Paul. The man had difficulties. Historians and theologians largely agree.[23]
>
> Would loving Paul be enhanced in devotees mimicking or otherwise taking on his personal psychological issues?
>
> (Captain *L)*

Back to the Man

No one needed to have been a psychic back then, in predicting that Paul's pain, if taken by devotees as anything more than a very dear person's personal cry for help, would fill the couches of psychiatrists throughout the foreseeable future. For himself and many among *The Way,* mega-levels of stress would be the norm. While thoughts of salvation would have been healing, they came at a fearfully high psychological price.

Added to this was that he had once been a member of the feared temple police. It was the same force that had investigated John and later arrested Jesus. It's highly likely that some of those Paul persecuted wound up crucified.

Supposedly, he had never met Jesus in the flesh. But it's possible that he had witnessed and, in his job as a censor of thought, he was employed in the despicable profession at the time, might have participated at some level in the execution itself!

The insight of a Jungian analyst isn't necessary in determining that while Paul's efforts were both heroic and sincere, along with stress, a heavy baggage of guilt had to have accompanied him. Evidence stands in that despite the empire's remarkable policies of religious toleration, Paul managed to get himself flogged on four separate occasions. They gave him 39 lashes each time (40 will kill you)! Shipwrecked, stoned, jailed, the target of assassins, run out of town, Luke had surely counseled (though no such evidence is recorded): "Paul, Paul, why do you persecute thyself?"

Rome spent a small fortune on Paul's personal security costs. But the government had no choice. His wealthy family had held the means to purchase not only his superior education, but also the Roman citizenship, which he had inherited. As a citizen, he had an entitlement to protection and once an entire regiment was needed to fend off those he had angered. Though he moved within the circles of the powerful, the privilege could be attributed to *old money*. The family's considerable income derived from manufacturing tents. Their chief customer was undoubtedly the Roman army itself. This same army had captured Athens (the Athenians had chosen to fight) and the scholar's extra precaution and even resentment, concerning Paul, was doubly understandable. This led to stress on all sides. And it was this stress which had lead to the divisiveness.

The problem wasn't theology.

The School of Athens

The learned of Athens, like those of Alexandria, would have delighted in a display of his considerable intellect. The dialectical fireworks, of which he was capable, were legendary. But despite their keen interest in things new to tell or to hear, they would hardly have found subjects concerning circumcision and celibacy of interest.

If Paul wanted their ear, he would have had to earn the privilege. They would not have asked questions casually especially to one who had attacked them so vociferously. Though it's doubtful, they feared going to Hell because of Paul (he was a little guy) there would have been, at some level in their minds, a voice reminding them that if they were, indeed, to go to such a place, then they may as well go down swinging.

Academics can be formidable. If you have ever faced the wrath of an enraged dean of the University of Maryland engineering school, dealt with the inquisitive mind of a Jess Stearn, tried to attract the attention of Ian Stevenson, Jesuits, and publishers, then you know the stresses and problems' Paul faced.

As to the problems these, were not due to the insensitivity of scholarly types, quite the contrary, most are very sensitive. At issue was that, like today, they're usually very busy with their own research and have little time to waste on indolent students and those proposing unsound ideas. Additionally, most in the profession have worked very hard to gain and maintain their reputations and need to be mindful of those wishing a free ride upon their academic coat-tails. (In this case, toga-tails.) Championing an-up-and coming scholar, or participating on the cutting edge of new ideas and concepts, has its rewards. On the other hand, the endorsement of folly results in reputations being destroyed virtually overnight.

Their examination would have required of Paul, a thorough and ready knowledge of Socrates, Plato, Pythagoras, and Aristotle. As a way of comparison, Pike's Masonic treatise referenced them no less than ninety-four times! But the evidence suggests Paul was knowledgeable and had a deep appreciation for their wisdom. However, the level of dialectic demanded would be stressful. But anyone, who had undergone a flogging for his beliefs, wouldn't have felt a polite discourse among Athenian academics to be threatening. The worst these guys could have dished out, other than a well-deserved cerebral *Charlie horse* between Paul's ears, would have been a C+.

But he was an able infielder and up to the task. He could field the rhetorical line drives of even the heaviest of hitters and turn their best shots into double and even triple plays.

He would have needed an in depth grasp of the Hebrew Scriptures. That he excelled in and revered their knowledge was unquestioned. He had the right stuff! It would be his first time in the big leagues. But he was a big leaguer!

His *ace in the hole* was that among academics, winning or losing was not that important. Foremost, then as now, is the quality of the game. Paul would only need to have played well, to impress upon his fellow intellectuals, that he had brains! As a result, a considerable reward would have been his (and that of the *Way*) in a warm invitation to walk among them, as an honored member of the *School of Athens*. He was worthy of such an honor.

But if a personal perception of low self-esteem were present, due to guilt and aggravated by stress, he might not have allowed himself such an accolade. Remember, he had once been of such a low stature, as a *policer of thought* that he had imposed upon the minds of others the most heinous of tyrannies: the denial that *you are gods!* It was the same tyranny that a later firebrand of equal intensity would "Swear upon the altar of God" to oppose. That, Paul would now be praised by those, who's thinking exemplified the highest, would have required of him, a heaping dose of self-forgiveness.

While he could preach forgiveness for others, he might not have been able to *walk the talk* and preach forgiveness for himself. Jung spoke of a psychological *shadow side.* In Paul's case, such a psychological process might have shadowed the inner vision of his own inherent worthiness as an unconditionally loved child of God. A child so loved that, despite Paul's past, he was being offered the same unconditional forgiveness that had been so easy for him to impart to others.

The lesson in this is that not only must we forgive others, but that we must also forgive ourselves. In Paul forgiving himself, his life might have come out differently.

Execution could have been avoided.

Unfortunately, his day with the *Greeks* proved to be a lost opportunity. But he was not alone in the loss. The result left the impression that he and they had quarreled. This surely led to the political easing out of valuable insights in the Scriptures and some serious errors of later mindsets. *Barbarous* mindsets, moving at the pace and precision of a rusty *Commodore 64* (during a Los Angeles brownout) they directed the sharp swords which drove Gnostic Christianity from Europe. The result brought about the *barbaric* thousand-year terror of the *Dark Ages*. Had the disaster been avoided, the world would have been far different than today. So much so, that the equivalent of *Columbus Day* (Viva Italia!) would be celebrated, not in honoring men returning from obscure islands in wooden ships, but celebrated in both men and women returning in spaceships from the planet Mars.

If only.

But *Forgive* wasn't heard that day in Athens. And in a world of should have; could have; might have; and if only: The loss of such an opportunity became, like so many other lost opportunities, another reminder that we as students, whether schooled in that of Athens, Alexandria, or in that of the *University of Hard Knocks* must keep on keeping on in our studies! For ultimately our curriculum, called life, leads too but one understanding: that salvation begins only with the *awakening* of the soul.

Once achieved, the return to God - through the forgiving thought of the *Christ Consciousness* can begin. But no matter how eagerly we might strive, the process can be long and arduous. Many of us have drifted far off course and as it is God's will that none should perish, we've got to pull together, lest someone is left behind. And so it is, that the race toward salvation is one that must be run not only with patience, but with the love Paul preached so long ago. While his experience with the Greeks might have left the impression that he and they were at odds, it just wasn't the case. But it didn't go unrewarded. The experience taught, that while everyone can hear the same *voice*, some listen as *wise* Greeks, and others listen as *unwise* barbarians. Unending efforts must continue, until wisdom and understanding reach the hearts of *everybody*. Then, all of humanity may finally open their eyes to see and open their ears to hear.

In the meantime, writers will write, politicians will politic and preachers will preach - as had Paul:

"*Greeks, Barbarians,* the *wise* and the *unwise,* for it is my duty to preach to *everybody.*"   (Romans 1:14)

Hear O Israel, The Lord Thy God is Love

"Though I speak with the tongues of men and angels, and have not love, I am become as sounding brass or a tinkling cymbal.

And though I have the gift of prophecy, and understand all mysteries and all knowledge; and though I have all faith, so that I could remove mountains, and have not love, I am nothing.

And though I bestow all my goods to feed the poor, and though I give my body to be burned, and have not love, it profiteth me nothing.

Love suffereth long and is kind; love envieth not; love vaunteth not self, is not puffed up.

Doth not behave itself unseemly, seeketh not her own, is not easily provoked, thinketh no evil;

Rejoiceth not over iniquity, but rejoiceth in the truth;

Beareth all things, believeth all things, hopeth all things endureth all things.

Love never faileth: but whether there be prophecies, they shall fail; whether there be tongues, they shall cease; whether there be knowledge, it shall vanish away.

For we know in part, and we prophesy in part.

But when that which is perfect is come, then that which is in part shall be done away.

When I was a child, I spake as a child; but when I became a man, I put away childish things.

For now we see through a glass darkly; but then face-to-face: now I know in part; but then shall I know even as also I am known.

And now abideth faith, hope, love, these three; but the greatest of these is love."

(1st Corinthians 13:1-13) King James Version

The Voice: How the Bible Reveals Reincarnation

Notes

1. Hoeller (1989)
2. Lamsa (1971)
3. Millar (1993) p. 50
4. Pagels (1975)
5. Pike (1871)
6. Ibid. p. 667
7. Ibid.
10. (4083-1)
11. John 3:16
12. Acts 27:24
13. Jefferson Bible (1989)
14. Padover (1970) p.1
15. Jefferson Bible (1989) P.39-41
16. Padover (1970) p. 167
17. Podover (1970) p.116
18. Heironimus (1989) p. 37- 43
19. Ibid p. 39
20. Jefferson Bible (1989) p. ix
23. Kranjenke (1976) p. 8-10
24. Padover (1970) p.119
25. (1208-1)
26. Romans 7:24
27. See A.N. Wilson (1997) p.30 - 35

On Course

Chapter 11

Others

In offering commentaries on beloved brother Paul, as many respectfully addressed his memory, Theodotus, a learned Greek of Gnostic thought, offered that the apostle's revelation: "Greeks and Barbarians, the wise and the unwise; for it is my duty to preach to everybody," recognized that Paul, "taught in two ways at once." Theodotus understood: "Each one knows the Lord in his own way: and not all know him alike."[1] The observation, as obvious in truth concerning human beings as were Galileo's observations concerning the stars, saw the good father branded as a heretic. Unlike the good astronomer, Gnostics, like Theodotus, have yet to have their names cleared.

This can be seen in the normally more open *New Catholic Encyclopedia* listing Gnostics as:

"Pseudo-Christians...anti-Christians...pagans, and one of the worst dangers faced by Christianity."

Other denominations often offer similar sentiments. Theologians term the early oppressors of Gnostics as *heresiologists. Thought cops* might be more appropriate.

This will not be an easy chapter. Faith, hope, and - *the greatest of these* - must stand as our waymarks in circumventing the painful rocks and shoals from a stormy past not yet left behind. Batten down the hatches!

Paul's work, as we've seen here and in mainstream history, was developed under arduous circumstances. Not so well known is that not all of his work was completed by himself. These portions are known as the Deutero-Pauline or *Pastoral* letters. Included among them are the epistles to the Ephesians, Colossians, and 2nd Thessalonians, which most scholars agree were not his. Virtually all agree that 1st & 2nd Timothy and Titus are products of the Paulian School, which came about after his death. Knowing that Paul, the man, never wrote: "I do not think it seemly for a woman to debate publicly or otherwise usurp the authority of men," engenders him a more sympathetic understanding in the twenty-first century."[2]

The Deutero-Paulines (Deutero means second) differ. But on most practical issues they appear similar to the authentic letters and are accepted as part of the Canon. The nature of these secondary sources was known back then and the reasons for their inclusion over other Spiritual texts, some certainly as valuable as are the Bible's other Books, and especially the *doctored* Paulines, is initially an enigma. It's understandable at first, as we'll see, in the *thought cops* looking the other way when it came to the *Paulian School*, but what later transpired is a sorry story.

It's important that a diplomacy leading to unity be established in the renewal of the reincarnation issue. Saint Constantine we need you. But it cannot and will not be left out, that the *reading right out* was ultimately a product of underhandedness and not a product of sincere <u>Spiritual</u> scholarship and discussion between those who would proclaim themselves as the mainstream, and those believers generally grouped as *Pythagoreans, Perennial Philosophers, Greeks, Essenes, Therapeutae,* and/or *Gnostics*.

Gnostic derives from the Greek word, *Gnosis*. Essentially it refers to an inner felt Knowing (as in *you are gods*) based upon insights, often experiential in nature, of higher levels of inner Spiritual understanding. Gnostics, were commonly called, *Knowers*. They grew in increasing numbers as Christianity became more institutionalized. While generally in agreement with the new religion's ethics and the necessity for organization and discipline that the dissemination of Christ's message required, *knowers* found that a simple adherence to blind faith, church ritual, doctrine, and community mores, as defined and enforced by authority figures such as Emperors, Kings, and even Bishops, was inadequate.

The purpose of the *knowers* approach, as father Theodotus had put so well, was to have *gnosis* or *knowledge* of: "Who we *were*, what we have *become, hence* we came, from *what* were we redeemed; what *birth* is, and what is *rebirth."* [3]

Like Jess Stearn's students, though generally jovial, these Pythagoreans/PerrenialPhilosophers/Greeks/Essenes/Gnostics/*Knowers* - et al were a tough bunch and surprising numbers held the equivalents of today's doctoral degrees in physics, engineering and psychology. Paul preached to a large spectrum, which included them.

He cautioned all in 1st Corinthians 1:20-21 not to get too uppity in worldly ways: "Has not God made foolish the wisdom of this world? Because all the wisdom which God had given was not sufficient for the world to know God, it pleased God to save those who believe by the simple Gospel."

Paul, here, addresses the value of his paranormal insights. He was not an anti-intellectual and an adversary to thinkers. Ask any Jesuit. As a learned person himself, he approved of Greeks, as well as the *Barbarians*, in their calling to spiritual purposes. It didn't matter whether this calling came by the *simple Gospel* (which in his time had yet to be assembled) or through the good intents of the many walking the same path.

Typically, like those addressed in Philipians 1:1, he honored them as *Saints:* "To all the *saints.*" With the same fervor, he urged them to use their brains and think:

"I don't want you to be ignorant."

Such saints, who in following in his footsteps, surely strove to follow the edict. Thus a true disciple would be one who, in addition to being a good person, would strive to overcome ignorance. It became customary for members of early churches to follow Paul's example and honor each other, *whether the wise* or *the unwise*, as Saints. As the process of canonization of Saints by specific religious organizations of its members, came about much later, the saints to be mentioned here might not coincide with those canonized in every church. It's in the same manner that Constantine's Sainthood isn't recognized outside the *Eastern* Church. In Rome, he's just another dead emperor.

But I think Paul would agree that God creates Saints, not churches. Churches merely recognize them. So if the churches don't, God still does! In understanding this, to their credit, Roman Catholic, Eastern Orthodox, and many among the Judeo-Christian/Islamic family of denominations have long celebrated All *Saint's Day*, or its equivalent, in commemorating *unknown* Saints. For this reason, it seems reasonable in suggesting that all sincere seekers of Spiritual truth may rightly be called *Saints.*

One such *Saint* in this context, is certainly Carl Jung. He had tirelessly sought to overcome ignorance through in-depth explorations of human consciousness and consequent healing. A great admirer of Gnostic creativity, in observing they had known, long before Freud: "The idea of the unconscious." Jung further declared, "It is clear beyond doubt that many Gnostics were nothing more than psychologists." [4]

Psychology's purpose is to initiate searching by its beneficiaries for self-knowledge. The process, in Jungian terms, is called *individuation.* The literal acceptance of - *you are gods* - for a Jung, would have been seen in the similar sentiment expressed in the third paragraph of Thomas' Gospel:

> "Jesus said ...When you *become to know yourselves*, then you will become known, and you will realize that it is you who are the sons [daughters] of the living father."

Individuation starts when one is ready to begin some deep thought in considering that if we ourselves are a very part and parcel of God, then unless we fully "*Become to know yourselves*," we cannot fully know God.

It had been Jung's foundation, which had helped to bring to light the miraculous discovery of over fifty undefiled Gnostic books. This occurred in 1945. As you recall, that's the same year the *sainted* Dr. Franklin had held, would be of such significance.

Saint Jung professed, as did *Saint* Cayce, that while existential and purely random events happen, things truly important more often come about, at their proper time and place, for all the right reasons. These, when they occur, are synchronous (or "in sync") with Spiritual intent. Jung labeled these as a *Synchronicity*.

You surely believe *sainted one*, as does this *voice*, that collective humanity needed in 1945, as it still needs, the *synchronicity* of the *Divine's* timely input. The world had just ended a long struggle in achieving a triumphal *New Age* of compassion over that of the combined twentieth century *Armageddons* of two world wars and the blood-letting of, Soviet-style, dictatorships. We can ponder whether the World Wars' resulted as the "final solution" the logic the *leaven* of the Pharisees leads to, and likewise, question if totalitarian material based dictatorships are the end product of the *leaven* of the Sadducees. Such questions make for divisive opinions and debates between those factions. Metaphysical types more often sidestep Pharisees and Sadducees. For most metaphysicians experiencing a synchronicity, be it as obvious as the great international celebrations following the close of World War II and the later collapse of the *Berlin wall,* or as subtle as the opening of an ancient jar in far off Nag Hammadi, Egypt, which just happened to have contained the Lost-Gospels of the Gnostics, the proper stance is to honor such events with similar rejoicing.

Commonly called the *Gnostic* Gospels, and sometimes the *Lost* Gospels, these were products of the great schools of *Alexandria*. Aristotle himself might have had a part in their establishment. Alexander *the Great*, as you recall, had long remained Aristotle's continuing pupil. Rivaling even Athens, Alexandria became one of world's foremost capitals of learning. It was here that not only was the wisdom of the East, and that of ancient Egypt valued but, as Stephan Hoeller, Jungian and respected authority on comparative religion notes, "Where Judaism met Platonism." [5]

Such was the interest that some two hundred-and-fifty years before Jesus, *Hellenistic* Egypt's learned ruler, Ptolemy Philadelphus, commissioned, as you recall, the *Septuagint*. Alexandrian scholarship continued to flourish and, years later, its many scholars, after what would have been a careful process of evaluation, free from missionary zeal, enthusiastically embraced the teachings of Jesus. One was Lucius Charinus. He had been a direct disciple of Saint John, the composer of the Fourth Gospel and direct disciple of Jesus himself. Another was Basilides, a professor of Persian and Indian religions; his teacher had been Saint Glacias, a direct disciple of *Paul*.

Yet another direct disciple of *Paul,* Saint Theudas, taught Valentinus. A Bishop, Saint Valentinus' moving ministry in Rome, where he often mentioned Paul as *brother Paul,* saw him nominated for the Papacy. That he had been of North African descent, rather than European, might have affected the election. Among the most moved and famous of his associates was not only the Paulian scholar, sainted Father Theodotus, but the enthusiastic, and fellow-sainted African, Father Origen: *I speak according to the opinion of Pythagoras and Plato*.

This distinguished background suggests, that the historic Paul had been a *Gnostic* himself. That scholars [6] are saying the same thing demand retractions and apologies for attacks against Gnostics:

"Pseudo Christians ... anti- Christians ... Pagans and one of the worst dangers faced by Christianity."

These are an outrage. Gnostic thought will become the *Godsend* of Christianity's future.

The appearance of their *Work* was one of the great finds of African biblical history, coinciding within a year or two of the more famous scrolls of the *Dead Sea*. The Dead Sea material generally confirms Cayce and Josephus and their accounts of the *Holy Land's* Essenes, though neither noted that as many, if not more, lived in Egypt. Most importantly, the findings lean toward a confirmation of Pythagorean/Perennial Philosophers/Greeks - et al linkages between Essene, Therapeutae, and Gnostic thought, including the preexistence premise. Dr. Hoeller notes: "The relationship of the People of the Scrolls to the New Testament, and beyond it to the Gnostic Gospels, is undeniable." [7]

While each might have had its quarrels over nuances of textural meaning, Gnostics, along with numerous other Christians pretty much agreed upon which side of the bread the butter lay, when it came to reincarnation. (Not all proponents of reincarnation were necessarily Gnostics.)

The lost Gospels importance is that for the first time, an unparalleled look, free from *thought cop* censorship and meddling, of the greatest minds of original Christianity can at last be seen. Incredibly, it's only been since the latter part of the twentieth century, that these works have been examined as they had been originally written. Previously, many had either been destroyed, mistranslated, or out and out altered, as Nag Hammadi makes clear, so as to make them appear ludicrous.

These Gospels needn't replace those of the traditional Bible. While Gnostic works would have been helpful, not one word of *the Book* needs changing. Historic approaches revealing reincarnation, and Paul's metaphorical preaching to the *Greeks,* when made clear, reveals enough. Though mentions will be made here, you'll need to do your homework through other sources, to grasp an in-depth appreciation of Paul's methods.

In brief, he had an uncanny ability, which would have made Jefferson proud, in communicating his encoded allegorical images to both beginners *(The Barbarians)* and the adept *(The Greeks)*. Recognizing that, *each one knows the Lord in His own way; and not all know Him alike,* Paul spoke with words that *each* could receive and act upon. When what was given was finally understood, usually through oral communication, more was offered, often from within the same passage, and sometimes within the same incarnation.

We've got to crawl before we can walk; walk before we can run; and run before we can fly!

There will be many wanting or needing additional navigational instruments, of course, and they will be well served with Gnostic guidance. When we reach port, if you *know thyself,* and wish to learn more about them, though she shies from reincarnation, you might want to try Dr. Pagels' wonderful *Work*. Interestingly, by chance, as in synchronicity, she studied Greek in college and as a doctoral student in Harvard Divinity School, discovered the *Gnostic Gospels*. They laid, still in their Grecian glory, stuffed in a professor's forgotten filing cabinet. They've formed the focus of her life's mission as a writer. Four of her books are listed in the bibliography.

You might also want to try the wonderful work of the Edgar Cayce study group program. It's been around for a long long, time and if you're of a more traditional bent in your religious training, you will find it a safe and instructive haven. Academic high powered, intellectual, even cynical, hard-nosed types, as in *Sadducee*, will find *The Course in Miracles,* meeting their most inquisitive of inquisitive inquiries.

There are more such sources of learning for sure, but these are the two I can recommend from personal experience. Remember, there are a lot of *wacko* cults out there. Take the *ole* captain's advice. You'll know them by their fruits. The litmus test is this: If they start making moves on your purse, private parts, or political persuasion - head for the door.

666

Among the youngest to live, but longest to be remembered of the saints and sinners sitting upon the throne of *Caesar,* history records his name as *Nero.* Like *Herod,* Caesar - pronounced *Kaiser* according to Miss Frazier, was a title. It was he, who in persecuting Paul's people and the followers of Peter, had wreaked such havoc among the tiny Jewish sect making up what would become the Roman Christian community.

Christians communicated Nero's name symbolically in the three infamous numbers, *Six, Six, Six*. Saint John listed them in *Revelation* (13:18) as symbolizing the *anti-Christ*. (Dr. Lamsa [1957] p. 1235 notes: "This number represents the Aramaic letters which spell *Nero Caesar,* namely 50, 200, 6, 50,100, 60, 200." The total equals six hundred sixty-six. As in Hebrew, each letter has a corresponding numerical value. In English, *A* could be assigned *1*. *B* - would be *2* - and so on. (Skilled code makers, like Freemasons and Jefferson, in varying the letter and numerical relationship, have confused their opponents for eons.)

Interesting, insane, and as bad a human being as history has seen, on July 19, 64 C.E. Nero set fire to Rome. Fiddling while it burned, he blamed the conflagration on the prophets, preachers, professors, pundits, plumbers, and plain people practicing and preaching principled lives, based upon the teachings of a crucified criminal.

A firebrand, praised by another firebrand teaching about a new life in: "The pattern in which it was *originally created*. Where there is neither Jew, Aramean, circumcision nor non-circumcision, Greek nor barbarian, slave nor freeman; but Christ in all." He went on: "Therefore as the elect of God, holy and beloved, put on mercy, kindness, gentleness, humbleness of mind, meekness, patience." [8]

Seventeen centuries later, as had Rome's rulers, the ruling elite of another empire would gaze aghast upon the declaration of yet another firebrand. Socially privileged, risking all, he declared a *New Order of the Ages*. This *New Order* was based after the pattern in which it was *originally created*. It was created for the purpose of giving gods on earth the right to live as equals because - as above, so below - *all are created equal*. This is why a truly free people recognize, that under democratically derived laws: "*There is neither Jew, Aramean, circumcision nor non-circumcision, Greek, nor barbarian, slave nor freeman.*" The troublemaker then went on to declare that as God cares and we're loved, we've been bestowed: Certain *inalienable* rights ... *among them life, liberty and the pursuit of happiness.*

> **A Sermon**
> ☺ Any among this crew having to ask what firebrand wrote inalienable "Rights and life liberty and the pursuit of happiness," goes over the side!
>
> (Captain L.)

Nothing New

The Roman elite would keep its eye on these people. A people, the elect of God, possessing an inner Christ in all have no need for an external allegiance to such an earthly contrivance as the Pax Romana and its divine emperor. Nor would America's "We the people," as they would so convincingly demonstrate, in rejecting the divinely appointed authority of the British Crown.

Free people quarrel. Whether right or wrong, it's just in their nature as part and parcel of the human condition. That they do so is probably a healthy sign. Early Christian's were healthy. Constantly quarreling, they gravitated toward two camps. *Knowers'* tended toward freer thinking and creativity. More conservative types, calling themselves the *Orthodox*, walked the straight and narrow. *Orthodox* meant straight thinking.

Heaven, Hell, and Reincarnation were issues, but not the only ones between the two sides. Sexual mores was another. *Celebrate* rather than *celibate* was more often heard among the *Knowers*. Sexual preferences were essentially a non-issue. This was a matter better left for individuals to decide. Especially individuals who in becoming less and less bound by the material world found themselves less and less bound to its material conventions and strictures.

Politics, and what should be *rendered unto Caesar,* also came up. Money, as always, had its place and as neither group were wealthy, both held services in the same places. This comment by Bishop Ireanaeus (*Bishop* meant supervisor) the second century's foremost *Orthodox* spokesman, bears this out. He said of Gnostics:

"They're full of blasphemy!" [9]

Their response, which Ireaneus, himself, describes here, was dismay and hurt:

"Why do *[straight]* Christians accuse us of malice, lies, arrogance and heresy? Why do they attempt to exclude us from common worship, and their bishops urge others to shun us as 'offspring of Satan' - when we ourselves confess the same creed and hold the same doctrines they do?"[10]

I love church communities. While I publicly don't divulge my membership or endorse a particular denomination, from personal experience as an inveterate people-watcher, I find the same subjects of Heaven, Hell, sex, politics, purse strings, and gossip about those *awful others* sitting in the next pew still *voiced* among the *Saints*. Some things never change, whether among *New Age California crazies* in San Jose, Baltimore, or Virginia Beach; devout Catholics; the most Episcopal of Episcopalians; the most Jewish of Synagogues, or the most fundamentalist of fundamentalist congregations.

While the good *supervisor's* comment might be heard in this light, that he went on, filling up some five additional multi-paged books of diatribes and bitter bites, suggests the gentleman *doth protest too much!* Endeavors that are truly *Spiritual* don't normally spark such negativity. Some of this stuff could have come about because he was simply stressed and unhappy. He endured a lot in seeing others suffer. Supervisor's stresses (most managerial *type A* types are constantly under duress) could have played psychological havoc. If he were celibate, the lack of a woman's nurturing companionship would be an additional issue. Envy might have been another in that, Gnostics generally weren't celibates. That sex is almost always divisive, when extremes are debated could have fueled further resentments.

Still, fear of death might have been behind most of it. Assured he had a direct passport to Heaven, he was a Bishop, and only needed to hang on long enough to get through retirement, would have been an idea defended with his every effort. And so it might have been. Most reincarnation type theories often rattle the cages of those proclaiming themselves among the *Elect*

The Storm

Yet, in all this, there might have been an even deeper issue. Always subtle, but always present, it's the *Six Six Six* factor. The *Gospel of Phillip* makes this most astute observation. A core belief among those in the know, it notes: "God created man and man created God. So it is in the world. Men make gods and they worship their creations."[11]

The god they created was known as the *Demiurge*. Satanic, it wears no red cape, has no pointed tail, and certainly no horns. Manifesting through the projected energies of humans, it takes on whatever form they desire.

Discerning the genuine *God*-within from the external *no other gods before me* type of deity, often misconstrued by some sects as the *jealous-*

God of the Ten Commandments, would be easy if these manmade creations looked like devils. But they don't. They speak with glib tongues and dress like the silk-suited, sued shoed, siding salesmen, I'd run across back in Baltimore.

Ireanaeus wouldn't have been the first to have, erred on the nature of God. The same had happened to the Romans of sixty-four C.E. Their religious laws declared Nero a god. At twenty-six, he projected the innocence of age, wore flowing robes, a purple sash, and often a sprig of olive leaves around his fat head.

When *666* heard noises were being made for a *recall,* in response, the *beast,* as *Revelation* remembers him, branded the Christian *crazies* as terrorists. Blaming them focused attention from himself and the burning city slums. When the heat died down, he garnished new support *gentrifying* the *hoods* and many making a killing in real estate. He knew he could get away with it. The Christian sect's small size and unpopularity in their homeland, where they were considered as *Jewish* heretics, wouldn't invite trouble from Herod Agrippa. Though Paul had met him personally, had Herod tried to help, his throne would have been in jeopardy, not from Rome, but from his own subjects. Agrippa II was not the *man of the grape,* but his son. When Paul had once asked: "King Agrippa, do you believe the prophets? I know that you believe." The last Herod responded: "With little effort you almost persuade me to become a Christian."[12]

That little if any, of his hundreds of thousands of influential, though tacit, supporters throughout the empire intervened, on behalf of their Christian brothers and sisters, wouldn't go forgotten.

Roman coliseums, despite their size, are intimate structures. I know. I've seen some. Spectators, in even the upper seats, saw gladiatorial combats with some degree of detail. Good gladiators were expensive to train and in high demand. They enjoyed *Rock Star* status and like today's television *wrasslers,* they were as much showmen as they were athletes. They weren't required to fight to the death and so long as they didn't take on a mortal wound or hadn't shown up for work too hung over, or still drunk from the previous evening's wine and wenching, and could put in a passable performance - they could count on a *thumbs up* from their fans. Survivors enjoyed a comfortable retirement or new careers as coaches. Common criminals and captured enemy soldiers, unfit for slavery, didn't do so well.

While Christians got picked up here and there, they generally could walk away so long as they acknowledged that the emperor was divine.

Gnostic's in believing that everybody was divine had little difficulty in rendering, as Jesus had said: "Unto Caesar what is Caesar's."[13]

Not so the Orthodox. Public executions in the coliseums were horrible. Sitting next to someone in church next day, who had gotten off, while a close family member had died - as a matter of deep religious conviction - would be remembered for generations. This would have driven an even deeper wedge between themselves and those *other* Christians. Roman spectators, on the other hand, because captured Christians were relatively rare and were routinely executed as criminals, might not have paid them that much attention.

Christian kindness and charitable works were noted on the streets, but those spiritually attuned enough to take notice, probably avoided the arenas.

The bloody spectacle of condemned criminals, enemy combatants, lions, and highly skilled gladiators, filled those places to capacity. Often emperors, like Nero, put such spectacles on for free. On those days, cheers cascaded among the masses.

He had a flair for show business and, as always, expected his newest citywide production to bring about, not only a triumph, but to deflect further suspicion from himself. Gleefully glaring from his throne, he signaled for the main attraction.

An extravaganza of spectacular proportions was expected,
but no such spectacle was to materialize.

Instead, what the fans got, in graphic detail, were close up views of the cruel deaths of everyday men, women, husbands, wives of the missionarys, and families, *like ourselves*: "Have we not the right to travel with a Christian wife, just as the rest of the apostles do, and as the brothers of our Lord and Peka [Peter]."[14]

While cheers were heard, most only masked the tears of shame Romans shed throughout their city's seven hills. From the arenas to Nero's gardens (now the *Vatican)* and even to the wealthy suburbs, though presented as criminals and ne'er do wells, the victim's innocence and the righteousness of their Spirituality - *Christ in all* - stood vindicated. In a silent still small *Voice,* united now (under God) male or female, Greek or Barbarian, Gnostic or Orthodox, *each knowing the Lord in their own way,* professing: *"Mercy, kindness, gentleness, humbleness of mind, meekness, patience."*

The Remnant

Lost were Paul, Peter and probably his wife, and much of the Church leadership and their followers. Along with them might have gone the chance for a more favorable resolution of the reincarnation issue. Also, along with this, went any clear claim to Apostolic succession. That is, a clear connection to those who knew Jesus and his disciples directly or the - beloved brother - Paul. The Orthodox would claim their Way was the only way as it had derived directly from he and Peter's leadership in Rome. Such a claim skated on thin ice in that they overlooked the many direct devotees, primarily Gnostic <u>Others</u> living in the provinces outside the city in places like Alexandria, Athens, and even Jerusalem.

I suspect the Roman Orthodox were able to replace their membership more quickly than they. New members rushing in, as a result of the obvious faith of those martyred, might have found the simpler straightforward approaches of *straight* teachings easier to grasp and therefore of more appeal. This new wave was mostly Roman. And as half the city's population were slaves (Germans, Gauls, British) with little or no education, there would have been proportionally less who were prepared to tackle the subtleties and sophistication of Athenian and Alexandrian approaches. One thing is certain; whether Orthodox or Gnostic, the tiny movement was no longer obscure and began to grow.

An additional five certainties were that near the end of the decade, six short years later, (2) Herod died in exile (about 71 – 72 C.E.), (3) Jerusalem - tragically - lay destroyed, (4) *666* committed suicide, (5) Roman political stability lay in a shambles as it endured the *recalls* of three emperors in a single year, and (6) within a few generations, men and women named their sons Peter and Paul and their dog Nero!

The Pagan

Some two-and-a-half centuries later, when Constantine converted, the first he sought would have been the church's leaders. Those he received would have been supervisors. Devout, though devout in error, they probably presented a Jesus and Paul with a voice reflecting not only unity, but representing the two somewhat differently than in earlier times. Nero's persecution, and those that followed, though not as severe, had hardened them to the reality that if they were going to carve out a safe niche within the empire, then they had better begin moving toward the center in presenting themselves as loyal citizens. This explains the motivation behind the Deutero-Pauline/*Pastoral* letters. Subtly downplayed was the immediacy of the Jeffersonian *New Order of the Ages,* and the indwelling messianic *Liberator,* who would manifest through the hearts and minds of all God's children – who like you and I - are the younger sisters and brothers of Jesus. Less obvious, even missing, would be the deeper meanings presented through allegory, simile, and metaphor *voiced* in the past.

Jesus now dwelled, literally, in the sky, accessible only through an external hierarchy of paternal representatives, supervised through an organizational hierarchy allegedly put together by Paul himself. If you wanted to get to heaven, you'd best fall in line as, after some two hundred years of church tradition, based upon Apostolic succession, only they knew *the Way.*

The *Way* wasn't to be the inward path of the *Gnostic,* but that of the straight and narrow, which included an assurance to Rome, as the Paul they had invented reveals here, that the *Orthodox* had no interest in meddling with the emperor's authority:

"Seek those things that are above, where Christ sits on the right hand of God.

Set your minds on things above, not on things on the earth"[15]

Neither Constantine nor his mom, were Christian insiders. While his dad had been an Emperor, Helena, his mother, had been born poor somewhere along the shores of the Black Sea. She converted in response to her son's dream and the visions he experienced. In seeking to verify them, she made pilgrimages to the Holy Land. The churches she had constructed still stand and so does the veneration many Christians place upon her as sainted, Mother Helena. Her major find was supposedly the actual cross upon which Jesus had been crucified. Constantine constructed a monument with her and himself holding the relic between them. This invites cynics to raise eyebrows, but this far-removed in time, among us who can, or even should, judge.

Just as difficult in discernment, is what their beliefs might have been regarding reincarnation. Had they possessed the *Unitarian* sensitivities and toleration of most throughout the empire, it mightn't have mattered. Most importantly, as both started out as *Pagans*, and as such were outsiders (as in naive outsiders) giving the Orthodox bishop's virtual *Carte Blanche* in administering the empire's coming religion finds a rationale.

An active Emperor and a military man, Constantine was too busy to do much else.

As an organizer himself, he would have resonated to the like-minded organization oriented mantra of executives and successful sales people everywhere - *keep it simple, salesman!* Helena and her son were not theologians and their, twenty-four/seven, schedules wouldn't have allowed them much time to consider, with any depth, the very deep and divisive theological *trouble making* issues that any well planned, silk suited, suede-sandaled representation of solid religious unity would have pointedly glossed over.

Constantine's dream leading to his conversion occurred on or about October 28, 312. By 313, his decree that the *Lawful* church are compensated, confirmed he'd bought the *Orthodox* agenda. These included tax exemptions for *orthodox* clergy, government construction of *orthodox* churches (including the Vatican) followed with envelopes stuffed with cash and letters of commendation. Supposedly signed personally, as if he had little else to do, they were routinely received by *orthodox* bishops. An innovation was a *faith-based* welfare system for the sick, poor, and those persecuted in the past.

A good idea but those supervising the program, *certain* bishops, of course received a commensurate salary and benefit package rivaling the C.E.O of a modern corporation.

Though Gnostic sentiments still prevailed among half or more of the believers, they were ordered to conform to orthodox teaching or surrender their places of worship. That old scores were to be settled saw prejudices toward Jews take form in legal restrictions. Fortunately, most of these laws went unenforced.

Dr. Pagels[16] is careful to quote scholarly opinion, that Constantine was sincere in believing the new religion should, while having some generalized basic framework, allow for free discussion. He had faith that reasonable people could agree upon what they disagreed and to agree upon those things that they did concerning religious doctrine. Once settled, they could then go on living normally in a climate of mutual respect and sisterly and brotherly love, as in, <u>*get a life!*</u>

That he'd been *had,* probably surfaced in the *666* mean-mindedness he would observe at Nicea. By that time, in realizing that what he'd bought had not been, *as advertised,* he could have done little more than to bring the bickering to an end in the hopes that the very broad based *Nicene Creed* would provide future generations a foundation for unity in the <u>***R***</u> word.

Nicea was not his only agenda. He was an Emperor, soldier and the son of a very dear mother. She bantered in and about the empire doing good works, living into her eighties. These demanded his attention. Theological nitpicking was strictly a back-burner issue. Moving the seat of government from Rome to Byzantium was a herculean effort in itself. Added to this would be the profound psychological challenges resulting from his deep Gnostic-like experiences, which would have been in such stark contrast to the daily duties he would routinely perform as the head of a totalitarian state. Maintaining stability required of him such things as assassinations and executions of persons such as his rebellious wife and a son. Subterfuge, half-truths, near truths, bold-faced lies – and aggressive warfare – these are the duty's monarchs must maintain to keep order. There is probably some special karmic exemption for them, as long as their actions aren't accomplished with malicious intent.

Time constraints and psychological conflicts like these, may have been behind the delay he imposed in having himself baptized. He remained a *Pagan* until he lay on his deathbed. On one hand he might not have wanted to be held accountable, as a Christian, for having committed the acts his job description called for. On the other hand, his holding back may have been intended as a reminder to certain *supervisors,* that while it was too late to stop what had been started; as a Pagan, he remained a *Divinely* deemed Emperor.

They'd have to fear him. Outside their control, he'd protect from persecution, the religious rights of the Pax Romana's *New Order,* he had hoped to establish. Like *Christ* Jesus, the *Apostle* Paul, *Father* Theodotus, *Mother* Helena, *President* Jefferson, and the *each one knowing the Lord in their own way: Saint* Constantine, in the final analysis and in possibly needing an additional incarnation or two or three or more, was a *real* Christian.

Other Teachers of Israel

Josephus said of Essene doctrines:

"Their doctrine is this: That bodies are corruptible... but that the souls are immortal, and continue forever: And that they come out of the most subtle air... and this is like the *opinion of the Greeks.*"[17]

A challenge to place the teachings of Jesus, John, and their followers outside the Essenes would need to start with biblical *voices* directly stating that holders of doctrines professing:

"That bodies are corruptible... but that the souls are immortal, and continue forever: And that they come out of the most subtle air, are like the teachings of "offspring of scorpions, those who strain at gnats, swallow camel..., blind fools, blind guides, and *Socrates was crazy!*"

Until then, the direct evidence of Essene/Therapeutae/ Pythagorean/Gnostic links still stand.

Simplicity. Beauty.

Such links point to the reality that reincarnation was the focus of the *born again* lesson Jesus taught - as you remember – to his student, Nicodemus. It's the same lesson Socrates imparted to Meno, and later, to the two troubled teens he had counseled just before being executed. You recall, of course, *word for word*:

"There comes into my mind an ancient doctrine which affirms that souls go from here into the other world, and returning hither, *are born again* from the dead. Now if it be true that the living come from the dead, then our souls must exist in the other world, for if not, how could they have been *born again?"*

Nicodemus was neither a scholar nor a teen. A good guy, though unschooled, he'd been more than likely an appointee of the crown. Such appointments were common among temple priests of the time. He could have been a retired contractor, plumber, sea captain, or the talkative brother-in-law of a big shot. Big shots in those days were either Pharisees, or Sadducees. The *Master's* expression of dismay during the discourse (John 3:10) that someone so high in the priestly ranks should know so little, seems understandable:

"You Nicodemus, are a *teacher of Israel,* and yet you do not understand these things?"

Yet, for nearly six-hundred years, despite orthodoxy's efforts, debate continued, between the inwardly focused intimates of Jesus and Paul and the Orthodox *teachers of Israel.* Cayce confirmed their initial purpose had been to reach the masses through taking shortcuts in simplifying the complexities of Christianity.

Cayce said of shortcuts in any approach to Christianity:

"There are none in Christianity." [18]

But it didn't matter. Some forty years after Nicea, when the *supervisor* of Alexandria, Athanasius, called for the burning of the Gnostic *Holy Text's,* the good monks, most likely of the Saint Pachornius Monastery, buried them in a cave. That Athanasius was able to get away with such a sacrilege, signaled that the production line set up to manufacture state-sponsored *shortcuts*, was at last in place.

The Pythagorean precepts of the earlier Christians were displaced, as streamlined teachings ignited overwhelming numbers of new converts. Proponents of reincarnation may see this as a stumbling stone. However, these might have provided a stepping-stone the West uniquely required in establishing its faith in a just and loving God. Still, had the *wiggle room* Constantine's creed allowed stood as the generalized guideline, which was highly likely his intent, and along with a standardized biblical text with some additional Gnostic *voices,* a better outcome, might have resulted.

A more stable, strong, prosperous, and most importantly, a less fearful, society could have resulted. But as history consistently teaches - absolute power corrupts absolutely.

There were few legal mechanisms for compartmentalizing the Empire's many diverse religio/political interests. Those in power found the many temptations to create a god in their own image, as in *666,* an irresistible enticement. The problem wasn't unique. It's found among any group of human beings - whether Persian, Chinese, Native American or those living along the shores of the Mediterranean.

When you examine the realities of how most lived before the *shot heard round the world* established the American experience, then you should be the first in line demanding your local school board teach, with the same fervency it teaches computer science, the more esoteric side of *The Place of the Soul's* - as in *Ka's* - history.

This includes the *Spirituality* undergirding its Constitution. Remember, its first concern was religious freedom.

While you're at it, send places like *Atlantic University* a big fat donation.[19] Your check, cash, money order, or even time, will help prepare graduates properly trained in communicating the long overdue *New Order* with that of the *Old* in the academic jargon academics, and subsequently, the nation needs to hear.

The Supervisors

The Orthodox as in all human endeavors had successes and failures. As for spiritual growth, they succeeded, though at a rudimentary level, in promoting for many a faith in a just and loving God. Now, as that's been accomplished, isn't it time to progress in the understanding that that faith can now stand rewarded in the knowledge today's scientific studies of reincarnation, reveal?

That is, the *Good News* of human survival is not only confirmed, but further revealed is a justice system of incredible intelligence and compassion.

Surely, this is the working of a fair and loving God.

To give you some idea of how efficiently run was the Orthodox outreach, its *supervisors* took a tiny movement that at the end of its first hundred years contained some thirty quarrelsome sects distributed among just seventy-five hundred members. By the time Saint Jerome came to prominence at the dawning of the fifth century (he exemplified Orthodox teaching), his *voice* ministered to a Christian population that had, by then, grown to over <u>thirty-three million.</u>

This was in an age when oxen moved freight over land locked communication and transportation routes at the speed of about fifteen to twenty miles in a <u>day</u> and the heartiest of mariners, during good weather, could make a hundred-mile fetch in about twenty-four hours.

To be evaluated is how well this thirty-three million figure, reflected God's and/or Constantine's intent.

God gladly got a return in *Prodigals*.

Constantine's ensuing empire, in becoming the sole agent for salvation, got tax revenues through human loyalties, though coercion played a part. Loyal subjects either followed the rules or were threatened with *Hell*. Hell was an innovation uniquely developed in its *Research and Development Division*. It was effectively used in building what could be called a giant *faith factory* manufacturing, for sincere seekers, dogma and methodologies leading to faith. Sometimes, though that faith turned out not to be the inward faith in one's own inner divinity – as a child of God and thus a part and parcel of the Divine itself - but the faith held in someone else's faith. Someone else's faith, which was based on the belief in the existence of an outside divine entity, separate from one's self.

Whether their theology was right or wrong, in terms of unit cost, the cost of converts' per drachma (after *Cathedral* costs and *Saint's* salaries were deducted) yielded those in charge tidy sums.

Despite this, though Orthodox and the later Christian *mainstream* explanations of life after death was, as today, not scientifically supportable and they failed miserably in mixing *church and state*, their efforts opened an initial path of salvation for many.

Many like Saint Jerome, to their credit, probably made little more than *minimum wage.* Good deeds matter more that good creeds and while one can lovingly agree to disagree with points of his creeds, it's easily agreeable that his deeds of faith, personal piety, and sincerity moved many. He translated the Bible from Greek to Latin, and without him the lost souls of his time might still remain lost. Though ultimately *Sainted,* as a human being he had an *unsaintly* shadow side.

The bottom line: He was a human being - *like ourselves.*

He once praised Father Origen as, "the *greatest* teacher of the Church after the apostles." 20

This had been the same Father Origen, as you recall, who had so eloquently written, "According to the opinion of *Pythagoras and Plato*." Despite other Papal Fathers support, when Jerome's boss, Pope

Theophilus, declared an ill-advised vendetta against the *greatest* teacher, Jerome proceeded to write in 402 C.E.:

"Now I find, among the many *bad* things written by Origen the following most distinctly heretical: ... That there are innumerable worlds succeeding one another in eternal ages; that angels, have been turned into, human souls; that the soul of the Savior existed before it was born of Mary; ...that in the end times ...Archangels and Angels, the devil, the demons and the souls of men whether Christians, Jews or Heathen, will be of one condition and degree... and will also be saved; ... and that this ...mass of... creatures with all their *dregs* left behind, then will begin a new world."

The dissertation ends in his reassurance that because such beliefs are heresies:

"We may have no fear that we who are now men may afterwards be born women, and one who is now a virgin may chance then to become *a prostitute.*"[21]

Unfortunately and incomprehensibly, such opinions would be used to persecute whole Pythagorean spiritual communities. Many were driven into hiding, exile, and as befell the large-scale denominations of gentle Cathars and Albigenses (good Christians all) complete extermination!

The horror found its roots in the Empire's latest dictator, Justinian and his wife Theodora. (She made big bucks as a courtesan before hitting the *jackpot* in the marriage.)

Through a series of sordid and divisive methods, they attempted to end the reincarnation matter in favor of the Orthodox at the Council of Constantinople of 553 c.e.

But, as many authorities disagree on the official outcome,[22] it's arguable that Origen, the Pythagoreans, and reincarnation were never condemned. Actually, only four issues seem clear: (1) though, she had died before the council came about, Theodora was not a theologian. (2) Justinian was not the Pope of the Roman Catholic Church, nor (3) the Patriarch of Constantinople of the Greek Orthodox Church, and (4) reincarnation was removed from study within the mainstream of the two religions!

Today, most clerics have been taught that reincarnation was banned and seldom seriously consider the issue. But, the forces of inquisition have long been silenced, and the challenge of modern scholarship and new biblical insights demand that discussion be reopened.

A Sermon

I submit the first questions in the Spirit of Elijah/John and the Brother/Sisterhood; that at the end of time when the last human being leaves the face of the earth and Archangels and Angels, the devil, the demons and the souls of men and women whether Christians, Jews, or Heathen, begin a new world of one condition and degree and will be saved, that of this mass of creatures with all their *dregs* left behind, will also include: Ireanaeus, Jerome, Justinian, Theodora, you, and myself? And won't each of us have been healed by the experiences of many lifetimes? And with us as *Sainted* prodigal daughters and sons won't all races, creeds, conservatives, liberals, *New Yorkers*, extraterrestrials, graffiti gremlins, and jaywalkers be included?

And most certainly will not only the men who afterwards were born women appear, but especially - to accolades and *hosannas* heard throughout the universe - the *virgin* Jerome had pegged: "that chanced then to become a *prostitute?*"

(Captain *L*)

Notes

1. Pagels (1975) p.5
2. 1ST Timothy 2:12
3. Pagels (1975) p. 30
4. Head & Cranston p. 152
5. Hoeller (1989) P. 79
6. Jung, Pagels, Hoeller, et al
7. Hoeller (1989) P. 38
8. Colossians 3:10 - 12
9. Pagels (1979) p. 32
10. Ibid p. 18
11. Hoeller (1989) p. 89
12. Acts 26:27-28
13. Luke 20:25
14. 1st Corinthians 8:5
15. Colossians 3:1-3
16. Pagels (2003) p. 174
17. Wars II 8:1
18. (5749-14)
19. P.O. Box 757 Va. Beach 23451
20. Head & Cranston p. 144-5
21. Ibid.
22. Ibid. p. 156-16

Chapter 12

The Holy Spirit

While exact definitions of the Holy Spirit may vary among the world's many faiths, I think this generalized dictionary description, should suffice for most:

"The active presence of God in human life."

For individuals feeling their faith compromised in considering reincarnation, the history of the *Holy Spirit's* role in the matter would be well to contemplate. This is especially important should one encounter authorities pushing the premise that the *active presence of God* was manifested through Emperor Justinian at Constantinople.

In such a scenario, a Protestant Christian could be reminded that councils such as Justinian's are generally not binding on the faithful. This typical disclaimer, seen here in the prayer book of the Episcopal Church, is clear:

"Forasmuch as they be an assembly of men...councils may err, and sometimes have erred." [1]

Roman Catholics may argue immunity in that they are not bound by the *Doctrine of Caesaropapism.* This roughly translates that a *Caesar* such as Justinian can impose religious views upon a Pope. In this case, the Pope did not call for the council. This is required before such a gathering can take place.

The New Catholic Encyclopedia notes:

"In the West European Middle Ages Caesaropapism was hardly a doctrinal possibility" [2]

The *bottom line* may be the NCE revelation that such a council can only bind the faithful if it meets the test for *Ecumenical* status. This requires proof of the Holy Spirit's presence.[3] The seeker might then consider that under anyone's Doctrine of Common Sense, that regardless of whether the Holy Spirit is Jewish, Muslim, Hindu, Buddhist, Protestant, Greek Orthodox, Russian Orthodox, or Roman Catholic, He, She, or *It* wouldn't show up for a church meeting where (1) its head, Pope Vigilius, refused to attend and (2) was illegally assembled and ruled over by a man who not only had poor Vigilius kidnapped from Rome and held captive for eight years, but mistreated so severely that he, *The Holy Father*, died soon after!

Justinian also *(Strike1)* prohibited priests from marrying, though he retained the right for himself; *(Strike 2)* forbade Jews to read the Old Testament in Hebrew; and *(Strike 3)* put forth policies which still split the mother church, even to this day. Further, he precipitated the *Dark Ages* in having the audacity to close down the Platonic Academies - that until that time had served the West for <u>Nine Hundred years!</u>[4]

Could such a *wretch* bring on the Presence of the Holy Spirit?

My *bottom line* was, and is, that reincarnation is a sectarian issue and not a heresy. I moved full ahead in thinking over that many original Christians embraced the Greeks, whom Josephus said were educated by Hebrews. As the sages based their faith in the Scriptures, which, for them, recorded the *active presence of God in human life;* my seeking Bible histories of returns by the deceased seemed like a good idea. If such existed, then the *normal means* of Socrates and Stevenson would pick them out. If *Biblical Cases of the Reincarnation Type* were found, then the insights of the first followers of Jesus would stand revealed.

So I proceeded.

Notes
1. Book of Common prayer (1978) p. 872
2. New Catholic Encyclopedia (1967) vol. II p. 1049
3. New Catholic Encyclopedia (1967) vol. IV
4. See Head & Cranston, (1978) & New Catholic Encyclopedia(1969)

**Kindly Pope Paul greeting well-wishers in 1964.
The irony, that such figures could be murdered over disagreements about life after death, is unfathomable.**

Chapter 13

The Procedure

Secure in the Holy Spirit, I set my course in this affirmation of Solomon:

"Commit yourself to the Lord, and he will establish your thoughts." [1]

I pursued Stevenson's procedure and pondered placing into tables, words that reflected not only the wisdom of little children, but also the wisdom of the Bible's most revered figures. If I could identify such words in the context of reincarnation, they might reveal verbatim claims of a past life or comments concerning the past lives of others. Finding the appropriate biblical entries would need to follow the same straightforward process of the lawyer or historian, that Stevenson's researchers use.

His staff lists pertinent details such as the name of the deceased the child claimed to have been, where they had lived, and the names and relationships of whom they had known. When available, birth and death records offer substantial proof of a past life. Neither hypnotists, psychics, nor other paranormal sources are utilized. However, the paranormal must be shown to have taken place. Evidence must meet Socrates' criteria. That is, the child's knowledge must be proven to have come from sources not normally available.

The research often takes place in isolated regions of Third World countries. This makes it easier to demonstrate that events which took place several years and some miles apart, could not have been communicated through telephones, the media, nor the normal social intercourse of modern urban areas. Interviews confirm parallel skills, behaviors, and the veracity of witnesses, especially when the child is called upon to confront those known in the past-life. That such reunions with lost loved ones can become extremely emotional is understandable. Stevenson noted he was personally unprepared for the gut-wrenching emotions he encountered in his initial research. And even danger. A child once said he had been murdered in his past life and named the killers. As they were still at large, extra precautions were taken. This insured both the child's and the interviewers' safety. As the incident had taken place in India, where reincarnation is accepted as the norm, the police did not dismiss the incident as a childhood fantasy.

The interviewers' profound *people* skills must stand acknowledged. However, once home in Virginia, expensive and time consuming hard work follows in reconstructing and analyzing the complex history seen in a case.

I would find the same in locating biblical cases.

Seeking and listing personalities' parallel skills, behaviors, and the veracity of sources seen in both biblical and secular history, like Stevenson's effort, was time-consuming hard work. Added to this was an especial difficulty in that nobody I knew about had done it before - using the Bible - and I couldn't seek out the advice of others.

Choosing the specific biblical personalities for study was readily solved in following Cayce's suggestion to start with Elijah. Suspecting that others linked with the prophet might have linked reasons for returns, I quickly saw enough clues to investigate more. Some of these were: Obadiah-Zecariah (John's father); the widow of Zarapeth-Elizabeth (John's mother); Ahab-Antipas; Jezebel-Herodias; Omri-Herod; Naboth-Agrippa; Joram-Necho; Ethbaal-Tiberius; Jehu-Josiah-Archelaus.

Cayce's confirmation on these wasn't to be found. This could be expected, as he seldom volunteered information that wasn't specifically requested. There would have been few in those days asking about biblical bad guys and gals! He also made it a point not to divulge a subject's past life information that might be detrimental. Who would want to know the specifics of a former life of questionable behavior?

Though these additional cases were important, they were not developed with the same vigor, as was Elijah/John. His made the point and there wasn't enough time or space for much else. My hope was either to personally pursue future research concerning these personalities, or to encourage others in a later endeavor.

As for Jesus, Cayce indicated His evolution in becoming the Christ involved some thirty separate incarnations. Six were biblical. The first was as Adam. This was followed by Enoch, Melchizadek, Joseph, Joshua and Jeshua. Cayce added that Mary's first and only incarnation was as Eve. My research, like Stevenson's, deals primarily with *regular folks,* that is, entities commonly ranked, as non-deities. Using dieties would negate the point that "regular folks" are not at all "*regular!*" However in deference to many Christians, who will surely find an interest, I have included an example in Joshua and Jesus in Chapter Seventeen. (Those seeking more might try Glenn Sanderfurs's *Lives of the Master.*)

These approaches differed from Stevenson, but they were similar in that they were expensive.

The expense came from time lost in not holding down a *real* job. I found that I couldn't just sell something with my usual acumen, and then return to the somewhat *space cadet* like state I experienced as a researcher of deep metaphysical material. Stevenson received a seven-figure grant from the Carlson Foundation, established by Chester A. Carlson, the founder of Xerox® Corporation. I had no funding and had long exhausted what monies I had brought to Virginia.

I stayed on course, regardless.

When Elijah was once in a similar situation, he was fed "bread and meat" by ravens, In my case, ravenous creatures would fly overhead on cold winter mornings, loudly *calling* and *quacking* to gobble up the *bread and meat,* I fed them. They knew they had an easy mark. Once Canadian geese, not only nuzzled up for food, but also allowed me to stroke them. In summers, sometimes herons roosted on the lifelines.

Miraculously, like Elijah, none of us missed a meal.

Unlike Stevenson, I never felt endangered. However, it would have been naive in overlooking that bloodshed, even warfare, has accompanied impassioned discussion concerning the Scriptures. Defusing such possibilities had been another reason for employing humor. It was also another reason for making contingencies, as had Elijah, if the need to disappear ever presented itself. I wouldn't expect violence from the academic community and the truly spiritual. At worst, they wouldn't read the material.

Fanatical types might act otherwise.

My tack also differed in that I never left the country, though a photographic expedition to the Holy Land's archaeological sights might have revealed additional evidence. Another difference was my utilization of paranormal sources, seen in Cayce's published gifts, though these weren't submitted as *prima facie* evidence. As for my own gifts, I'm a talker - as in *mouth of the South!* A writer, photographer, plumber, mariner, and as they tell me a "*good guy"* (though, "*good for what"* has yet to be established). If some measure of personal intuition is present, it's probably because I seldom researched without preliminary meditation and prayer.

This may or may not have differed from Stevenson. In his eighties at that time, he'd retired and remained reticent about his spiritual convictions for the rest of his life. Others replicating his research often reveal theirs. This is a good idea as potentials for hidden bias might be lessened.

Ultimately, my task would prove to be neither *rocket science* nor *New Age*.

The Pity Party

Initially, a member of the thesis committee discouraged the endeavor. He feared that I might run into the same deadlock others had encountered in having their insights on reincarnation read right out, or that I would have to throw in the towel in admitting that the Scriptures had been so deeply tampered with, that firm conclusions couldn't be drawn. Dr. Danner was a practicing minister and held his doctorate in theology. He also believed in reincarnation. His sincere skepticism had to be doubly heeded.

However, I pressed on.

I felt shot down, two fold, in reading that Stevenson also felt that reincarnation was in the Bible, in some arcane form, but that even he couldn't figure out how. I felt like Casey. Not Edgar Cayce, but the mythical Casey *at the bat*, of baseball fame. The hometown hero had played till the bottom of the ninth. Like him, though down by two strikes, I still stood to take another swing.

The proverbial *full figured* lady was yet to sing.

Ego aside, I pondered concluding the Master's thesis with a concession that the best of theology and science couldn't find convincing evidence. It was a valid conclusion and I could still get my degree. I had already put a lot of time into the project and began to accept that I wasn't getting any younger. I began thinking I should put all this business about writing on the back burner and start making *hay* while the sun still shines and start saving for retirement.

I couldn't live, as mom had said, on *moonbeams* forever.

After retiring, I could begin all over again.

Is nothing new?

I looked over my retirement portfolio and pondered my position: Should the thesis make its point, would it ever provide an income as a best seller if turned into a book? Stevenson was backed by a large philanthropic grant and was a tenured professor at a major university; *Atlantic University* could barely meet its payroll, let alone provide a pension for its professors or alumni. Would social security and my children support me?

I began having a first class *pity party*.

Then I pondered *where* my - *post* retirement - days might be spent. At that, a still small *voice* began to speak. Instinctively I girded up my loins, as had Job. Like he, I knew I was in for four solid biblical chapters - count em - 38, 39, 40, & 41, of unanswerable questions like: "Where were *you* when I laid the foundations of the earth."

Mercifully, only one query was put forth:

"Does *Brinks*® make deliveries to the graveyard?"

Back on Course

Before the next pitch, I had to learn new skills and retrain my thinking. Typists are expensive and learning to type, at fifty, took some time. That was the difficult part. The impossible centered on my religious convictions concerning the Bible. In the past, I had usually looked for the warm fuzzys in Scriptural study and adopting the cold and dispassionate methods of the new approach would prove problematical. Change, of most any nature, is always a problem. Especially, if one is as stubborn as I. I needed to adjust my approach to that of history and modern theology.

This was because both Stevenson and today's theologians use similar historic approaches. If my research were to be convincing, I would need to *walk the talk*, and learn how to communicate in a similar fashion. It bears repeating: it made the most sense in thinking that the more my methodologies paralleled their methodologies, the more convincing would be the findings.

Historic Approaches

Among theologians, as you recall, historic approaches have been on the increase for about the last seventy-five years. The development of modern archaeology, in particular biblical archaeology, and such discoveries as the Gnostic Gospels and the Dead Sea scrolls have made it possible to assemble information rivaling that of secular history. Proponents of historic approaches feel that faith must ultimately stand upon Bible histories of real people, places, and events. In this respect, the Bible's place is unique among the world's sacred literature.

Most sacred literature records divine directives revealed by sages such as Muhammad, Confucius, or Lao Tzu. Some books of the Bible use the same approach, of course, and similar poetic license of myth, simile, metaphor, and allegory must be accounted for. Examples can be seen in biblical books such as Job and Jonah. While Job might have, like Casey, been a mythical figure, Job's virtues of patience and faith still live on.

Jonah likewise. Accepting his being swallowed whole by a whale presses the modern reader, until they come across Dr. Lamsa's insightful gems. But even if a seeker has yet to see these, like Job's, Jona's message is timeless, especially if he returned, with the same reluctance, to continue God's work as had Peter. Seeing these as accounts, which might not have historically happened as reported, but imparted important lessons as I heard one Rabbi explain them, made sense.

The explanation presented no challenge to my faith.

But, over all, the Bible is different in its primary claim as a book of history. Its primary task is to reveal histories of *the active presence of God in human life.* As the *active presence of human beings* is likewise revealed, discretion in discernment is a must. Unless poetic license and its corollaries are implied or directly stated as such, Bible stories are to be understood as based upon fact.

While proof of Solomon's women might not exist, well-read Bibles, bolstered by proofs from secular history, and archaeologists' well-placed shovels, have pretty much established that he was real -likewise, King Ahab. Though an accurate count confirming his seventy sons might be lacking, he was a historical being, as was his infamous wife, Jezebel.

Herod and even Pontius Pilate were real.

I had to set aside my views and see the Bible as a historic collection of works addressed to readers in cultures and times, quite different than today's. I also had to assume that few, if any, of the authors were consciously aware that their creations would someday become *canonized* as our Bible.

Hard-nosed historical accuracy was to be maintained.

But as a metaphysical person of faith, I also had to maintain that the *active presence of God* permeated the material. The task seemed no different than that of Socrates or Stevenson, if the *active Presence, is* defined as *paranormal.*

The dead returning is about as *paranormal* as it gets.

Such paranormality is certainly attributable to God's presence. If it is not attributable to such a *Presence,* then to whom else or what else can the dead's return be attributed? If the Bible records the same types of activity, as seen in Socrates and Stevenson, then these activities must surely come from the same source. It seems that such actions should be seen as quite normal, but oddly, most view them as *paranormal!*

Semantics aside, I decided that the best way to maintain this *Presence* was to let the Bible speak for itself. I would not ignore what it said, nor ascribe to it what it didn't say. I attempted this using verbatim verse, as much as was practical and found there were no shortcuts in making the Bible relevant for today. The same approach also seemed appropriate for sources such as Socrates, Aristotle and Origen.

That the placement of both ancient and contemporary commentaries might be distracting and discourage a broader readership was also considered. This was not a concern of the thesis. My general command of academic writing had long pleased professors. The problem would become paramount in rewriting the material for a book such as this. Of course, no such book would be forthcoming, unless I could make a solid biblical argument for reincarnation. But also, no such book would be forthcoming unless a publisher could be convinced that a lot of people would read it.

The Dream

In pondering whether a popular readership might find a super-slick version featuring a "crystals and carrot juice" approach to a best seller on reincarnation, of more appeal; I decided it was best to stick with using direct quotes. Letting go and letting God reveal The Word seemed best. This would also respect the common sense and sincerity of anyone who might read such a book. While a reader friendly approach would be attempted, even in the thesis, I wouldn't pretend that what transpired would be easy weekend reading.

However, I hoped that the experience would be inspirational.

Another reason for using direct quotes was in considering who might read them. *CNN/Gallop* consistently reported that 96% of its respondents believed in God and about 27% of these accepted reincarnation. A goodly group *(pun intended)* surely shared an interest in the Bible. This would be a lot of people.

However, 73% browsing the biblical section of a bookstore probably wouldn't believe in reincarnation.

Religious sensitivity would need a careful consideration. I suspected that few outside of the metaphysical community were aware of the issues. But once aware, the academic and religious rank and file would want to read the wisdom of the West's wisest minds. The introduction of more universal brains like Plato, Schopenhauer and Einstein, to offset mindsets such as Iraeneus and Justinian, might prove helpful.

> ***A Sermon***
> ☺ Ireaneneus and Justinian were full of *blasphemy*.
>
> (Captain *L.*)

The Prize

Direct quotes from within our own traditions and, in particular, from within the universal Judeo/Christian tradition of the Holy Land presented in an Islamic friendly manner and of the very universal Judeo/Christian and Islamic friendly Edgar Cayce, would further lead to an easier acceptance by the mainstream of our culture. The approach would better insure the Work being accepted as an opportunity for Spiritual growth, rather than being dismissed as more New Age nonsense, or just another politically correct assault on Western beliefs.

Reincarnation in the Bible was not yet, and is still not, a high profile issue. But this will change. The inevitable scientific impact of Stevenson will one day make it so. His discoveries are worthy of a Nobel Peace Prize. I suspected reincarnation would be a front burner issue in the coming century. I hoped my research would prove helpful.

The Sleeping Prophet

As to Cayce as a prophet, his Work has seen criticism concerning prophesies of earthquakes sinking California into the sea. Clearly this has not happened and, quite rightly, questions doubting his status as a true prophet have risen. However, a deeper look suggests many misunderstood such predictions.

The confusion centered upon Cayce's metaphorical meaning.

The same confusion can often be seen in biblical study. Metaphorical mention of Solomon's seven hundred wives and Ahab's seventy sons referred to Godly gifts, as understood by the patriarchal people of the times and not necessarily to physical realities. (The use of the number *seven*, in metaphysics' usually symbolizes something of divine nature.)

Cayce's metaphorical mention of earth shattering California earthquakes concerned personal problems faced by himself, others - you're problem is <u>like</u> an earthquake - and coming world events he saw throughout the nineteen-thirties and early forties, leading to World War Two. Later date *earth changes* might have referred to the vast worldwide transformations in spiritual, cultural, and technological events, he predicted for today.

Prophecies, which don't come to pass, should not necessarily be dismissed as errors, especially if they were prefaced with a suggestion to work either for or against a fulfillment. The measure of Cayce, as a prophet, should be based upon how he motivated people toward positive acts. In the Bible, Jonah faces a similar evaluation. God instructed him to tell the people of Nineveh that their evil ways would bring destruction. Its occupants changed and avoided a disaster. Many good people, in hearing Cayce, went to California to join the good already there to *pray away* the problem.

Among them was Jess Stearn himself. He anguished over possibly over alarming people, in his coverage in the *Sleeping Prophet*. He needn't have. That the citizens of Nineveh and California, separated by centuries and continents, avoided big league class prophesied disasters, established that even the most *bonafide* of such prophesies can be changed through positive human effort.

Nineveh being spared didn't label Jonah as a false prophet and the same regard must be given to Cayce on California. Prophecies only reveal the future in the way that blueprints only predict how a structure is going to be constructed. *Free-or will*, like the architect's pencil, can make changes in the twinkling of an eye.

As to architecture, Cayce challenged conventional history, especially that of Egypt's Great Pyramid of Giza and Sphinx. As to that pyramid, speaking as a builder, there's - *No Way* - such a precise structure could have been built so quickly with copper hand tools and hard labor. Laser cutters and a lifting device of some sophistication had to have played a part. That an advanced civilization was responsible, as Cayce offered, is still the best explanation, despite the evidence presented in the, otherwise, very excellent *Nova* television series.

You should be able to get a tape or DVD at your local rental place. That other pyramids were constructed using the methods they presented, are valid. However, their assertion that each of Giza's two and a half million multi-toned stones were set - <u>every two and a half minutes</u> - is, with all due respect to Drs. Hawass and Lehner, implausible. Pharaoh Cheops' claim that he built it during his own lifetime is ludicrous. It took a hundred years, in the twentieth century, to build Washington's National *Cathedral*. If Cayce's right, Atlantean high-tech techniques took about as long in building their cathedral-like structure, long before Cheops was even born!

The pyramid's purpose wasn't to gratify the two-bit tyrants' ego - his only relic is a figurine just a few inches high - hardly the mark of someone who could have even *spelled* pyramid, let alone build one. Cayce calmly asserted that the monument is to remind civilizations, like ours, that others as smart as we, got here first.

Nothing's new.

It's both a symbol of caution - they self-destructed, and so can we. It's also one of hope. They placed hope's symbol in the monument's deepest chamber. The laser precision of its original limestone facade, while impressive, holds within it the greatest of all symbols soothing humanity's deepest fear. It's the empty sarcophagus. The structure never housed the dead. The assurance is from ourselves, to ourselves. Yes we've walked on this planet before. It explains that while great calamities may come and go: *There is no death!*

Life is eternal.

The Sphinx reminds us that we are infinite beings created in the image of God that are living in finite bodies. But we are not our bodies! The weathering on the sphinx's sides, according to some studies; date it more in line with Cayce. He said both monuments were built about ten thousand B.C.E. Save your *Atlantean* money boys and girls - in both technology and relics, Atlantis shall rise again!

Bias

I felt secure I could defend Cayce, Stevenson, and my many sources as relevant. But I still had to be aware of personal biases and keep things as mainstream as possible.

Three fully credentialed Ph.D.'s were covering my tracks and it wasn't easy writing for such mighty minds. They were not only smarter than I was, but their professional reputations would be on the line could I convince them to endorse what I had written. Any hint of a "wacko" approach would end the ball game. I would have to make sure my hind loins were well girded.

I was convinced that direct quotes and *historic* approaches would cover the bases. That is, until I hit into foul territory. My major source, in studying the Bible as history, had been a small work by theologian Vernon Teeples. I had carefully followed his advice and had no problems; until I was hit with what I felt was an untenable position.

He noted that one must accept that some ancient writings, which include the Bible, contain revisions of fact, or fictional narratives, which are not always truthful. Sometimes their intent was benign, as seen in Job and Jonah. But sometime their intent was to serve the propaganda purposes of the ruling elite. As language changes, as we've seen, such insertions are easy to spot by those trained in ancient linguistics.

I backed up *full astern!* I had no difficulty in accepting benign intents to strengthen moral messages, nor in accepting that the megalomania of a Pharaoh Cheops or a Caesar Nero could influence how history remembers them. Egyptian and Roman records have been known to gloss over the truth. But I could not accept such mischief in biblical accounts. Like Stevenson, in his early inquiries, this was an emotional obstacle for which I was unprepared.

In dealing with such, an alien supposition, I began to question the value of historic approaches. Rather than confronting them, I explored a more traditional approach. This consumed precious research time, in what I would realize was a futile attempt to avoid a major test of my faith. I feared that the combination of close scrutiny demanded of Stevenson's and historic methods might compromise the cohesiveness of the Bible. I had felt it was my purpose to uphold biblical verses and not to break or confound them. This was the root cause of my dilemma. I ventured further and found a waypoint. Teeples described it as *bibliolatry.*

This needs some explanation.

Islamic and Judeo-Christians mention Moses cautioned his flock to avoid idolatry: "You shall have no other gods before me." [5]

Teeple's explained that the Bible could become an idol (as may any external object or ism) should one perceive it as the Godhead. The caution helped in realizing that while I was a person of faith, I also had a bad case of *bibliolatry*.

The antidote was *wisdom.*

In meditating, the door to wisdom opened and I began to see the Bible as a navigational tool, not unlike what a ship's captain uses to determine position. In realizing that as beacons, buoys, and charts are not, in themselves home port, neither is the Bible - or at least one's personal grasp (as in *demiurge*) - God incarnate.

Seen as a good instrument, the Bible helps captains of personal destiny know their relative positions and plot correct courses to righteousness. Thus equipped, I began to rewrite some one hundred twenty-five pages of polemics and platitudes. These had been interesting, but lacked the tough scrutiny needed to satisfy modern demands. In retesting the waters, I developed an inner guidance system. This made it possible to steer, in new ways, through the coming currents, calms, and storms of the Scriptures.

The system allowed for unfettered expressions of emotion and opened feelings, which sometimes were not of the *goody two-shoe* variety, associated with biblical study. I expressed them in the bellicose vein of Elijah, as nautical expletives which would have made even Justinian blush. I had never felt outrage in reading the Bible before. While initially disconcerting, I grew to feel that such feelings would keep me on a true course to *God's* Word.

Thus, I felt anger was proper in reading of events when praised as virtues, that upheld injustices. In recognizing *hard* feelings as warnings of Spiritual imperfection presented as *The* Word, I sought to steer with the greatest precision. My fear was that I might miss such navigational markers and, as in a sin of omission, feel my vessel bump bottom in not addressing them. Prior to this, my fear had been the same fear that bibliolatry congers up, known as *fear* of God. Fortunately, Dr. Lamsa[6] pointed out that the biblical idiom "fear of God," is better understood as "respect," as in, "respect for God." (Josephus described Roman soldiers' respect for Jerusalem's temple as, "holy horror.")

In my developing processes, I had felt some measure of being less than respectful, especially, in considering that someone as evil as Justinian could have taken liberties with the Bible. My difficulties were relieved in realizing that others had sailed these seas before me. They too, had experienced similar problems in balancing faith, scholarly integrity, and common sense. Fortunately, in their explorations, reliable charts were created and navigational markers placed.

Admiral Cayce couched this advice:

"The Bible has past through many hands. Many that would turn that which was written unto the meanings that would suit their own purposes, as ye yourselves often do."

The *Spirit* of the Word is what's most important:

"But if ye will get the *spirit* of that *written* there ye may find it will lead thee to the gates of heaven ... Read it to be wise. Study it to understand. Live it to know that the Christ walks through same with thee."[7]

High Seas and Curve Balls

It would have been difficult to accept that the Bible might not bat a perfect thousand; but suppositions must change in light of new evidence, no matter how painful. However, I felt that even if discrepancies were present, biblical truths would still stand. Like Cayce's Work, the Bible's value is best measured in how it encourages people towards positive acts.

I later discovered that the Bible has its own systems of self-correction. This was often seen in the psychic abilities of its prophets. Their paranormal *Work* makes up about thirty to forty percent of the Bible and their statements go far in reinstating *thousand percent* suppositions. An example of self-correction is seen in taking another look at Jehu. How can anyone forget: "And Jehu drew a bow with his full strength, and smote Joram in his back, and the arrow went out at his heart, and he sank down in his chariot."

There's little reason to doubt the account's accuracy. The problem is that Jehu's act was seen as Godly. But shooting his king in the back hardly seemed proper for a spiritually directed soldier. To let the issue slide would be ignoring the Bible's insightful coverage of human beings. And as error and fraud often accompanies the *human condition*, a failure to discern between *The Word,* and that of a scribe, as has been seen in comments concerning Cheops claims as a pyramid builder and Cayce's earth changes, can lead to confusion. Also, as Stevenson had found necessary, issues of error (and *boldfaced lying*) are always the first consideration in reincarnation type cases. He used the scholarly term: *Motivated error of memory and recording.*

It still means, *bold-faced lying!*

As to Jehu's piety, and how the Bible corrects such misconceptions, we must examine events, which took place after the tyrants' death. He died during the 7th century B.C.E. About one hundred years later, in the late 7th and early 6th centuries, the prophet Jeremiah appeared. He saw Israel's deity, *Yahweh,* as the omnipotent creator of the universe. Humanity experienced the *Presence* in inner-felt ways, as would the Gnostics. *World-class* holy persons at about the same time as Jeremiah arrived at a similar enlightenment. They were Lao Tzu, Confucius, and Buddha.

Though stated in different languages, their universal concept saw God's love as open to all. The understanding came to the Holy Land through Jeremiah. Yahweh was a being far beyond that of the mountain deity, or wrathful god of war, that the Israelites had so often fathomed as their protector. The new Yahweh was *love* incarnate, and as such, loved each of its creations equally. No particular peoples or places, such as Jerusalem, were placed above the rest.

Jeremiah saw Jerusalem's coming destruction. He offered that one of the reasons for the coming calamity was that certain books of the Bible, of his day, had either been altered or misread.

These were not the benign embellishments of a Job or Jonah, but embellishments that would delude Jerusalem's people into thinking their salvation lay in strict conformity with certain laws and traditions of the past, and in rigid religious ritual. Jeremiah's concern would have centered upon an alleged newfound version of the book of *Deuteronomy*. Deuteronomy, as we have seen, spelled out portions of the laws of Moses.

This new version was supposedly discovered during the renovation of Jerusalem's temple, under king *Josiah*. Jeremiah psychically pegged the document as not entirely that of Moses. Many scholars agree.[9] Jeremiah didn't subscribe to the polite polemics of scholars - *motivated errors* - and termed such action, *the lying pen of the scribes*. He faulted Jerusalem's *wise men* for allowing the outrage:

"How do you say, we are wise and the law of the Lord is with us? Lo, surely the *lying pen* of the scribes has made it [the Bible of his era] for falsehood.

The *wise men* are ashamed, they are defeated and caught because they have rejected the word of the Lord, and there is no wisdom in them." (Jeremiah 8:8-9)

In leaving out the term, *lying,* the King James translation is a little kinder:

"The *pen* of the scribes is in *vain.*"

It means the same.

The Jerusalem version is as painful as the Aramaic in maintaining Jeremiah's unvarnished directness. *Jerusalem* is rooted in the *Work* of Saint Jerome:

"How dare you say; we are wise, and possess the Law of Yahweh?

But look how it has been falsified by the *lying pen* of the scribes!

The *pen* obviously wrote for the house of Josiah. Had Jeremiah been a historian or a psychiatrist - *voicing* the above would have seen his execution. The house of *Josiah,* like that of *Jehu,* had a similarity in killing off those who differed:

"*Jehu* slew all that remained of the house of Ahab in Jezreel, and all his great men and his kinfolks and his priests."

(1st Kings 10:11)

"*Josiah* slew all the priests of the high places, who burned incense upon the altars."   (2nd Kings 23:22)

Jeremiah, because he was a *prophet,* was exempt from such atrocities. Dr. Lamsa, as a United States *citizen,* though his Aramaic translation is not always found in traditional biblical bookstores, was likewise immune, despite his spelling out this controversial idiomatic understanding of Jeremiah's passage:

"Scribes *forged* some of the passages of the Bible." [10]

Jeremiah's endless struggle against Josiah's warlike stance, and that of his loutish offspring, made the prophet's life miserable.

He had counseled them to seek peace.

As to Josiah personally, on the surface, his intent would seem to have been a calling to repentance, and a returning to the laws of Moses. As to why parts were *forged,* as Aramaic and Latin so uncompromisingly put it, Jeremiah's raising a paranormal red flag indicated Josiah, and those on his payroll, had more on their minds than a devotion to the *Lawgiver.*

It must be remembered that, after the death of Solomon, Israel split apart. Ten of her twelve tribes moved north and the remnant remained in *Judah.* Judah and Israel constantly quarreled and even warred between themselves. When Israel was destroyed by the Assyrians, with Judah's blessing, much of what survived to become Israel's history, was *penned* by her enemies in Jerusalem, Judah's capitol. (Israel's capital was *Samaria.*) Josiah, I am quite sure, had a hand in the revisions, and most likely, the later Assyrians. (A divided Middle East would be easier to control.) These revised histories became books of the Hebrew Bible. Tainted, as were Paul's *Epistles,* they encompass 1st and 2nd Kings, Chronicles, Joshua, and Samuel.

These not only cover Jehu, but Solomon, Elijah, Ahab, Jezebel, and all the kings of Israel and Judah, from Saul until the fall of Jerusalem. As only the southern kingdom survived to return relatively intact (Israel's *ten tribes* of the north were all but obliterated) it is not surprising that the north received such *bad press.* While no one person physically survived to counter, as we've seen and will continue to see, archaeology and intuition has.

The northern region became *Galilee.* Those later living there were called *Samaritans.* All Israelite kings were attacked, and even Solomon reprimanded. The Scribe *Hatchetjob (*my inner sources tell me that was *her* name) had concluded that Solomon's love life had offended God. The numbers he maintained of wives and concubines weren't a problem. *Heaven's* complaint concerned so many of the beauties having hailed from foreign capitals!

Worse yet, Solomon even let them practice the religions of their homelands. The final outrage was in honoring their beliefs, with an occasional presence at their worship services! The *pen* intimated that love, racial equality, and religious freedom had been the reason for Israel's split.[11] King Solomon, the wisest, virulent (and from this lascivious salty soul's point of view) the most blessed son of *Bathsheba* and *David,* would normally have rolled off a heavenly cloud, in a belly laugh, at such a deduction.

Unfortunately, such scribal meddling created profound problems for *Heaven,* the children of Israel, Judah, the Middle East of today, and the history of the world. It was no wonder that Jeremiah had gone *ballistic*. Jesus, himself a citizen of *Galilee*, sided with Jeremiah in saying of such scribes:

"Woe to you *scribes!* For you have taken away the keys of knowledge; you did not enter, and those who were entering you hindered." [12]

As to Jehu, *oddly,* such scribes let him remain relatively unscathed. Their major reprimand concerned his not having massacred more *infidels*.

Despite *the keys of knowledge,* which Josiah's <u>good press</u> sought to *hinder,* Jehu was <u>bad news</u>. His military coup not only saw the takeover of Israel's legitimate government and the deaths of priests, but all Ahab's seventy sons. Jehu's callousness is further noted in archaeology's suggestion that he had been Ahab's own brother (see Chapter 17)! Jehu established three generations of loutish and warlike offspring, whose ineptness, so like that of Josiah's brood, led to the kingdom's downfall.

Questioning why such a *lowlife*, who would also incur the wrath of at least two prophetic sources was idolized by Josiah, whom an arrow would later *smote* - just like Jehu's victim, sparked my curiosity. Obviously, Josiah and his supporters sought to prove, through their *lying pens*, that Israel's problems hadn't resulted from the sinfulness of its present administration. Those sins had been committed in the past by those transgressing laws of the newly discovered *Josiah* version of Deuteronomy. Such sinning had infuriated the wrathful God of old. If Josiah could show that Judah's current problems were attributable to past sins, he could avoid criticism of his failed policies.

This can explain the rewrite of history, biblical forgery, and generalized metaphorical misrepresentations. An example might stand in this passage:

> "I the Lord am a zealous God, visiting the *offenses of the fathers* upon their children to the third and fourth generations." [13]

According to *the word of Josiah*, in blaming his failures upon the *offenses of fathers* that were being passed on to him, <u>as an innocent victim</u>, he could cover up any consideration that his phony personal piety and political stupidity, so like *Jehu's,* was the real root cause. Later leaders would have reason to maintain Josiah's myth. Initially, it would dissuade their subjects from revolt, and after the failures of the crown, confuse the followers, as to whom they owed their allegiance.

This avoided *regime change!*

Later generations would be deluded into thinking that the metaphorical understanding, *sins of fathers are passed to sons,* meant that God punished innocent children for the transgressions of their ancestors. This concept led toward the doctrines of *Original Sin* pushed with such irrational fervor in later times.

Reincarnation, as the better understanding, explains that the metaphorical *fathers* are the actions, which we as humans, regardless of gender, create. The results, or *children*, are the fruit of those actions. Jeremiah's insight and the calamities created in history, by *the word - <u>according to Josiah</u>*, lead me to change my supposition. It was he, rather than Justinian, who initiated the *reading right out*! As to the literal belief that God punishes innocent children, *The Word,* according to <u>God</u>, as asserted in the very same book Josiah shamed, shames the scribes:

> "The fathers shall not be put to death for their children, nor shall the children be put to death for their fathers; but every man shall be put to death for his own sin.   (Deuteronomy 24:16)

The short-term results of Josiah and Jehu saw *holier than thou* religious issues surface. While the kings might have hoped to exploit them, bloody civil unrest at home and disastrous diplomatic isolationism abroad resulted. It was lost that Solomon's multiple marriages symbolically represented peace treaties, between Israel and her many Palestinian, Oriental, and African neighbors. (Additionally, concubines, in the context of the passage, might have referred to the other dictionary definition, suggesting that such folks could also be non-sexual or *social partners.)*

Solomon's treaties had brought unparalleled prosperity and security.

That spirituality and practicality often go hand in hand, seemed to have been overlooked. The new policies insured that populations were polarized and allies alienated. This gave super powers opportunities for expansion. When first Assyria, and later Babylon, stepped in, Jehu/Josiah's defense plan had been to sic Yahweh on them, as one would sic an angry pit bull upon an intruder. It was a foolish expectation. God respected no persons or places, above the rest. Divine love was both unconditional and equal. Jerusalem could not exploit its especial position, as the capitol of the *chosen people*. For God not only loved the Israelites, but Arabs, Africans, Assyrians, Babylonians, Chinese, Egyptians, Ethiopians, Phoenicians, and later, even *Romans:*

"Hear, O Israel: the Lord thy God is one Lord." [14]

Biblical cases, I was sure, would also provide examples of biblical self-correction. Such cases would likewise expose the folly of a Jehu, who would *live by the sword,* or a Josiah, who would have the audacity to change the Scriptures. I suspected his easing up on Jehu was because he'd been Jehu! This would explain so many of their similarities, including the bizarre circumstance of Josiah's death (to be seen in Chapter Seventeen). If their cases revealed a *father* and *son* relationship, in past and later life circumstances, such a case would expose, as a fallacy, that peace can come to the Holy Land (or any other place) through brutality, or that one can blame their personal circumstances upon the actions of others.

Jeremiah's fearless mind maintained my faith, that the wide-open course of historic approaches could not confound or confuse the Scriptures. Like Cayce, Jeremiah was not the only prophet to suggest seekers use discernment. And like Cayce, Jeremiah had no problem in using paranormal gifts to clear confusion, when error or *the lying pen* was presented as *the Word of the Lord*.

Though I was forced to accept that obstructions lay about, knowing that the Bible revealed its own markers of self-correction, saw a newfound confidence. I girded up my loins in humbleness, awe, respect, and wonderment.

Link to Jeremiah.

His oracles, like Cayce's, were penned by others. This seal might once have adorned such a *Work*. The inscription identifies its owner as having been Baruch, the prophet's scribe (see Jeremiah 45:1). Baruch's apparent fingerprint stands embedded to the left.

Rigging for heavier weather, I kept an even sharper watch. I no longer feared a compromise in my relationship with God. If I got into shallow water, I reckoned a distress call (practiced as prayer) would result in the presence of a more powerful vessel. Such a *Vessel* would pull this hapless mariner off any shoals of mistake he might encounter.

Passages, which aroused anger, or doubt, were now pursued with the same diligence as those producing joy. In maintaining a course between these extremes, I determined deeper insights, not only about the Bible, but also about myself. The extremes let me know where I stood as an advancing soul.

When anger was felt in gory passages that were once seen as Godly, then I knew I had made headway. If truth touched me with positive feelings, my heading was likewise correct. Thus, I surmised that, applying the close scrutiny demanded, not only of historic approaches - but of all approaches, including those which involve feelings - was to honor the Bible as a document worthy of one's best inquiry. To do less was to fetter its message.

The *Divine* is limitless, and so should be our questioning.

I knew that while my insights wouldn't read like Sunday school sermons, they would withstand the high seas and curve balls of critical debate. As to personal bias, I offered my complete *confession*, warts and all, in an effort to lessen possible errors in objectivity.

The Captain's Confession

"Personal belief is a factor, which is probably inescapable in this type of research. While the use of guidance, through prayer and meditation, has been practiced, I have conscientiously sought to remain unbiased and have limited my personal opinions to well-worded occasional quips and tiny sermonettes. These are best considered as off the record in the reader's evaluation process. But, biases may still be present. Thus some understanding of my personal background may be necessary, lest unacknowledged currents increase potential for error.

Though I bear the name of a prominent frontier family of Eastern Kentucky's *Bible belt* and possess an accredited university diploma, a substantial portion of my formative years was spent growing up in a tough Baltimore city neighborhood. This background, coupled with experiences in the *College of Hard Knocks* as a home improvement contractor, professional plumber, and waterman, may sometimes color these pages. Out of respect for lessons learned from this past of pain, practicality and growth, I have respectfully inserted some of their associated jargon and vocabulary.

As to religion, I am a Christian seeker. Reincarnation as a rational realization, maintains my inner knowing but constantly tested faith. I also possess a lifetime membership in the Association for Research and Enlightenment.

To account for my close feelings with the personalities, soon to be presented, my children submitted a hypothesis. They concurred I was old enough to have known Elijah, or at least John the Baptist, personally. Thus any sensations of *deja vu*, that I experienced, were undoubtedly attributable to a memory befuddled by old age.

The Captain's Kids
Since this photo, they've become fine young adults. At Puberty, I dealt with teen type family friction in reminding them, that as they had chosen me as their father, *before birth*, it was too late to complain. Thus the fatherly - and so Solomon like – directives of wisdom being heaped upon them would continue.

They complained anyway.

I most reverently decline any past-life identification with famous persons of the Bible. I am the *mouth* - not the *Voice!*

In Old Testament times, I was surely a Phoenician seafarer, studied art at Elijah's school on Mount Carmel, and attended classes at Plato's academy.

In the New Testament, during the construction of King Herod's waterworks, the marvel of the age, I might have consumed a few beers with his head plumber, in their discussion. More importantly, I probably knew Saint Luke in some capacity.

A psychic, in reviewing my more recent past lives, said I was once a British captain who fought pirates off Virginia's east coast. He stated my previous vessel 'was larger, had guns, and was more ably manned than the one you now possess.' Though I was sure I had once been a pirate, who fought British captains, the psychic's insight rang of truth. As I had paid him with good money marked, *in God we trust,* I assumed that his services were just as genuine.

Accordingly, as a penitent sailor experiencing some karmic demotion, either from a past life or past mid-life indiscretion, I hereby acknowledge, in true humbleness, all conscious personal virtues, blemishes, and biases." (Captain *L*)

Notes

1. Proverbs 16:3
2. 1st Kings 17:16
3. See Charlesworth (1988)
4. See Teeples (1982)
5. Deuteronomy 5:7
6. See Lamsa (1972)
7. (262 - 60)
8. See Sachar (1965)
9. See Snaith, Sockman and Calkins (1954)
10. Lamsa 1971 p. 42
11. See 1st Kings 11
12. Luke 11:53
13. Exodus 20:5
14. Deuteronomy 6:4

Chapter 14

Shore Leave

Let's *heave to* for now and take a minute to evaluate positions. If you've been pretty much in agreement, concerning reincarnation in general and in the Bible, you should breeze right through. Most of your works been done. The purpose for this pause is to allow for a self evaluation as to which direction you might want to go - either in shoring up your present beliefs, or in considering changes.

Benjamin Franklin used the following approach in making decisions of all types.

He would make a list giving the reasons why he would go forward on an issue. Then he listed the reasons why he wouldn't. He added them up, considering the quantity and quality of the entries, and made his decision. I've alphabetically listed some of the names we've seen supporting reincarnation and provided spaces for the opposition. You'll need to list your own people if you're a materialist or instant creationist or undecided. Only you know your beliefs and you should know the sources behind them. If you're not sure, you can read and reread and add or subtract from the lists, or do a little homework on your own. When you fill in the blanks, be kind. Don't put someone like Al Capone in the materialist column if you oppose materialism or Himmler and Tojo in the reincarnation section to gain a cheap shot - if you oppose reincarnation.

Remember, you're dialoging - not debating.

Be fair. Use objectivity and place only those who consistently promoted their positions through writing, teaching, or other significant activity. Capone, Himmler, and Tojo were tried as common criminals. I doubt that not one of their Italian, Chinese, Filipino, Jewish, or American victims was lectured a deep discourse on materialism, instant creationism, or reincarnation.

Listed next are two dozen plus, among the supportive souls seen so far. As for Muhammad, I'm placing him on the list now, so as to assure Muslim readers - up front - that they're being included. He hasn't been discussed yet, as he wasn't a biblical figure. However both his faith and the religion, which he founded, were Bible based. His followers offered sanctuary to the Pythagorean and Essene descendants escaping the *Orthodox* purges of the dark ages.

A thousand years of advanced civilization resulted.

Today's Islam is made up of some seventy sects spread throughout predominately third world countries from western Africa to the Philippines. Its two largest sects are Sunnis and Shiites. Shiites, Sufis and Druse are among the major groups professing reincarnation. An additional movement is the Wahhabists. They're among those against reincarnation.

Established in what is now Saudi Arabia at about the same time as the establishment of the American *Constitution,* Wahhabism has been the kingdom's official religion since the days of the dynasty's founder, King Ibn Saud. Perceptions of Islam's militancy, second class treatment of women, virulent anti-Semitism, and an insistence upon rule of Mosque and state (called *Sharia Law),* with its disturbing revision, according to figures recorded in the United Nations, of slavery,[1] are rooted in Wahabi teachings. These make it difficult for the more moderate sects to advance the religion's appeal.

It's an internal struggle moderation must win.

At stake is Islam itself. For should open mindedness fail, its best and brightest, in being forced outside the Muslim mainstream, as had Christianities best and brightest - the Pythagoreans - been forced outside the Christian mainstream, many Muslims will likewise have to look elsewhere for spiritual sustenance. This could throw the billion souls now embracing Islam at the mercy of a fanatical leadership bent on leading them toward a disastrous backward step. Religion and politics don't mix in free societies. Like communism, such attempts have failed whenever and wherever they've been attempted.

Whether drawn to God/Allah, Jesus, Muhammad, or Vishnu, all of good will must work for a peaceful resolution. It doesn't start by pointing fingers. Our own past has also seen sin and who among us could cast a stone at Muhammad's intent. He led a desert people to learn about God's goodness through observing nature and taught them the similar *born again* sentiments of Jesus:

"And [Allah] sent down rains from above in proper quantity and
He brings back to life the dead earth, similarly ye shall be *reborn.*"

(Al Koran Chapter 25 - Sura Zakhraf - Meccan Verses 5-10-6)

As there is no *canonized* version, noting the translation is important. Just as important are Cayce's notations that the word *Jews,* when referenced in the Bible - and most likely the Koran - referred to the authorities and not to the people, nor their descendants. Only bigots look for anti-Semitism in the Holy books!

As for today's terrorists, these Ku Klux Klan types are no more the spokesmen for the Islam of Muhammad than were Milosovich (of Kosovo's forgotten headlines), Hitler, or Himmler, the spokesmen for the Christianity of Jesus. The same sentiment stands for Togo and Buddhism.

Common criminality, rather then religious fervor, links them. As for the likes of Osama Bin Ladin, his henchmen, and the late Saddam Hussein - a materialist minded *Stalinist,* and probably not even a Muslim - Muhammad intended this message for them:

"Those who doubt immortality are dead and they do not know when they will be *born again.* Your God is peerless and those who have no faith in the ultimate have perverse hearts and they want to pose as great men."   (Sura 14:2)

God will not be mocked.

In today's climate, spreading the lessons of reincarnation through the story of a revered figure like Elijah, who returned as John the Baptist to lose his head as a criminal - because of past life acts of religious intolerance - is paramount. That religions and national identities can change in later incarnations is critical. Yes, you can die white, Anglo, and Anglican and become *(born again)* a Hindu in India. A Muslim might return Jewish, and someone Jewish could come back black and so on and so on …and!

Play Ball

Below are the three columns. They're not unlike the rosters of sports teams. Choosing which team you might want to join, once you've listed and looked up *whose who,* ought to help you decide which direction you might want to take.

I've unbiasedly named the reincarnation proponents *All Stars* as they're *all stars.*

Materialists, or *Sadducees,* sadly appear shortened as *Sadds.* Though bravely leading lives in the *here and now,* when the time of the *here and now* of death arrives, it often arrives - for them - as a *here and now* of sadness.

Instant creationists exhibit *prayer and praise*. As *prayer and praise* are heard in heaven, *prayer and praise* are heard here. Especially *praise* as *Voiced* by Jesus: *You are gods.* Those that *listen* become *All Stars*. Until willing to see and hear, as the children of Jerusalem Jesus: "longed to gather as a hen gathers her chickens under her wings"[2] - you'll be teamed up with the *The Chicks.*

Hope no one's offended. *Bias* will be *bias.* (Har Har!) Be good. If not - be careful! When you get back, we'll *shove off.*

Reincarnationists	Materialists	Instant Creationists
All Stars	***The Sadds***	***The Chicks***
1. Aristotle	1. Fidel Castro	1. Ireanaeus
2. Buddha	2. Saddam Heussein	2. Josiah
3. Mr. Edgar Cayce	3. Adolph Hitler	3. Justinian
4. Mrs. Gertrude E. Cayce	4. V. Lenin	4. O. Bin Ladin
5. Dalai Lama	5. Chairman Mao	5. Ms. Theodora
6. Dr. Albert Einstein	6. Karl Marx	6.
7. Saint Elizabeth	7. Ms. M. M. O'Hare	7.
8. Dr. Benjamin Franklin	8. Joseph Stalin	8.
9. Mahatma Gandhi	9.	9.
10. Jeremiah the Prophet	10.	10.
11. Christ Jesus	11.	11.
12. John the Baptist	12.	12.
13. Carl Jung Md.	13.	13.
14. Mary Mother of God	14.	14.
15. Muhammad	15.	15.
16. Origen of Alexandria	16.	16.
17. Saint Paul	17.	17.
18. Bishop James Pike	18.	18.
19. Plato	19.	19.
20. Pythagoras	20.	20.
21. President F. Roosevelt	21.	21.
22. Socrates	22.	22.
23. King Solomon	23.	23.
24. President G Washington	24.	24.
25. Ms. Martha Washington	25.	25.
26	26.	26.
27.	27.	27.
28.	28.	28.
29.	29.	29.
30.	30.	30.

Pop Quiz:

Benjamin Franklin's Masonic lodge was located in Philadelphia, where he served as its *Grand Master.* The lodge was named after a famous biblical personality prominately prefaced with the mention - *the Voice* - in all four books of the Gospels.

Can you name this person? (For the answer, see item 3 in the notes below.)

Notes

1. See *N.Y. Times* Sept. 5, 2000; *Boston Globe,* Sept. 18, 2000 and numerous notations on the Internet and other media.
2. Luke 13:34
3. If you had to look here for the answer, shore leave is denied!

After swabbing the decks, varnishing the topsides, pumping out the holding tanks, and wiping down the bilges, you'll need to *read again*: 1st Kings chapters 16 through 22. Then, *again read,* chapters 8 - 10 of 2nd Kings, the 40th chapter of Isaiah, the Book of Malachi, the 1st chapters of Mark, Luke, and John, and the 3rd, 4th, 11th, 14th, 17th, and 21st, of Matthew. This will do for starters.

Upon receipt of your fifty-buck donation to Atlantic University, *shore leave* will be reconsidered.

Shore Leave.

Chapter 15

The Grand Slam

Welcome back.
Stow you're gear and we'll *shove off*.

Homeward Bound.

In reviewing the *procedures* my game plan evolved. Presented would be a historically accurate portrayal of biblical events using *over the counter* mainstream sources. You've seen these in the previous chapters, some of which will be reviewed again and, as a glance at the *Suggested Readings and Bibliography* chapter bears out, nothing, *off the wall* was to be submitted. Historic accuracy and scientific resources would be next at bat. The combination of the three would (in American baseball terminology) "load the bases."

But established biblical tradition and secular skepticism would field a formidable defense, and no matter how many playing points might be on the "bases," scoring can only occur when these merge to form a persuasive final consortium or "home plate" of reasoned conclusions.

Scoring would begin with the relatively straightforward establishment that cases similar to Stevenson's "reincarnation type" stood recorded in the Bible. Next would be demonstrating that the context of the scriptural metaphors lined up in support of reincarnation, as easily as we saw in those concerning *sins* of metaphorical *fathers* and *mothers* being passed down to their creations, that is, in their next lives, as in *children*. Such a combination of history and metaphor, which when combined with the rest of the evidence, would be the *grand slam* which would win the ball game. The *full figured* lady could then commence to sing.

I re-entered the batters box. It was time to **Play ball!**

In comparing Elijah and John, I looked about for the same features seen by Stevenson. While each of his cases is unique, the most common occurrences are: (A) Predictions of rebirth; (B) Announcements proclaiming the decedents return: (C) Statements made about the past life by the subject; (D) Birthmarks or birth defects which correspond with fatal wounds received in violent deaths (a typical example, is a birthmark located on the reborn, which is in the same location where the deceased was struck!); and (E) Unusual similarities linked with the deceased.

Applying feature (A) of Stevenson's scientific method (i.e., predictions of the deceased's return), I found two such occurrences in this case. The first is Isaiah's foretelling Elijah's return. It was written, as you saw in Chapter Two: "the voice of him that cries in the wilderness prepare the way of the Lord, make straight in the desert a highway for our God." [1]

The second is Malachi's final prophecy of the Old Testament: "he shall prepare the way before me...the messenger of the covenant, in whom you delight...Behold I will send you Elijah the Prophet ... And he shall *turn the heart* of the fathers to the children and the heart of the children to their fathers." [2]

The mentions of *parents*, which could easily mean metaphorically - *past-lives* - and *children*, metaphorically meaning - *present-lives* - reaching a resolution in their hearts - as in *forgiveness* for a transgression, present themselves here quite readily. Was this to be the *Covenant*

The Grand Slam

the *delightful messenger,* Elijah, would one day *voice?*

You bet!

In announcing a deceased's return (B), scientific cases sometimes record the occurrence taking place in the dream of a family member. In Elijah's case, Saint Luke recorded that John's father, Zechariah, received the news in a dream-like vision. The Kings 18:37 and Malachi's theme and variations of *turn* and *turn the hearts of parents and their children* were presented with such reverence, that the words were reserved for repetition by, none other, than the *Voice* of an Angel of the Lord:

> "And the angel of the Lord appeared to Zechariah... saying ...your wife Elizabeth will bear you a son, and you will call his name John...And many Israelites he will cause to *turn* to the Lord their God.
>
> And he will go before them with the spirit and power of Elijah to *turn the hearts of parents to their children*"

For further insights on Elijah's spirit returning in a full- fledged *spirit*, *mind* and *bodily* return as John, check, if you haven't already, the Appendix. (see Item 3)

At the babe's circumcism his mother, Elizabeth, who identified Mary as the mother of Jesus, insisted little Elijah be named John, rather than Zechariah. She challenged patriarchal tradition:

"He shall be called John." [4]

This may indicate a form of encodement, linking the names. Pythagorean sects of Judaism and Freemasonry, called Cabalists, are said to know of such matters. As many of their traditions are secret, the matter must end here.

The Gospels honor Zechariah as the first male in the New Testament to be filled with the Holy Spirit (Luke 1:67), the first human to confirm the Old Testament's last prophecy, and the maker of Christianity's first:

> "And you boy will be called the prophet of the Highest; for you will go before the face of the Lord to *prepare his way.*" [5]

Herodian "Real Politick"

Unfortunately, as Stevenson often found, families face difficulties in reincarnation cases if publicity occurs. According to Cayce, when news of the claim reached King Herod, kindly Zechariah was slain.

The problem for Herod was that a child presented as Elijah

returned would be expected to proclaim a Messiah. This Messiah could then claim the throne of David. While this might be acceptable as a spiritual endeavor, any king not of the Davidic lineage, as was Herod's case, could not for long tolerate such a rivalry. Two fears being that the lad could be kidnapped by zealots and tricked to pick one of their own, or Zechariah, who was linked to David through his marriage to Elizabeth, have a personal ambition.

Fraud, then as now, is the first consideration, especially when returns by the famous are featured.

Herod's kingdom, as we've seen, was the strategic geographical hub of Asia, Africa, and the Mediterranean. Friction was incessant, as its powerful neighbors sought, like today, their own interests. As a means of achieving those interests, strife between Palestinian peoples was often encouraged. When divided and weakened, incursions of outsiders could be counted upon to create mischief. Herod *the Great,* though taking his throne by force, had ruled for over thirty years. He had maintained a hard won period of enviable diplomacy, relative peace, and prosperity. This had not been seen since the days of King Omri and his son Ahab.[6] The two had been able to reunite Israel's factions, after the death of Solomon, and the subsequent establishment of Judah. Miraculously, Ahab reunited them. However, the two split after Jehu's coup.

Separation of church and state would not become politically practical until our era. Herod had little room for error in keeping the political and religious issues, which had split Israel and Judah, from returning. Such issues would light off yet another powder keg of unrest and upset the delicate domestic and diplomatic balance he had established.

Though Jewish in his beliefs, that he was an Iduemean Arab (his father having been converted at the point of a sword) and not native to Jerusalem made his task more difficult. Despite Herod's restoration of Jerusalem's temple, ambitious building programs, brilliant defensive works (in the style of Omri) and an advantageous alliance with the Roman *superpower* to the west, his subjects were often blinded by the zealot's fanatical pursuit of isolationism. Many seemed unwilling to understand Persia's continuing danger. Siding with the Mediterranean community, while it had its costs in Roman excess, was Judea's best option, or so Herod and his many supporters felt.

What Herod feared in John was that history might repeat itself and some political amateur would proclaim himself *King of the Jews*. This could divide the people and repeat the scenario, which had led to the likes of Jehu and Josiah.

A disgruntled warrior, as we have seen, Jehu (sometimes pronounced *yahoo*) had usurped the throne. He had claimed Elijah's heir, the Prophet *Elisha,* had secretly anointed him. Anointing a king in secret seems highly unlikely, as such ceremonies were usually performed in public, as they are today. This leads to the suspicion that, Jehu was fooled by an Assyrian agent in disguise.

Citing religion as a pretext, Jehu killed off, not only the entire Omri dynasty, but Jezebel, Ahab's aged widow. She had become the queen mother of both Israel and Judah. It had been her son, Joram, whom Jehu had, smote in the back. Jehu went on to kill her grandson, Ahaziah, the king of Judah.

Like the Herod's, the Omrid's family tree is complicated.

Jehu not only reopened the rift between Israel and Judah, but also ended the western treaty with the powerful Phoenicians. *Ethbaal*, their king, had been Jezebel's father. When Assyria invaded, Israel was weak with civil unrest. This, Assyrian agents had surely helped to maintain (in Herod's time, similar persons might have been about). With few allies, Israel was easy pickings.

However, Omri's brilliantly designed defenses took the invaders over three years to breach.

An Assyrian monument notes Ahab, with a massive coalition of Middle Easterners, which even included an Arabian contingent of 1000 camels, had inflicted a pre-emptive strike not unlike the twentieth century's *Desert Storm*. Like the Iraqi dictatorship of Saddam Hussein, Assyria claimed a victory. However, historians suggest both suffered a setback.[7] The battle occurred at Quagar in 855 B.C.E. Curiously, the Bible makes no mention of Quagar or of such a battle.

Though ugly as homemade *sin*, Jehu, as Ahab's *mighty man*, had distinguished himself in riding with Israel's six mile long corps of 2000 chariots. Constructed of iron in Egypt and bankrolled by the Phoenician treasury, the devises represented the cutting edge of the time's technology.

Fueled by grass, they could pass anything but a pasture.

With a power plant developing enough traction to pull a *Bud* beer wagon, its four barreled intakes, coupled with a fully tuned two-port exhaust system - at the crack of a whip - could achieve a zero to thirty time faster than a twentieth century *Harley*. The Assyrians, along with ducking arrows, took notes. Not only of Jehu's' sideburns flapping in the breeze, but of his I.Q. and (in looking up 2nd Kings 9:25) his position:

"After Ahab."

The combination of stupidity and envy resulted in another Assyrian monument. It depicts his foolish face bowing down, in homage to their king (see Chapter 17). This invites speculation that bribery, rather than the spiritual guidance of prophets, profited Jehu.

These monuments have only been discovered relatively recently. But a third, whose inscription Herod might have known about, told of what befell Israel's nobility:

"Noblemen I impaled alive."[8]

Herod had fathered fifteen children and would never have allowed his own to suffer such a fate. Nor himself! No Herodians were to hang, crucified, for any cause. He probably experienced a karmic *knee-jerk* in ordering the hunt for John. As a father, I doubt that he stomached killing kids. It was probably these types of actions that affairs of state continually thrust upon him, which led to his mental ruin and death by stomach cancer. He later felt forced to kill the infant Jesus, though unsuccessful. At the height of his insanity, Herod succeeded in killing some of his own family members.

Josephus reported an Essene holy man, in a happier time, predicted Herod's rise in a positive light:"Menahem smiled to himself, and clapped Herod on his backside with his hand and said..., 'However that be, thou wilt be king, and wilt begin thy reign happily, for God finds thee *worthy*."[9]

That God found Herod *worthy* indicated he had skills in containing chaos, as had Omri. Containing chaos is necessary as *New Covenants* won't likely manifest in chaotic times. This adds to the evidence that, while Herod became *good gone wrong*, he was once Omri.

Fortunately for John, when the prophecy came true, Herod sought Menahem for another reading. Herod asked about the longevity of his rule. Upon hearing that he would hold on for thirty years, in an age when even Caesar's lasted from only about two to ten: "Herod was satisfied with these replies and gave Menahem his hand and dismissed him and from that time he continued to honor all Essenes."[10]

But there had been an additional element in Menahem's

prediction: "for thou wilt excel all men in happiness, and obtain an everlasting reputation, but wilt forget piety and righteousness: and these crimes will not be concealed from God."[11]

The element also proved correct and Herod's rule degenerated. Despite his later paranoia and the imposition of a police state, Herod kept his word to the Essenes. Their enclaves would remain immune from scrutiny: "The Essenes also as we call a sect of ours were excused from this imposition."[12]

This explains why John and Jesus could never be located, despite a secret police, which even the later K.G.B. of the old Soviet Union had envied. Some 70 years later, the worst fears of Herod were realized in Judea's fall. The disaster served, neither God, Jews, nor the Mediterranean community.

Herod's brilliantly designed defenses, as had Omri's at Samaria, took Jerusalem's invaders over three years to breach.

Heavy hitters like Herod call to mind this aside in Plato's *Republic*. It regards another *heavy hitter,* named Odysseus. (The Romans knew him as Ulysses. His adventures make up the Odyssey.) The scene opens, in the spirit world, with a lecture to those beginning their next earthly incarnation:

"A new generation of men [and women] shall here begin the cycle of its mortal existence. Your *destiny shall not be allotted to you*, but *you shall choose it for yourselves*."

Plato pointed out what by now should be old hat:

"Virtue owns no master. He who *honors* her shall have *more* of her, and he who *slights* her *less*. The *responsibility* lies with the *chooser*. Heaven is guiltless."

He offered a good reason for not judging others:

"When Odysseus came up to choose, the memory of his former sufferings had so abated his ambition that he went about a long time looking for a *quiet retiring life*, which with great trouble he discovered lying about, and thrown contemptuously aside by the others. As soon as he saw it, *he chose it gladly*."

Like Odysseus, Herod was a fallible human called to formidable tasks. He had heavenly choices, but lost sight of them. In doing so, he became good gone wrong. His earthly choices saw, inevitable consequences in his suffering the paradox of worldly ways.

He became both the world's master and its victim.

After a time of karmic cleansing, he hopefully developed the wisdom to gladly choose, as had Odysseus, a *quiet retiring life.* May they both rest in peace. Hopefully, they're real Christians by now, whether Greek, Jewish, Arabian, wise, unwise...

Heavenly "Real Politik"

Obadiah had made a heavenly choice to hide God's prophets at Mt. Carmel. Heaven's heavenly hitter, Edgar Cayce noted that Zechariah, like Obadiah had secreted another of God's prophets: "Mary and Elizabeth were members of the Essenes you see and for this very reason Zacharias kept Elizabeth in the mountains and the hills."

Zachariah knew the Essenes were off limits from Herod's police. "Hence, these were being here protected were in Carmel, while Zacharias was in the Temple in Jerusalem"[13]

As a decoy, he knew what was to come:
> And about the dawning of the day, Zacharias was slain.
> (Apochryphal Book of James 23:4)

The widow of Zarapeth cared for Elijah. Most likely, she returned as Elizabeth, to become John's widowed mother. After her husband's death, she soon died. John was adopted by the Essenes. Like their counterparts, who raised today's Dalai Lama (Free Tibet!), the Essenes chose to insure John's proper education.

The Essenes knew of the Elijah prophecies, the events surrounding John's birth and the coming arrival of Jesus. I suspect, that like Tibet's Monks, they still scrutinized the precocious rascal.

An imposter could never accomplish Elijah's mission.

Their Mt. Carmel location was near the sea: "the original place where the school of prophets was established during Elijah's time."[14]

Elijah's time was about five hundred years before Plato's Academy. I don't know if the school's diplomas were embossed in gold; but I'll bet the graduates were counseled:

"Those who have the light should declare it unto others."
(Off the Record)

Cayce went on to confirm that, like Stevenson's kids, the tiny Baptizer remembered his past-life at an early age and even wore a distinctive garb like Raphael would paint. John continued his studies throughout the world until:

"He came as a witness to testify concerning the light."[15]

The First Gospel said of him: "For this is he of whom it was said by the prophet Isaiah, The *voice* which cries in the wilderness, Prepare the way of the Lord, and straighten his highways."[16]

The second Gospel reinforced the first:

"The *voice*, which cries in the wilderness." [17]

The Third concurred:

"The *voice* which cries in the wilderness."[18]

Though Herod *the Great* was long dead, a charismatic being like John would, predictably, draw an investigation. You'll recall the Fourth Gospel recorded inquisitors from Jerusalem asked John:

"Are you Elijah? And he said, I am not." [19]

We've seen the label: "*Motivated error of memory.*" Here, the merry mariner was *motivated* to report an *error* in the Elijah *memory.* While the *error* might not measure up to the expectations of an Essene Holy Man, remember that the portrayal of weaknesses in great beings often reinforces the authenticity of the total account.

There was no error in Saint Peter's call to *attention:*

"For we have not followed cunningly devised fables."[20]

John is shown in all this as a very human human being.

It appears that when he was sure he had convinced the thought cops he was crazy (a term familiar among reincarnation researchers), John quickly *remembered* Elijah's *motif* on their leaving: "I am the *voice* of one crying in the wilderness, straighten the highway of the Lord."[21]

The verse makes for a unanimous Gospel agreement on John as Elijah. It also illustrates the third (C) of the five major traits of Stevenson's cases - *statements made about the previous life* - that are also shown, as seen here, in the Bible! As for (D) *corresponding birthmarks*, Elijah didn't suffer a violent death and one would not be expected. (It's rare when all five appear in one case.) We'll see a dramatic example of a biblical birthmark case in Chapter 17. In reference to (E), the *unusual similarities*: Stevenson said at least six combinations linked with the deceased need to be shown, to go beyond the laws of chance. Being sure the same mathematics applied in ancient times, I began to look for seven. As seen in Solomon's 700 wives, Ahab's 70 sons, and Stevenson's seven figure grant, seven is a nice mystical number and, as used here, is one more than needed to establish a statistical significance.

In making entries in the tables, my first observation was, as you recall, that (1) both possessed unusual wilderness skills:

"The ravens brought Elijah bread and meat in the morning and bread and meat in the evening; and he drank from the brook." [22]
John subsisted on, "locusts and wild honey." [23]
(2) Then I noted what was said of Elijah's unique clothing:
"He was a hairy man of girth *with a girdle of leather about his loins*." [24]

Uniquely, John the Baptist was the only New Testament figure with a similar sartorial taste:
"John wore a dress of camel hair *with a girdle of leather fastened about his loins*." [25]

**Detail from the Alba Madonna.
Raphael's rendering of the very young Baptist reveals: "a dress of camel's hair."**

A third (3) divulged their ability in gathering crowds:
"And *all the people* came near Elijah." [26]
John excited: "The whole province of Judea."
They rushed out: "To John the Baptist." along with:
"*All the people* of Jerusalem." [27]

See the Appendix (items 14, 17, & 18) or take my word for now: (4) both were *world class* orators, (5) drank no wine and (6) neither had girlfriends. As the Old Testament said Elijah was a *delight* and Jesus said the assertive waterman was the one in whom: "you were willing to *delight*." [28]

I suspected (7) they had a pretty good sense of humor.

By now, I had reached the statistically significant number seven and more followed. The Scripture's unique approach in historically establishing *unusual similarities linked with the deceased* seemed surprisingly clear. I termed the technique the *Biblical Past-Life Motif (BPM)* and submit the repeated verses and *catchwords*, which I italicized, were deliberately placed by an intelligent *Presence*. I.e. "the active *presence* of God in human life"

Rounding the bases, I could hear the *full figured* lady sing.

In humming along, I contemplated my long love affair with grand opera. Carmen presented herself, but the spell was short lived. Richard Wagner came to mind. Then I read that he also believed in reincarnation and had worked out a similar method of presentation in an opera:

A "Grand Opera," *of the reincarnation type*?

Though never completed, it was titled, *Die Sieger*. He applied a unique variation of his famous *leitmotif*. A *leitmotif* is essentially an accompanying musical theme uniquely identifying each character. It's played whenever the person it identifies appears or is mentioned. The technique was used by the famed film producer, Stephen Spielberg, with great success in his movie, *Jaws*.

Jaws was a rogue shark. Whenever the monster was to appear, a unique musical accompaniment conspicuously announced its arrival. Wagner had the deceased person's theme or motif played, whenever the *reborn* person they had become appeared on stage:

"The simple story of "Die Sieger" assumed significance by having the previous life of the leading characters merge into the present existence by means of an accompanying musical *reminiscence*. Having immediately realized how to present clearly this double life through simultaneously sounding music, I applied myself to the execution of the poem with particular devotion." [29]

I suspected he got the idea from the Bible. Wagner's astute eyes for poetry and drama could easily have picked up Elijah's poetic *reminiscences,* such as *prepare the way* and *girdle of leather,* whenever any mention or appearance of John occurred.

I submitted that the *motifs* explain how the Christians of Essene/Pythagorean persuasion fathomed their faith. Being a Christian, of the same opinion, I was curious to see what Jesus - recorded as a witness who knew John personally - might have said about his cousin as a *born again* Elijah. Jesus is unquestionably the New Testament's highest authority and a confirmation would bolster the context of reincarnation in both the *motifs* and *The Word*.

My first entry in the tables shouted out:

FOR All THE PROPHETS AND THE LAW PROPHESIED UNTIL JOHN.
AND IF YOU WISH TO ACCEPT IT, HE IS ELIJAH WHO WAS TO COME.
HE, WHO HAS EARS TO HEAR, LET HIM HEAR. [30]

My first reaction was to type:

"JESUS SAID IT - I BELIEVE IT - THAT ENDS IT!
(Off the Record)

As the table was assembled, it began to look like this:

> **Table 1**
> **Tabulations of Biblical Statements**
> **Direct Statements of Jesus Identifying John the Baptist as Elijah Biblical Past-life Motifs are Underlined.**
>
> 1. For this is he of whom it is written, behold I will send my messenger before your face to <u>prepare the way</u> before you.   **(Matthew 11:10)**
>
> 2. For all the prophets and the law prophesied until John. And if you wish to accept it, he is Elijah who was to come. He, who has ears to hear, let him hear.   **(Matthew 11:13-15)**
>
> 3. But I say to you Elijah has already come, and they did not know him, and they did to him whatever they pleased... Then the disciples understood that what he had told them was about John the Baptist.   **(Matthew 17:12-3)**
>
> 4. He said to them," Elijah does come first to prepare everything; and as it is written concerning the Son of man, that he will suffer much and be rejected. But I say to you that Elijah has come, and they did to him whatever they pleased, as it is written of him."   **(Mark 9:12-13)**
>
> 5. This is he of whom it is written, Behold, I send my messenger before your face to <u>prepare the way</u> before you.   **(Luke 7:27)**
>
> 6. He was a lamp, which burns and gives light; and you were willing to <u>delight</u> in his light for a while.   **(Luke 5:35)**

This is He

I found no direct sayings of Jesus, or anyone else, arguing that John was not Elijah! Also, the return occurred during the Master's lifetime and, therefore, the verses do not refer to a second coming:

"For all the prophets and the law prophesied until John." [31]

In fact, because the verses so conspicuously state the purpose of Elijah's return was to *prepare the way,* critics who say John was not Elijah, also dispute the key claim of Jesus as the Messiah. This is so, because: "Elijah must come first." [32]

The Hebrew Bible's prophecies prompted the New Testament's great concern with the establishment of Elijah's return as John the Baptist. All references regarding the two are constructed with great care. At stake is the promise that Jesus was the Messiah. Those siding against the Elijah/John reincarnation connection run a great risk in undermining the credibility of Jesus. It makes for more sense that a far greater reward is to be found in simply reading the Scriptures - as they are written - and reconsider reincarnation, rather than doubting Jesus and risk having to seek out the nearest Ashram, Synagogue, or Mosque, for a new religion.

Remember, on such a major point, Jesus said:

"The Scripture cannot be broken" [33]

The Scriptures remain unbroken in consistently carrying the message of Elijah/John. They never state that John the Baptist appeared in the *spirit* of Elijah in the context of the Old Testament's *Elisha*. (He was the prophet who carried on Elijah's work). It was said of Elisha:

"The *spirit of Elijah* rests on Elisha." [34]

If applied to John, then surely Jesus would have used a similar wording such as "John appeared *in* the spirit of Elijah" or "the spirit of Elijah rests, on John the Baptist." But the Bible doesn't dance around the issue in these passages. Those attempting to wiggle off this point would have to rewrite the Hebrew Bible and make it say "Behold, I will send you someone to 'prepare the way' who will *exhibit* the spirit of Elijah," or words to that effect. They would also have to rewrite the Gospels, placing into the mouth of Jesus a *one liner* such as "the spirit of Elijah *appeared* as John the Baptist and reincarnation is *baloney!*"

John is clearly presented as, "he *is* Elijah ... this *is* he ... and ... Elijah *has* come." Nowhere does the Bible blast reincarnation and never issues a commandment - *thou shalt not believe in it*.

Likewise, it makes no mention of *baloney!*

A Sermon

☺ *The first rule of theology is,* thou shalt not ascribe to the Bible what it does not say nor shalt thou deny what it says!

(Captain *L.*)

The Chariot

There is still the important issue concerning Elijah's passing. Again, some of this is review, but as any teacher will tell you, a little

The Grand Slam

review is often a good idea. We've covered a lot of seaway since the second chapter and you've just gotten back from shore leave. Maybe a cup of coffee is in order or, better yet, green tea?

The *shore patrol* told me you had a good time.

Elijah's passing is honored in 2nd Kings 2:11 with the appearance of a "chariot of fire and horses of fire," and his being taken "up by a whirlwind into heaven." This raises questions on the uniqueness of his demise and rebirth, and the determination of his *humanness* must be answered.

In reference to his demise, we've seen history honor Mithra of Persia, Romulus, the founder of Rome, and Caesar Augustus with bodily departures. Dr. Lamsa notes the idioms regarding Elijah respectively denote "speed and a glorious manifestation" and "a glorious departure from this life." But regardless of the nature of the "glorious departure from this life,"[35] Jesus stated in Matthew (11:11) the Baptist was: "Among those born of women."

Dr. Lamsa mentioned the phrase denoted mortality: "A human being with limitations, weaknesses" [36]

That Elijah was bodily taken to heaven, and therefore, did not die, is difficult to establish in both history and theology. While accomplishing great feats, as *a human being with limitations and weaknesses,* he incurred enormous criminal liabilities.

Murdering others over religious issues can never be condoned, whether in the past or in today's *911* world. As neither terrorism nor religious fanaticism warrants a free ride anywhere other than to Hell, a difficult second look, as in *lying pen,* is in need. Though risking Jeremiah's wrath, I'll use the term *questioning pen.*

Jesus, as we've seen, identified Elijah, *being born of woman,* as John. If the case were otherwise, Jesus would have told us so. If Elijah were taken bodily aloft, then how come he didn't return in the same manner? It would seem the usual way for those things to work. This risks a retort that Elijah didn't return. Such a supposition suggests Jesus was an imposter and a liar, unless divine intervention is cited. But Elijah being, *the least in Heaven*, most likely wouldn't have been that deserving. As the preponderance of evidence indicates his return and Jesus saying of John, *he is Elijah,* a look at the possibility of Elijah's physical death might be the better course, at least for Christians.

This requires of the *questioning pen*, a closer look at that scenario. Elisha was its only witness. [37]

Though he was reportedly pious, no one else was around to corroborate his story. Usually the *two or three or more* rule applies in cases involving first hand accounts.

There should have been plenty.

The fiery spectacle of horses and whirlwinds, accompanying the lift off of an extraterrestrial ascent, would have been seen for miles. In a like manner, though their senators swore up and down both aisles of the forum, that Augustus departed in a similar manner - history doesn't record a single Roman citizen seeing such a spectacle either.

Most likely, Elisha simply buried Elijah and eulogized his passing in the customary language and manner of the times. The process of mytholigation followed, providing meaningful lessons to future generations, which is its good purpose. But Elisha might have had a hidden agenda of ambition as well. This is seen in the account leaving him as Elijah's undisputed heir.

Elijah headed up a powerful political force.

In Israel, prophets lived among the people and like today's Islamic clerics, wielded power. The monarchy couldn't ignore them. To the south, Jerusalem's priests worked within the Temple, which was always close by to the ever-watchful eye of the king.

Worship wasn't permitted outside its walls.

This not only insured a steady flow of pilgrims, which helped to maintain the city's always busy innkeeper's industry, but it also insured that whatever was preached, could be controlled.

While priests had little power, Elijah, as head of the *Son's of the Prophets*, represented a forceful faction. That someone of the stature of Elisha might have harbored some measure of ambition, beyond the norm, might be an emotionally difficult supposition for many reading the Bible, but biblical history is often quite candid in describing difficulties in its personalities, whether saint or sinner.

Ambitions are seen in Elisha's demand: [38]

"A double portion of your spirit [authority?] be upon *me*."

The response to such ambition was prophetic displeasure:

"You have asked too much."

Its premature nature, as Elijah was still alive, is seen in his blunt call for patience:

"Wait for *me*." [to die?]

Like Ourselves

You'll recall there are no direct statements naming Elijah as a god and this statement by James, the brother of Jesus:

"Even Elijah, who was a weak man *like ourselves* prayed earnestly." [39]

In the minds of most reasonable people, and certainly for those believing Jesus, compelling evidence should by now be seen supporting Elijah's return in the Bible. Additional evidence, seen in the Appendix and in Chapter 18, will add even more.

The question then, which immediately arises, is that if he is *like ourselves,* as James notes, and is no different than other mortals, and can reincarnate, then cannot others do the same?

Concerning a question this critical, differences in translations should be examined.

Referring to Elijah's mortality, Aramaic translates: "Elijah who was a weak man *like ourselves*." Jerusalem's Latin uses: "Human being *like ourselves,"* and King James states: "He was a man subject to life's passions as *we are*."

Seemingly, this prepares the way and makes a highway of Biblical information certain concerning other humans. That is, if Elijah is a weak man *like ourselves*, or a human being *like ourselves* or as *we are* - and can reincarnate - then as a normal course, cannot other Bible persons, Stevenson's kids, saints, sinners, and other human beings - *like ourselves* or *as we are?*

Notes

1. Isaiah 40:3
2. Malachi 3:1 and 4:6
3. Luke1: 11-17
4. Luke 1:60
5. Luke 1:76
6. John 1:7 Sachar, 1965
7. See Herzog & Gishon, 1978
8. See Keller, 1956
9. Antiquities XIII-10:5
10. Ibid
11. Antiquities XIII-10: 4?
12. Ibid
13. (5749-8)
14. (5749)
15. John 1:7
16. Matthew 3:2B3
17. Mark 1:3
18. Luke 3:4
19. John 1:21
20. 2nd Peter 1:16
21. 1st Kings 17:26
22. Mark 1:6
23. 2nd Kings 1:8
24. Mark 1:6
25. 1st Kings 18:30
26. Mark 1:5
27. John 5:53
28. Head & Cranston p.328
29. Matthew 11:13 – 15
30. Matthew 11:13
31. Matthew 17:10
32. John 10:35
33. John 10:33
34. 2nd Kings 2:15
35. Lamsa (1971), p. 14 - 15
36. Ibid-p. 64
37. See 2nd Kings 1:7 – 11
38. Ibid 1:2 - 6
39. James 5: 16 -18

Chapter 16

Conclusions
```
Innings:    1 2 3 4 5 6 7 8 9
All Stars:  777, 777, 777
Sadds:      0000000000
Chicks:     0000000000
```

The close similarity with Stevenson's cases shows Elijah/John's reincarnation experience as a common denominator of the *human condition*:

Comparisons of Spontaneous Cases of the Reincarnation Type and the Biblical Case of John the Baptist.

Recurring Features: **Correlation:**

1. <u>Paranormal Predictions of Rebirth</u>:   Yes
Bible verses were unquestionably written beforehand.

2. <u>Paranormal Vision or Dream Declaring a Return</u>:   Yes
The vision of an angel heralded the returning of Elijah.

3. <u>Prenatal Response</u>:   Yes
The unborn Elijah/John prompted his mother to see Mary as the mother of Jesus (Luke 1:44). Modern mothers sometimes craved foods favored by the previous personality!

4. <u>Corresponding Birthmarks</u>:   No Evidence
Elijah died nonviolently and none would be expected.

5. <u>Statements About The Previous Life</u>:   Yes
"I am the voice of one crying in the wilderness."
Verifiable statements about the past life are more frequent in spontaneous cases.

6. <u>Associated Unusual Behaviors</u>:   Yes
The frequency of the numbers goes beyond chance.

7. <u>Recognitions of Those Known in a Past life</u>:   Yes
John's link with Antipas and Herodias is obvious.

8. <u>Little Memory Between Lives</u>:   Yes

The *active presence of God in human life* is shown in secular and biblical case histories of real persons, places and events in this world.

9. <u>Gender Change</u>: No Evidence
Future research may reveal such cases in the Bible and new insights on homosexual behavior.

10. <u>Emotional Responses of Participants</u>: Yes
 Highly charged as would be expected.

11. <u>Attitudes of Witnesses</u>: Yes
 Subjects beliefs regarding reincarnation varied.

12. <u>Family Consequences</u>: Yes
Most tasted inconvenience, boredom, loss of privacy, and expense with publicity. John's family felt tragedy.

13. <u>Ranges of Memories</u>: Yes
Most children curtailed memories between age five and eight. Some, like John, preserved them.

14. <u>Changes in Past and Present Circumstances</u>: Yes
Stevenson noted a *promotion* rate of 28.6%, *demotion* of 45.6%, and *no change* rate of 26.2%. The Biblical cases close to Elijah show 30.7% *promoted*, 30.7% *demoted* and 38.6% *no change*.

15. <u>Group Returns</u>: No Evidence
Common in the Bible and Cayce. Research limits may prevent proving such events in scientific cases.

16. <u>Geographic Considerations</u>: Yes
Many returned within the same general geographic and political boundaries, as in their previous lives.

17. <u>Short Intervals Between Births</u>: No Evidence
The median interval revealed in 616 cases taken from ten different cultures was fifteen months. John did not appear until nearly 850 years after Elijah's passing.

18. <u>Changes in Religion, Race, and Nationality</u>: Yes
Such changes can upset the bigoted. Prejudiced Hindus and Muslims in modern India felt this. (see Mills, 1990). In the next chapter, a dramatic Biblical case will see a Jewish king return as an Egyptian Pharaoh.

19. <u>Cases Involving More Than One Return</u>: No Evidence
Stevenson's cases are limited to single incidents, making biblical linkages unfeasible when they occur. Cayce (262-81) notes numerous returns are the norm.

20. Frequency of Violent Deaths Yes
Stevenson saw a 53% rate, in a sampling of one hundred and sixty four solved cases. Of the 13 major previous personalities counted with Elijah,

53.8% died violently. (Unless noted, all cases are from Stevenson (1987).
21. <u>Similar Theological and Moral Questions</u>:   Yes
Both types of cases are worthy of one's best inquiry.
22. <u>Purposes for Earthly Returns</u>:   Yes
Three major factors appeared: violence, childhood fatalities, or lives leaving unfinished business.

Discussion

In the table, only five comparisons seem at variance: (1) Corresponding birthmarks and birth deformities. These offer compelling evidence for reincarnation. (As Elijah died nonviolently, another Biblical case will be offered in the next chapter.) (2) Biblical gender changes of the type, which had so, concerned Saint Jerome. (I'm sure they exist, I just haven't found any yet.) (3) The long spans between returns of Bible personalities versus the eighteen months or so for Stevenson's (it may be that today's larger populations allow for sooner returns; also, lives cut short may be a factor. Violent deaths were about the same, though Stevenson reported more childhood fatalities). (4) Few in his cases return in groups and links between family members are seldom seen. (The Bible and most esoteric traditions reveal quite the opposite. Scientific restraints would seem to make such cases unsolvable. A scientist cannot overlook that a child could have known about a past life through the *normal means* of family members and peers offering information.) (5) That only one pair of links are shown in our era, while more numerous occurrences happen in the Bible, can be attributed to time. (*The Book*, as devotees of Islam refer to it, covers centuries and Stevenson's studies only about a generation.)

In addition to the table, consideration must be given to historic evidence seen in scientific archaeology. The places, events, and many of the those described have left tangible proofs of a past existence. These are, or will be, noted as we proceed. The suggested readings and the bibliography offer more. The personalities' psychological behaviors appear reasonable, in most instances, given the time's sociology and the circumstances the participants confronted. (While some liberties have and will be utilized in reconstructing past events and behaviors, the cases, though enhanced, neither stand nor fall on these reasoned speculations.)

Biblical, metaphysical, and secular sources are cited as sharing a measured congruency in reasonableness, that the events recorded reflect historic realities, except for certain redactions, as scholars have noted.

But for now, it is reasonable to assume someone named John the Baptist appeared in the first century c.e. and practiced a ministry of great impact. Many identified him as Elijah returned. Among those making that claim were Jesus the Christ, the angel Gabriel, Zechariah, Elizabeth, and the additional commentaries of Saints Matthew, Mark, Luke, and John.

In Biblical Cases I listed these five formal findings:

1. The direct statements identifying John the Baptist as Elijah returned reflect sources of impeccable authority. The credentials of the Messiah, four saints, an angel, a martyred priest, and especially Elizabeth - John's mother - must bear a considerable impact in any reasoned or intuitive evaluation.

"He shall be named John" (Luke 1:60)

2. My investigation of the New Testament revealed no direct counter-claims to these informants' statements concerning John the Baptist as Elijah returned.

3. The Edgar Cayce material concurs in its similar claims and insights that Elijah returned as John the Baptist.

4. The remarkable similarities with major features of, "Spontaneous Cases of the Reincarnation Type" would seem to reinforce assertions of Biblical support for a reincarnation hypotheses.

5. Reasonable psychological behaviors, sociological, and historic evidence seem supportive to the possibilities and probabilities presented in the reconstruction of events.

A later chapter debated alternative theories to reincarnation. Two classes were *normal* and *paranormal* explanations. Major *normal* issues were:

(1) Fraud: (this was rare and will be discussed in Chapter 18.) Dr. Stevenson was a fully credentialed psychiatrist and professor. He published primarily in the academic and scientific press. As such, he endorsed the testimonies of his subjects. Likewise, I endorse the testimonies of my subjects: Jesus the Christ, Saints Matthew, Mark, Luke, John... I pray they endorse this testimony).

(2) Genetic memory theories: (the children and the personalities they claimed to have been, like Elijah and John, were not genetically related);

(3) Cryptomnesia: (memories absorbed from outside sources which delude a person into thinking they came from within.) These were scarce and as most made their claims before age three, the kids

could not have lived long enough to have absorbed such complex and compelling memories. (Parental and caretaker *brainwashing* affecting John's self identity will be seen in chapter 13.)

Paranormal alternatives, such as extra sensory perception and possession by discarnate entities, were likewise addressed using Stevenson's similar reasoning. The two were discounted seen in the matter-of-fact nature of the children's discourses and they're exhibiting no evidence of personality changes or mediumistic tendencies. (Stevenson was a recognized expert on mediums.) No sound reason could be determined as to why or how an outside entity, whether alive or deceased, would target children with such detailed information, let alone imprint them with birthmarks or deformities. Furthermore, when localities had been changed after a subject's death, upon returning, they were unaware of such changes.

As for Elijah, it would seem a difficult alternative hypothesis to accept that he waited 850 years at Mt. Carmel, for a child of proper intellectual and physical stature to randomly present himself, so that the prophet could possess such a specimen for his mission. Reincarnation, in both secular and Biblical cases, would seem the most plausible explanation.

Those wishing a more scholarly formatted look may wish to obtain copies of *Biblical Cases 0f the Reincarnation Type*. Most forms of payment will be shamelessly accepted. The unrepentant are reminded to include an extra 10%

Photo by: Susan Mann. Costuming by: Judi Flowers.
This Means You!
Looking authoritarian, a certain familiar face appears as a "Wiseman" in a worldwide televised Christmas Day production.
Who among us might have enjoyed dressing (as did the captain) like this in some present or past lifetime?

Home Waters.

Chapter 17

Other Cases / Other Lessons

Other Biblical personalities will now be scrutinized. These will further demonstrate that Elijah's *born again* experience was not unique, reveal an example of a fatal wound with a corresponding birth mark or defect, and establish from both a spiritual and scientific viewpoint, the admonition:

"Love your neighbor as yourself." [1]

The role of reincarnation will further be seen in addressing fraud and correcting misunderstandings concerning God's presence in biblical history. As promised, Joshua and Jesus will be cited.

The first case concerns Jehu. In my opinion, he was the baddest of all the Biblical bad guys. Of his many crimes, the most heinous was his takeover of Israel's government. It was ruled by the *House of Ahab*. Ahab's family home was located in the town of Jezreel. In having its aged queen mother, Jezebel, who was of Phoenician extraction, thrown from a balcony and trampled under his horses, he wiped out the vital alliance between Israel, Judah, and countless Palestinian communities. This included the racially and religiously open-minded Phoenician nation.

Isaiah termed Phoenicians the "honorable of the earth" (Isaiah 21:8) and Solomon entrusted them to build God's temple (see 1st Kings, ch. 5). Jehu declared his actions resolved long-standing issues of religious, racial and gender discord in a Godly fashion. While such issues plagued the region and the world, as they do today, prophetic sources have, for nearly twenty-eight hundred years, rendered unanimous messages of dissent concerning the Godliness of Jehu's solution:

"I will avenge the blood of Jezreel upon the house of Jehu."
(Hosea 1:4) (9th century B.C.E.)

"Adolph Hitler...stands much in the position as did Jehu."
(3976-13) (Nov. 4, 1933 C.E.)

Among Jehu's major *motifs,* in addition to being ugly as homemade sin and stupid as a stone - as in *Yahoo* - were such depictions of him as a reckless driver of chariots and a braggart.

You'll not forget his *smoting* Joram in the back:

"And the arrow went out at his heart and he sank down in his chariot."

Then he inflicted multiple wounds upon Joram's nephew, the feisty Ahaziah, King of Jerusalem and grandson of Ahab and Jezebel. Mortally wounded, Ahaziah:

"Fled to *Megiddo* and died there."

Where:

"Ahaziah's servants *took him in a chariot* to Jerusalem, and buried him *in his own sepulchre*." [2]

Paybacks are hell was Jehu's lesson in his return as Josiah, twenty-four chapters later. This is seen in a similar verse, following *Jehu/Josiah's* death. It occurred in the same city of Megiddo:

"And Josiah's servants *took him in a chariot* dead from Megiddo, and brought him to Jerusalem and buried him there *in his own sepulchre*." [3]

In *Biblical Cases,* I had left it undecided as to who had avenged *the blood of Jezreel upon the house of Jehu.* Of the many, eligible, able, and eager, either Joram or Ahaziah seemed the best candidates. But only one of the two feisty fighters could have returned as the feisty Pharaoh Necho. As Ahaziah had died violently from multiple wounds, he would most likely have been the one to carry their results over as birth deformities in becoming:

"Pharaoh the *lame* King of Egypt." [4]

At the time, he made the best example of a birthmark/deformity case in the Bible. I sifted through a lot of grizzly material to see if Necho's mummy still existed. Trust me, unwrapped mummies aren't a pretty sight. The idea was that if his remains could be found, then there might be some evidence of lameness. On the outside chance that if he had been the born again, Joram who's arrow had, "*smote* [Jehu/Josiah] at Megiddo, when he saw him there," [5] a prominent mark on Necho's mummified back and chest might open the eyes and ears of many.

To date, I've been unable to ascertain the status of Necho's mummy. But about two years ago, while whiling away a perfectly good day in a Palm Spring's bookstore (reading books for free) I stumbled across a tiny picture of his image. I checked for photo credits in the index and found the relic resided in a museum in Philadelphia. The un-retouched photo they sent made the hairs on my beard bristle. When back in Virginia, I got to see the real thing in a traveling exhibition, in of all places, the College of William and Mary.

The synchronicity saved me a long drive north. I photographed the reverse side to see if a prominent mark, as well defined as that on its chest, could be determined.

Overall, the statuette is intricately detailed. If a birthmark is indeed depicted on the lower back and a more pronounced depiction appears on the high side of the subject's chest, these could indicate the past-life victim was hunkered down in urging his horses to flee. Exit wounds are typically much larger than entry one's and an arrow entering low on a forward leaning figure would likely exit high.

Reverse View: Pharaoh Necho.
Photo of the reverse side is by the author.
"And Jehu drew a bow with his full strength and smote Joram in his back, and the arrow went out at his heart."

(Photograph courtesy of University of Pennsylvania Museum of Archaeology and Anthropology.)

Frontal Photo: Pharaoh Necho the Lame King of Egypt.

While a definite entry wound like mark exists on the reverse side, it could have come from an air bubble in the casting process. The frontal mark, because of its prominence, appears to have been deliberate. If it were, then it must have been a brave sculptor to have included it, and maybe not such a bad Pharaoh to have allowed himself depicted, not only kneeling, but with such an intimate disclosure of what was probably an unattractive physical feature.

Those guys were usually raised with big egos.

Not all will agree that this represents adequate evidence.

However, most should agree that whatever it is that's there looks a like what adequate evidence ought to look like! The probabilities of such a mark appearing by chance, if it is indeed an actual representation of a corresponding wound, according to Stevenson's calculations, would be one out of one-hundred sixty.

When birthmarks correspond with entry and exit wounds, of which Stevenson had many cases, then the probability that they appeared by coincidence jumps to one out of twenty-five thousand!

Impressive.

As *Joram/Necho*, he exacted a precise, karmic justice for the murders of his nephew, mother, countless relatives (and the many who would later suffer), upon the reckless and braggadocios driver of chariots, *Jehu/Josiah*.

Additional evidence from Josephus helps build the case:

"I suppose it was fate [Karma] that pushed Josiah on to his conduct, that it might take an occasion against him; for as he...rode about in his chariot...from one wing of his army to an other, an arrow put an end to his eagerness for fighting." [7]

Love your Neighbor as Yourself

The spectra of a Jewish king's return as an Egyptian Pharaoh sends a clear message regarding the futility of ethno-centric zealousness. Such an understanding, when it is seen through reincarnation in the Bible, should bring forth better relations between Egyptians and Jews. They both revere The Book as the foundation of their faiths. The same must be said for Bible believers everywhere, as they discover the new insights offered out of these ancient accounts. All must understand that biblical and historic data, coupled with Stevenson's findings and Cayce's revelations, illustrate that an individual's racial, religious and national identities can cross over in later lives.

Jesus noted we should *love our neighbors as ourselves*. This case illustrates, as did Stevenson's Lebanese study of a neighboring man and women finding their confrontations even more intense in his return as her son. The universe allows us no alternative. We must love our neighbors now, as in future lives, they can become ourselves!

Fraud

In studying reincarnation, whether scientific or biblical, fraud is always the first consideration. Examples of fraud in the Bible are, as we have seen, hot button issues. They often risk futile proof-context methods to defend and reader's faiths stand threatened. Reincarnation offers a solution in that dire consequences are seen in the later lives of those who attempted fraud, in altering or interpreting the Scriptures, to suit their own ends.

Jehu/Josiah provides a good illustration. Like Jehu, Josiah also claimed issues of religious purity in his wholesale extermination of differing faiths.

So intense was his fanaticism that he even slew animals:

"And Josiah slew the horses which the kings of Judah had given to the sun." [8]

The best and the brightest, which had exposed him for the *666* he was, came next:

"The men with familiar spirits and the wizards." [9]

The effort backfired. In failing to maintain the diverse resources of a pluralistic society, and allies such as the Phoenicians, Josiah saw the demise of the region:

"So Judah *was carried out of their land*." [10]

The House of Jehu experienced the same:

"So Israel *was carried out of their land*." [11]

Justinian's similar means saw the glory of Athens move to Islamic regions and establish a thousand-year enlightenment. While Justinian's cathedral still stands, it was once a Mosque and is now a museum. It hasn't housed the vestments of Christianity for centuries. (The Renaissance was born in Italy with the return of the Platonic academies. Constantinople fell at about the same time.)

Religious persecution was obviously not the will of God as these examples illustrate. You can see why the major movers of our American Constitution heeded these lessons. The result, as you recall, was the first amendment's guarantee of religious freedom.

Another lesson of Jehu/Josiah and Justinian is that Godliness only manifests itself through Godly ways. Risking fraudulent means, mislabeled as religious, invites an assurance of personal and civil self-destruction.

It is important then, to read the Scriptures and history with caution, when ungodly acts are seen as Godly. It's not that the verses are fraudulent, it's that their *intention* for the more evolved reader is to reveal fraud, and without historic objectivity and the measuring stick of reincarnation, confusion can present itself.

As many examples are present in the book of Kings and Chronicles, which detail much of Elijah and those about him, an accurate evaluation requires a considerable effort in weighing myth, legend, and earthly reality.

Assyrian hegemony cannot be discounted. It was in their interests to keep the region in turmoil. By dividing, they could conquer. That they were successful in destroying or doctoring original sources accounts for the centuries of war and political chaos that today, still ebb and flow throughout the turbulent region.

This must be set aright.

A change in tack is called for. In this hi-tech age, a good start might be in launching, a satellite broadcasting twenty-four-hour seven days a week messages, not so much about reincarnation and history (though not a bad idea) but the basics of mutual forgiveness, and the mantra, *Love one another*. At the same time, a similar system should be launched over our own skies!

The Perfect Crime

Like the child remembering the perfect crime Stevenson reported, Josiah, made king at age eight, might have wished to embellish his own past-life crimes. In his immaturity, he could have ordered his scribes to honor Jehu's acts as those of a spiritually directed heavenly hero. However, Josiah failed to grow up and his record reveals, not the active presence of God, but the active presence of humanity!

Josiah's tampering, and its magnifications by outsiders, has undoubtedly biased certain aspects of the accounts to make his own actions, and the theology which he claimed motivated them, stand in a better light. To his dying day, he sought salvation in rigid religious ritual and the assessment of divine retribution for breaches of contract between his predecessors and God.

Josiah saw Jehu as God's agent, visiting Ahab's offenses, in killing all seventy of his sons. But Jehu's fervor forces a question: Did he seek Heaven's long-term reward, or Assyria's immediate reward of money and power?

"He slew all that remained of the house of Ahab in Samaria." [12]

Jehu's accomplishment at Samaria ultimately gained for Assyria, what its army failed to achieve at Quagar!

As Jehu/Josiah, he had another chance. In correcting his errors, a new kingdom could come about insuring human happiness and freedom.

He lost the opportunity in faulting all but himself:

Jehu.
Ironically, this only known image of an Israelite king is labeled *Son of Omri*. He bows to Assyria's chief.

"For great is the wrath of the Lord that is kindled against us, because our fathers have not hearkened to the words of this book" [the forged copy of Deuteronomy]." [13]

If Jehu/Josiah's actions had been Godly, would not reincarnation and his own yardstick show his children living good lives? The first child to sit on the throne died as Joram/Necho's captive and the second was executed in Babylon.

Ignorant lust to control others, though hidden in false piety, as Jehu demonstrated, results in similar scenarios. Josiah's acts saw the murder of children, priests, and *burned men's bones:*

"He slew all the priests of the high places, who burned incense upon the altars and *burned men's bones* upon them" [14]

The same was seen in inquisitions. Twentieth century self-styled social utopias saw similar sins in Stalin, *Khmer Rouge* and Kosovo killing fields, Saddam Heussein's atrocities and Nazi crematoria. Josiah's demise illustrates a clear message to the *Yahoos* of past and future generations:

"Whatever a man [woman] sows that shall he [she] also reap." Seen in the light of reincarnation, the Scriptures retain their consistency and *cannot be broken*. They reveal the frailty of free-willed human souls caught in webs of self-created cause and effect situations. Thus illuminated, the Bible maintains, as has been seen in Plato - God's innocence: *Heaven is guiltless.*

But Plato is overshadowed. This is seen in the biblical depiction of God, who while innocent - cares. Only a caring God would have made an outreach to insure reconciliation with Its' creations. The outreach is seen in the exposures of criminal acts, when mislabeled as Godly, in the Scriptures. Whether actually committed or not, if such were allowed to stand uncorrected, a Soul's journey of return would be prolonged. This was why another child, a *babe*, would be sent to correct the crime of another.

Joshua

This case concerns the mighty man who, in humbleness, would evolve to perfection and correct, through forgiveness, the calamities created by the perfect crime.

Joshua became that gentle *babe* who was to come.

In preparation for the famous battle of Jericho, *Rehab* the *harlot*, (*Rachel* in some translations) provided protection for Joshua's soldiers. She was promised safe passage for her family and herself during the coming cataclysm. Once the walls came tumbling down, Joshua made good on the promise and she dwelt among the children of Israel. The closing verse states she did so: "even to this day." [15]

Harlot back then often labeled innkeepers, and not necessarily prostitutes. Such a one was to return, though never given the biblical title of *harlot*. However, among many traditions, Mary Magdalene, even to this day, still retains that label. In Middle Eastern tradition, some sects have their women wash their husband's feet upon his return:

"Then Mary took a cruse containing pure and expensive nard, and anointed the feet of Jesus" [16]

Yet still others, as we've seen, honor this Mary as:

"The disciple Jesus loved."

Joshua, reportedly, crucified five kings.

However, as Josiah had adulterated the text, and based on what has been seen in this guy, such crucifixions might not have occurred. Likewise, not only was Ahab not so bad, but also Joshua might have been innocent. And the kings. In simply defending their own territory, they wouldn't seemingly have committed:

"Acts worthy of death and *crucified* on a tree." [17]

Joshua might not have mocked them:

"Put your feet upon their necks." [18]

Nor commanded:

"At the time of the going down of the sun they took them down from the trees, and cast them into a cave...and laid *large stones* at the mouth of the cave." [19]

While historicity might have been compromised, it's irrelevant here. What matters is that God, the Scriptures, and Humanity were reckoned in truth. Unlike Josiah, no one blamed others. Joshua had been a *prince of war*. Returned as Jesus, the *Prince of Peace,* whether having been guilty of *wickedness* or innocent, He had to set the record straight. For no misunderstanding or misinterpretation of that written of Joshua, could ever be construed as an excuse for committing atrocities.

Such a devotion to Scriptural truth, lead to the atonement for our sins:

"And when they had *mocked* Jesus they...took him out to *crucify* him."[20]

The rest of the account is found in the closing chapters of each Gospel:

"And the Scripture was fulfilled which said, He was reckoned with the wicked." [21]

The body was laid in a tiny *cave:*

"Which was hewn from a rock and they rolled a *large stone*, and placed it against the door of the tomb and went away." [22]

Notes

1. Mark 12:31
2. 2nd Kings 9:27-8
3. 2nd Kings 23:29 - 30
4. 2nd Kings 23:29
5. Ibid
6. Stevenson (2003) p. 97 & p.110
7. Antiquities X-5:1
8. 2nd Kings 23:11
9. 2nd Kings 23:24
10. 2nd Kings 25:21
11. 2nd Kings 17:23
12. 2nd Kings 10:17
13. 2nd Kings 23:20
14. 2nd Kings 22:13
15. Joshua 6:15
16. John 12:3
17. Deuteronomy 21:22
18. Joshua 10:24
19. Joshua 10:27
20. Mark 15:20
21. Mark 15:28
22. Matthew 27:6

Chapter 18

Back to the Case

Jehu/Josiah's scribes said of their master, "He did that which was right."[1] If true, then us regular folks, whether *Greeks or Barbarians* (as always) are in a lot of trouble.

But wouldn't we be in even more trouble in disrespecting the religious beliefs of others, practicing prejudices of all types and varieties, including gender bias, and the long litanies of barbaric behaviors, which those who have acted after Josiah's example have forced upon Western and world history?

In Biblical Cases, I offered no, magic formulas for correcting such injustices, nor any methods for securing the individual soul's salvation and have not done so here. That's because right thinking and truth, concerning God's Word were not and are not to be found in books, isms, gurus, or sources and experiences outside one's innermost self. Especially yours.

Despite Deuteronomy's never being seen by Moses, the message still stands that God speaks equally to Greeks, Barbarians, the wise and the unwise on issues of the soul. Cayce quoted the thirtieth chapter's verses (12-14) more than any in the Bible. It bears repeating here, as all need to remain reminded that, *The Word* is: "Very near you, in your mouth and in your heart, that you may do it."

Determining good begins in individuals listening. Knowing what needs to be done to hasten an individual's enlightenment, and as a consequence, the enlightening of the world, is already known at the soul level.

Inner awakenings, followed by good group actions, whether from the cultural left or right or in between, will bring the best result.

As to Jesus and *why me* type questions concerning people's unique circumstances, which seem to appear for no reason, His answer would remain as that given to Nicodemus. While in today's parlance Jesus might say, "What goes around comes around." In the Bible, His message remains etched in an eloquence seen in Solomon:

> "The wind blows where it pleases and you hear its sound; but you do not know whence it comes and whither it goes; such is every man who is born of the spirit."[2]

Recalling Chapter Four's geography lesson on the world's roundness, Solomon said: "The wind blows toward the south, and turns about the north; "It whirls continually, and returns again according to its circuits." [3]

Though good geography, geography was not Jesus' intent. The intent was to impart to Nicodemus, the rationale of reincarnation. *What goes around comes around* reminds us that the seeming chance happenings on this always interesting and enticingly addictive planet really result over the same issues, encountered by the same souls as, as the verse concludes:

"There is nothing new under the sun."

This recalls the last episodes of the Baptist's life.

The Tetrarch of Galilee

Long before John began his ministry poor old Herod as Cayce called him, had died. But some years previous, as Josephus noted, the king made an unusual choice in deeming his youngest son, Antipas:

"Worthiest to be made king." [4]

Antipas had only two years of study in Rome, before his father's death. Subsequently, as a young teen titled *Tetrarch of Galilee*, he demonstrated such skills in statesmanship that Rome awarded him the dynastic title, *Herod,* in 6 C.E. (They must have marveled in the Socratic axiom: "But if the child did not acquire the knowledge in this life, then he must have learned it at some other time?")

Though never officially a king, the common people reflected their respect in referring to him as such. Saint Mark (6:14) honors him: "Herod the King"

His rise was without bloodshed; however, his older brother, named Archelaus (pronounced yahoo) initially thwarted him. Unfortunately, *old Herod*, at the height of his insanity, had made a last minute change in his will. It named Archelaus (he was as *stupid as a stone*) as king of Judea. Archelaus (a *braggart*) insisted, despite the royal family's protest, that the new will was legitimate. His lawyer convinced the Roman court that *old Herod's* loyalty to Rome proved he was sane! While the lawyers harangued and harassed each other, (an attack on Herod's sanity could be construed as an attack on Rome itself) without warning, the boys' mom dropped dead.

An advocate of law, always, Antipas set aside grief and disappointment. Despite the tears he could not dare to have shown in public, he would work with what he ultimately was given.

Tiny Galilee approximated the borders of the old Israel of Elijah and Ahab.

Like his father and King Ahab, Antipas was a city builder. Creating Tiberius, his capitol, it overlooked the Sea of Galilee. Middle classes, slaves whom he personally freed, and the poor were attracted by opportunities for jobs, free housing, a sound economy, a stadium, places of worship - including a major synagogue - and a ruling council in the mode of the democratic Greeks. Ahab's government contained a similar parliamentary body known as *All Israel*. While *life, liberty and the pursuit of happiness* wasn't entirely achieved by Antipas, of the world's places where God would want his *first born* to live (like the U.S.A.) *the land of Galilee* was appealing. It was also safe from the likes of a Jehu/Josiah/Archelaus:

> "When Joseph [the guardian father of Jesus] heard that Archelaus had become king over Judea...he was afraid to go there; and it was revealed to him in a dream to go to the land of *Galilee*."

Roman rule soon saw Jehu/Josiah/Archelaus banished. His continuing brutality offended the empire's affirmation as protector of its members. This is an example of the, seldom reported, positive side of the *senate* and *people* of Rome's role in Palestine.

Archelaus' replacement, *Pontius Pilate*, suffered a similar fate. A major cause might have been his misunderstanding of the intensity of the *Good?* Herod's desire to see Jesus set free. Though Herod gets bad press on the issue, scholars (see Hoener, 1980) suggest his public adversity toward Jesus was to appease Jerusalem's mob. Herod sent a symbolic message of innocence to Pilate, seen in the royal robe placed on Jesus. Herod could do little more. He was outside his territory, having come to the city to worship in its temple. The robe's purpose was not to mock Jesus, as has been the popular misperception - precipitated by and large by Josephus's hatred of the Herods - but to validate Jesus' stature as a spiritual leader back in Galilee. Herod had a reputation for looking after his people. That Pilate got that message is seen in this insight the astute Saint Luke left in Herod's defense.

> "I [Pilate] have found no fault in Jesus ...*nor even has Herod*; for I sent him to him; and *behold*, [the robe's symbol of royalty indicating] he has done nothing worthy of death." [6]

More evidence is seen in Jesus having lambasted Jerusalem's authorities, but the only statement He made about Herod was to call him "*that fox.*" *Fox* in Aramaic means *shrewd* which aptly describes both Ahab's and Herod's styles. It might have been this shrewdness in *real politick,* which saw Herod suggest to Emperor Tiberius, who replaced *the risen* Augustus, that Pilate be recalled.

Tiberius was Herod's close mentor and a *soothsayer.*

He was like Ethbaal, Jezebel's father, who had been Ahab's close mentor and a *soothsayer*. Josephus declared Tiberius had often proclaimed a policy of keeping governors, such as Pilate around, no matter how corrupt. Tiberius figured those in power had already stolen as much as they needed. A replacement, in having to start from scratch, would steal even more in starting out fresh. That he changed his mind, indicates some behind the scenes persuasion.

The Marriage

But Herod had a problem. At age sixteen he'd been awarded an Arabian bride in an arranged marriage. That she was an Arabian wasn't the problem. The problem was that the arrangement saw no children. Like Rome, and most governments of the time, the question of an orderly succession of power wouldn't successfully be solved until some one thousand seven hundred and seventy six years later - as a fruit of the American Revolution. In the meantime, as Herod was nearing fifty, he was pressed to produce an heir.

Cayce commented upon celibacy in Biblical times:

"They didn't take vows of celibacy!"

Following up, he said:

"Not to have children during those periods was considered to be ones not thought of God."[8]

The first phrase is refreshing to those spiritually minded, who do not feel that a call to *God's Work* needs to be accompanied by a corresponding call to celibacy (celebration, would seem the more appropriate accompaniment). The first entry would also indicate the high probability that, procreation, was attempted by the couple. The second sees their unfortunate lack of children indicating that Herod, despite his remarkable position, had left some serious unfinished business behind as Ahab:"And Ahab the son of Omri did evil in the sight of the Lord above all who were before him."

Had Herod retained conscious memories of the past life, the rigors of his career had probably pushed them aside. As a child, his Samaritan mother might even have discouraged them. Suppressing children's unwanted past life memories is common in the East today, and back then, was probably the same. She would have known that a child listed as having been as bad as Ahab, would have a heavy burden to carry - even if the mention could be dismissed as another fabrication, or near truth, of Jehu/Josiah.

Karma or *sins of fathers* was probably not a consideration for Herod and his advisors. Infertility on his part would be unthinkable and a solution would be in seeking a new bride.

As fate would have it, the love of Herod's life, Herodias, stepped into the picture. It seemed an incredible attraction and romance by any measure. She had long divorced her inept first husband. Now - at *thirty something* - with a ready made heir and proof of further fertility in her daughter *Salome*, she made an ideal candidate.

Herod obtained permission from Rome to divorce his first wife. Jewish law forbade his marrying his brother's ex-wife; but he might have argued that as he was only his half brother - an exemption could be made. (Their father had maintained a harem of ten wives and the boys didn't share the same mother.) That Jesus never condemned Herod and Herodias' marriage may lend some sway to the argument. While it might also have indicated divine compassion, it more than likely indicated karmic collusion.

But according to the, forever snooping, Josephus, a snag developed.

The first was Herod's first wife. She had learned of the plan before he could appease her family and herself. Disgraced, she returned home to her father, the wily *Aretas of Arabia*. He owed Herod a lot of money, and might have seen a way to get out of debt in the squabble. He threatened a border war at Perea, near ancient Gilead, in whose defense Ahab had died. Aretas probably planned to back off, provided pride and the money matter were settled. That there had been a historic coincidence in a certain Arabian king, the wily Bar Haddad, having once tried a similar tactic on Ahab, suggests even more karma.

It was during the height of the delicate diplomatic negotiations with Bar Hadad/Aretas, that another snag developed. Despite Herod's efforts to avoid an ecclesiastical scandal, a certain voice was heard to cry:

"It is not lawful for you to marry your brothers wife."[10]

Herod knew of John's six-month ministry along the Jordan. Under more normal circumstances, the remark might have been dismissed as an ill-considered remark by a crank. However (1) history taught the dangers of popular preachers in politics. John could anoint a new king as had been reported of Elisha long ago. (2) War was eminent and Herod needed to impress Aretas with a show of Galilean unity. (3) The Parthians, or Persians, ever looking to de-stabilize the region, in assassinating John would see Herod blamed. (4) John might have had a personal ambition for the throne. Such considerations, forced Herod's hand:

"Herod feared lest the great influence John had over the people might put it into his power and inclination to raise a rebellion (for they seemed ready to do anything he should advise)." [11]

Negotiation with Aretas found Herod moving to Marcherus, a fortified castle to the south. He dared not risk John's ability to talk his way out of captivity and:

"John was sent a prisoner, out of Herod's suspicious temper, to Marcherus, the castle."

Further, Herod couldn't risk the consequences of yet another snag:

"Herodias was bitter toward John and wanted to kill him." [12]

Many, in seeking Herodias' favor, could have harmed him. Herodias' behavior must have been puzzling. Her extreme embitterment made no sense. As a *Royal* and the granddaughter of a priest, she would hardly have strayed from the normal protocol of ignoring a slight by one, of whom many about her had said: "He is crazy." [13]   Herod had ruled for twenty-five peaceful years until his karmic wind returned *according to its circuits* in Ahab's two troublemakers: Jezebel and Elijah. Herod was now in the unenviable position of having to maintain domestic tranquillity at home, while upholding job security at work. As to domestic tranquillity, he might have relied upon the norms of expensive presents and the poetry of a romantic, such as Solomon:

"How beautiful are your breasts, O my sister my bride! How much better are your breasts than wine!" [14]

As for job security, Herod was a hard worker, and he knew his business. Surprisingly, he still found time to visit John. Herod seems to have found him delightful:

"Herod heard him gladly." [15]

The Captive

But this was not to say that John was content. While he might not have been placed behind bars, any type of confinement would have pained him. Experiencing stress, the classic behaviors of one suffering a narcissistic personality problem surfaced (See item 27 in the Appendix). Such a sufferer often requires constant attention and admiration. Sometimes they fish for compliments, in putting personal achievements down, hoping someone will step in to bolster their self-esteem, with a complimentary retort. In 1st Kings 19:10, Elijah had fished for praise from God in denying the obvious success seen in bringing the Israelites – as in, to turn - back to Yahweh worship. They were hardly forsaking God's Covenant:

"The children of Israel have forsaken thy covenant."

At other times, the sufferer praises those they admire, and then criticize them. Mark 1:7 noted John praised Jesus, "One who is mightier than I am." John's later contradictory remark, in Matthew 11:3 suggests such a narcissistic extreme:

"Are you the one who is to come, or are we to expect another?"

Jesus understood.

He never took offense and bolstered John's self esteem with such praise as: "He is Elijah."

Jesus sent him other messages of kindly encouragement:

"And blessed is he who does not stumble on account of me."[17]

Good treatment is seen in John's disciples having access to deliver such encouragements. Cayce commented that one such messenger had been his older sister. She had teased John, as a youngster, about his Elijah garb. With maturity, she served the Essenes and John's later ministry. That the Gospels did not mention a sister would not be unusual, given the times male mind-set. Dr. Lamsa[18] mentioned that Middle Eastern women, even in the 20th century, might have five or six girls, but would still be called childless! Elizabeth's similar description, before John's birth, while deplorable, would seem the norm. As an aside, Cayce pointed out the Essene's high regard for women:

"This was the beginning of the period where women were considered as equals with the men in their activities, in their abilities, to live, to be, channels."[19]

As to John and Herod, both were learned men. Herod knew the Greeks, Hebrew history, and spoke Arabic, Aramaic, Greek, and Latin. As a builder, he was acquainted with the Pythagorean theorem. Cayce [20] described John as an intellectual who emphasized the letter of the law rather than, as had Jesus, its spirit. Nevertheless, John was witty, well traveled and:

"Acquainted with the teachings of those groups in Persia, India, Egypt and even the Hebrews and in the activities in Olympus and the isles of the sea."[21]

Socrates and Plato would have found him an able colleague.

Likewise: Herod. Ahab had been a patron of scholars and Herod's city of Tiberius still stands as a learning center and holy site. At some point, Herod must have realized that this astute individual had engineered his own arrest. Herod would also have ascertained that John wasn't crazy. No ordinary hermit or *street preacher* could have sustained such a vast ministry nor commanded this very busy king's attention. Had John designs on the throne, he would have avoided capture or put up a *firefight*. The implications of Elijah's garb were obvious to anyone having even the slightest grasp of Hebrew history.

Herod's inquisitive mind would by now be wondering what were the motivations behind this most distinguished of captives. He wouldn't have accepted it at the time, but John was hardly the one being held captive.

The issue was that only Herod stood between John's destiny with Herodias and everyone knew it was unlikely that Herod was going to let her get at him. To overcome this, John would need to somehow persuade Herod to change his mind. This might have required John to convince Herod he was the genuine Elijah and to remind the king of his own mission in fulfilling the Scriptures.

While Herod could easily have been impressed with the intensity of John's claim, accepting it as fact, would need some deliberation. Like today's researcher, his first consideration would be fraud: He would be satisfied in seeing John's lifestyle. It was like that of many holy men and riches and power hardly motivated him. The Herod's were respectful of Essenes, even Archelaus had sought their council, and John's spiritual credentials were impeccable.

Fraud hardly seemed an issue.

If not fraud, then could the Essenes have unintentionally brainwashed John into believing he was Elijah? Was his father's claim merely that of an old man's fantasy, which the Essenes reinforced? Herod, had he suspected John's intent, would mull this over, not knowing that twenty centuries later, after thirty years of research, Stevenson would generally dismiss such cases. One was a case in Turkey, where a father claimed his son had been John F. Kennedy.[22] The townspeople supported the notion. However, the claim was not long lived and Stevenson had never found, except in reincarnation type cases, children who claimed another personality, as a unified aspect of themselves, over a period of time. Psychotic adults may make these claims but psychosis is rare to nonexistent in children.

Herod knew John's history didn't exist in a vacuum. His education would reveal an intricate relationship with learned Essene elders and masters of both East and West. His role with Jesus was also a factor. Essenes, like Tibet's monks, were not fools and would never have risked their reputations, revenues, and very lives, unless sure their charges were authentic.

Herod would not have had the insight of science or these other considerations of the future: Evidence of *Skinner boxes* and similar methods of psychological behavior modification have yet to be found in the ancient world. Twentieth century genetics and the material based nightmare of Communism never produced such beings as a John the Baptist nor others of similar stature. That is, Nazi experiments in genetics did not produce an Einstein or Joe Lewis.

Soviet behaviorists never successfully picked someone at random and taught them to become a Rachmaninoff, Tchaikovsky or a Tolstoy and the genius of Lao Tzu is not expected to appear this year, as a result of such efforts, in the People's Republic of North Korea. As no one taught the unique being, *Mozart* music nor a *Babe Ruth* to hit, no Essene behavior modification effort could have picked just anyone and taught them to be Elijah or Jesus.

The essence of humanity is Spiritual. We are unique individuals and no soul, or *psi component* (to use a term from parapsychology) can be made to become someone that they are not.

John was Elijah!

The Encounter
At Marchurus, Herod in having a little time from his busy schedule would call upon John for some enlightening and delightful conversation.

In the days of long lost Israel, when something important needed doing, Ahab called upon Obadiah:

"Who was *the steward*."[23]

In Ahab's later incarnation, the king would send for:

"Chuza *the steward* of Herod."[24]

Like Obadiah, Chuza would promptly respond. His wife Joanna had been healed by Jesus and what was to occur at the coming birthday celebration probably came from what *the steward* would have sadly shared.

Herod, in waiting, gazed out over the steep ramparts. Built by his father, like the defenses of Masada and Jerusalem itself, it was impregnable. In the same manner, so was Samaria. Restored, again by Herod's father, it was originally built by Omri, Ahab's father. Unique, and still visible in those structures today, are the massive hewn stones, called ashlars, with a distinctive ridge carved around their edges.

His birthday (the big *Five-0)* found him contemplative, as are most men at that milestone in their lives, if for only an instant. At the peak of his career, thoughts about past triumphs and the uncertainties of the future would occupy his mind. Riches, retirement and a coming life of ease would displace the stressful issues he would have to deal with once back at work. For now, a relaxing drink and a little banter with his witty guest was sufficient.

Just then, a still small *voice* would prompt Herod *to turn*.

He stood, face to face, facing a *big-guy*. Cayce described him:

"A figure, rough with the strong characteristics of a man, with the hair not too long but ruffled with a beard, with a staff resting across the limb...and the dress of camel's skin or hair with a girdle binding same about the body."[25]

There would be a pause. Then the memories flashed back eight hundred and fifty years to the wily Bar Hadad, and the *Siege of Samaria*.

The Memory

"Thus says Bar Hadad, Your silver and your gold are mine; and the most attractive of your wives and your children are mine also.

And the king of Israel answered...I am yours and all that I have."[26]

Trapped, *that fox* was in a jam. Despite his foxiness, and strategies of stealth, Ahab had found himself inside Samaria cut off from his main force. Stalling for time, he consulted with the city's elders to rally their support.

Ahab was a parliamentarian and not a tyrant:

"And all the elders and all the people said to him, Do not hearken to him nor consent."

Backed by *All Israel* and the people, Ahab's defiant response remains the slogan of today's Israeli army:

"The one who ties a knot is not more able than the one who can untie it!"

The Jerusalem version reads:

"The man who puts on his armor is not the one who can boast, but the man who takes if off!"

The modern reader roughly translates both:

"Don't count your chickens before they're hatched!"

Just then, a still small voice prompted Ahab to turn. He stood, face to face, facing a *big*-guy.

"A figure, rough with the strong characteristics of a man, with the hair not too long but ruffled with a beard..."

Then came that *voice:*

"And behold, a prophet drew near to Ahab king of Israel and said to him, Thus says the Lord...I will deliver Bar Hadad's army into your hands."

The two, after carefully conferring, saw an opening upon which their respective *paranormal* and *normal* minds could agree. (Likewise the stickler for translations. Both the Jerusalem and King James Bibles translate Bar Haddad as Ben Haddad. But because he was a *drunk,* the Lamsa translation of *Bar* instead of *Ben* seems more appropriate):

"*Bar* Hadad was drinking old wine...he and the thirty two kings who were come to help him"

Ahab gave the order:

"And they slew everyone his man...and Bar Haddad the king escaped."[27]

Forewarned, Ahab prepared for their return. This time, Bar Hadad was captured. The battle of Aphek occurred at the famous Golan Heights. It's still strategic. Abab's reputation, among Israel's enemies, shames and exposes the *lying pens* of revisionist scribes. They should have been asked, like some of today, whose side are you on? Revisionists said of Ahab:

"There was none like Ahab, who sought to do evil."[28]

Israel's enemies would have slain *every one his man* - especially scribes - had Ahab failed to defeat them. They played for keeps in those days.

Ahab's adversaries, outside his own country, said of him:

"The kings of Israel are merciful kings...perhaps he will spare our lives."[28]

A man of chivalry, Ahab is shown sparing their lives and personally embracing and saying openly of their wily king:

"He is my brother."[30]

Also shown is a man of diplomatic skill. He needed Bar Hadad as an ally in the coming battle with the Assyrians.

Elijah was surely the nameless prophet heard helping Ahab defend Samaria and the Golan Heights. Ahab's success lay in his abilities of stealth. He often fought in disguise and *foxed* his enemies with military intelligence Elijah might have psychically provided.

Quagar likely saw such stealth.

Apparently unaware of Elijah and Ahab, Assyria listed Bar Hadad as Palestine's chief. Remembering that he was a *drunk* (aptly named *Bar)* and that he was twice defeated by the *daring duo* suggests he was a decoy. I suspect *Bar's* task was to duck, while Elijah prayed and *that fox* fought. A similar situation was seen in this popular song of World War Two vintage:

"Praise the Lord and pass the ammunition."

Assyrian aggression was set back for many years.

When in error, Ahab would heed his chaplain: "And the word of the Lord came to Elijah the Tishbite, saying, Have you seen how Ahab has humbled himself before me?"

Jesus praised the faithfulness of another good soldier: "Not even in Israel have I found such faith as this." (Luke 7:9)

As had Ahab's troops listened to Elijah, Herod's troops also heard John: "Do not molest any man, and do not accuse any man: your own wages should be enough for you." (Luke 3:14)

That same figure, *with the strong characteristics of a man*, would again prompt they and the king *to turn* towards God. John's mission was to rest on the axiom that, like all good soldiers, Herod had ears and would hear.

The Pitch

The Scriptures stated that only Elijah could testify to the Messiah's return. Likewise, only Elijah could make amends for his errors. It was therefore necessary for him to have himself presented to Jezebel/Herodias. The marital slander and predictable arrest got her attention. As she was unlikely to have forgiven him, he knew death would result. His mission to fulfill the Scriptures had reached its zenith at the Baptism, but its completion lay in what was to follow.

John needed Herod on his side. This required the *voice* of a superb salesman. Like my old man, John pitched with the best.

In a recruitment effort, John might have started his pitch in relating a custom he observed in India. As today, in the India that John had visited, Buddhist masters continually confronted their students on how to deal with the destinies (or karma) of others when such individuals touched their lives. Visualizing a drowning person struggling beneath a bridge, the problem was worded: "If it is that person's karma to drown, should those on the bridge act to save them or stand aside and allow the drowning person's karmic destiny to fulfill itself?"

Upon hearing such a question, Herod would counter that, as a king, his personal hands were tied and matters of state would take precedence. Thus his action would depend upon how such a rescue might serve his kingdom.

This first-hand encounter with the dynamic and rational John, so convinced of his past-life that he would die for it, would also have impressed Herod. John was impressive. So much so, that Herod had caught the Baptist's drift right away. Herod was also impressive. He knew, at some level, he was being asked to allow the karmas of John and Herodias to come about. From his rational side, he'd offer that in John's case, he would be kept in safekeeping. Harming him now might topple the king's reputation and lead to the type of civil discord, which could cost him the coming war and even his crown.

The dialogue could have taken place at some subconscious level, such as in a dream. Perhaps it didn't take place at all. If it did, I envision John addressing Herod's reluctance in asking, "Whom do you serve: The kingdom of God or the kingdom of man?" Had Herod said he served God and made his kingdom a reflection of the kingdom above (a concept that was, highly likely, held by Herod: "As in heaven so on earth") an opening was created. This opening could trigger Herod to a righteous, though politically incorrect and *non-rational* decision. A *non-rational* decision is not to be construed as one that is *irrational.* Herod was always a *rational* type and never one to take any action based on some off the wall *wacko* proposition: John was not a *wacko*.

Drawing upon a future event (I'm sure John possessed prodigious ESP), or recalling a past conversation with Jesus, John's final closing attempt would begin:

"And as Jesus passed by, he saw a man who was blind from his mother's womb.

And his disciples asked him, saying, who did sin, this man or his parents, that he was born blind?

Jesus said to them, Neither did he sin nor his parents. But that the works of God might be seen in him. I must do the works of him who sent me."

Tying the plight of those on the bridge with that of Jesus and Herod, John would ask, "Whose karma is being presented to whom? Is it the karma of the one drowning and 'the man born blind' or is it that of the observers?"

For Jesus, the issue had been clear.

It was his own karma in witnessing the person's plight. "Sins of this man or his parents" wasn't an issue. The issue was in what Jesus was observing. He saw in the blind man a karmic opportunity to *do the works of God* and followed through with a positive act.

The blind man saw.

John might have closed the deal in reminding Herod that, as a king, his position was as unique as it had been for Jesus as a healer. As only Jesus could have made the blind man see, only Herod could interject the kingly guiding principle, *as in heaven so on earth* and help bring about a Scriptural fulfillment. Resolving the *situation ethic* would test the best of Herod's inner self.

By now he would be suffering *buyer's remorse*. He would ask himself, *why me?*

His answer would be in exploring his own earthly mission. The process might have been at a level of which he was unaware. As a builder and statesman, a logical side ruled and he would want to spare John; yet, there would be a *still small voice* pushing him to go against his norms of human logic. John might have hinted that while the outcome would be seen as a negative, *The Work* required Herod to stand aside and let Herodias have her due. Herod needed no reminding that faith was required. His reward wasn't going to be:

"That which is Caesar's."[33]

But that of heaven:

"He who receives a prophet in the name of a prophet shall receive a prophet's reward."[34]

John had planted the seeds of his mission's success; the rest was up to a higher power. It was time to *let go and let God*

The One in Whom You Delight

John might have speculated upon Herodias forgiveness. If she were able, then the saga of Ahab, Jezebel, and Elijah could be put to rest. It might free her and Herod to bear Galilee children: Another Ahaziah, Athalia, or Joram. Herod could maintain in them, the diplomatic skills of peace. They in turn would bring forth little foxes, which would not only bring great joy to their grandparents, but also outwit the Roman juggernaut for a millennium.

John would be left to seek the simple pleasures of the *good life* Odysseus had sought. Like Odysseus, John was also like ourselves and, at some level, yearned for the same human condition of home, health, security, companionship...

Marrying a nice Phoenician girl, and trading his camel skin for a toga, he could get a *real* job. Starting in sales, he'd rise to the top:

Transportation - JORDAN JOHN'S CAMELS:
"Used but not abused!"
Fast food - JORDAN JOHN'S BURGERS:
"Lightening fried!"
Designer clothing - JORDAN JOHN'S JEANS:
"Buckles! Belts!"

Little Johns and little Johnettes?

John would listen for a *still small voice*.

Knowing that such scenarios didn't happen, in even the most syrupy of Synagogue school sermons, he was not surprised in hearing his own prayer uttered long ago.

"Oh Lord, take away my life; for I am not better than."[35]

Chortling, he reminded himself, that prayer is always answered even if its eight hundred fifty years in coming. He'd remember the lesson - next time.

He still had options. He could get a pardon from Herod and seek exile. He could ask God for a postponement, as would Jesus:
"Let this cup pass away."[36]
But John, without asking, knew what was coming:
"If I must drink it, let it be according to thy will."[37]

John might have shed a tear, a tear for what could or should have been. But not for long. *Pity parties* weren't his forte. He was the one, "In whom you *delight!*" His broad smile returning, I imagine his humming these lines from a Persian poem, as he bade Herod farewell.

The poetry would be attributed to the Sufi Muslim mystic, Rumi:
"I died as a mineral and became a plant.
I died as plant and rose to animal,
I died as animal and was man.
Why should I fear death?
When was I less by dying
  Yet once more I shall die as man, to soar with angels blest;
  But even from anglehood I must pass on."
               (From The Mathnawi)[38]

The Daughter of Tyre

Herod's birthday soon saw the arrival of Herodias. As expected, she had an agenda for John. Her method might not have been formulated; but, she was sure luck would allow an open window of opportunity.

Whereas Elijah's downside had been as an errant *Avatar* and Ahab was one to let issues blur when affairs of virtue and national security clashed, Jezebel's anger drew her to revenge. She had been one to whom many promises were made, but few kept.

She had been the *Daughter of Tyre* spoken of in Psalm 45. Without doubt, it was sung at her wedding to Ahab[39] As a teenage princess, she had been asked to give up her idyllic life by the seaside:
"Hearken my daughter and incline your ear; forget also your own people and your father's house."

She would cement the treaty, through an arranged marriage, to the *warlord* of her nation's eastern ally:
"Your arrows are sharp; let them pierce the heart of the king's enemies, and let the people fall under you."

However, every luxury the age could offer would be hers:

"The king's daughter stands in glory, the queen stands at your hand in gold of Ophir."

The trade off was she would never sail the seas and share the adventures *sea people* cherished. Her loss was Carthage, Cadiz (the future port of Columbus) Yucatan, Europe, circumnavigating Africa: Vikings...

Her choice was *The Work*. She chose to serve Phoenicia's people and those of Israel. Recall archaeology's findings: many Israelites worshiped both Yahweh and the nature deities.

"All the glory of the king's daughter is from within."

She would find inland biases burdensome:

"So shall the king greatly desire your beauty, for he is your Lord: make obeisance to him."

And the daughter of Tyre shall *worship* him."

Fat chance!

The Seal of Jezebel.

Four mirrored images of Hebrew letters spell out her name: JZBL (vowels weren't used then). The first two appear just under the winged disc (the symbol of immortality) and the latter two at the base.

When pressed into wet clay, the images read correctly. They marked Jezebel's *Work*.

Nevertheless, Ahab had his appeal:

"You are fairer than the children of men; grace is poured into your lips...

You love righteousness and hate wickedness; therefore <u>Ahab</u> *[later scribes scratched out his name]*, your God has anointed you above your fellows."

On those times when, as in all marriages, domestic tranquility was to go awry, she could count on expensive presents and Solomon's poetry to set things aright:

"How beautiful are your breasts, O my sister my bride! How much better are your breasts than wine!"

She already had *looks* and money and the many suitors a king's daughter would normally possess. Her *bottom line* would concern the well being of future children and her reputation. Children of the rich often possess anything they please, by virtue of inherited wealth. The only thing they can gain on their own merits is a good reputation.

A good reputation was important to her.

Two promises closed the Psalm. The first assured a good future for any children:

"You shall make them princes in all the earth."

The second addressed her reputation:

"I will make your name to be remembered in all generations; therefore shall the people praise your name for ever and ever."

"Baloney!" she muttered, when she first heard it. As a child, her priestly grandfather had probably read the psalm aloud. In deference to his love of the Scriptures, she would have kept her feelings to herself.

She never forgot.

The first was her death. Knowing she was going to die, she remembered to properly prepare herself. As the Queen mother of both Israel and Judah and believing, as a Phoenician[40] she would look as fashionable in her future life as she had in the last:

"She painted her eyelids with kohl [mascara] and adorned her head and looked out a window."[41]

Recalling that the traitorous Zimri had once taken the throne, but had held it for only a few days, her final words were aimed at the *beast* entering her courtyard far below:

"You Zimri, murderer of his master."[42]

Expecting the *voice* of a wimp - bending like a reed in the wind - the world's first *Yahoo* could do little more than bellow back:

"Throw her down. So they threw her down; and some of her blood was sprinkled on the wall, and the horses entered and trod her under foot.

Then he went in to eat and drink."[43]

As Jezebel, all her children had been murdered. She was thrown to her death and in Herodias day, as today, Jezebel's name was placed on wanton women. And on the subject of reputation, the murderer of her prophets got away, scot-free, to enjoy the reputation:

"The one in whom you *delight!*"

Her remembrances continued.

When Ahab returned from Mount Carmel and told how Elijah had defeated her prophets at the altar and killed them, she never forgot having to hide her grief. She had to set it aside so as to console her terrified children. Their funny uncles weren't coming home for diner.

They had eaten together, like family, at the same table.

She remembered how she didn't buy the story of the miraculous fire nor the reasons for the rains, which followed. The impressive thunders were soon to come anyway. Righteous prayer was always answered, whether worded by Archangels and Angels, Heathens, Greeks, Barbarians, the wise, the unwise, and even Israelites!

Her father, Ethbaal, had already prayed:

"When Ethbaal made supplications, there came *great thunders*...By these words he deigned the want of rain that was in the days of Ahab."[44]

Like the Senate of Rome at Augustus' rising, *All Israel* was present to witness the mountaintop miracle. Their official communiqué, she suspected, was a fabrication concocted to cover up nothing more than a cold-blooded execution. Was this the price Elijah and his followers demanded for siding with her husband in the oncoming battle with the Assyrians? Was Elijah's public run before the king's chariot making a statement to the people that they were united in the coming fray? Preemptive strikes are often *hard sells* to populations enjoying periods of peace.

Why were her simple priests such a threat?

Like all Holy-men, they stood on the same side with the *Sons of the Prophets* when it came to God's goodness, didn't they? Yes, her people saw the *Divine* as a collective entity and utilized differing rituals. But what did it matter whether they professed there were ten gods or no gods? They didn't pick people's pockets or break their legs. Was it money? The long drought would have hurt the economy and lessened the tithes. Was some sort of sex-thing behind the killings - like envy? What was wrong with sex and spirituality being seen in the same light? Were Elijah's followers, just another cult. Were the issues the usual *quick cash, private parts* and hidden *holier than thou* political agendas so typical of such groups?

At the least, an invitation to join in a covenant with the God of Israel would have been the better option. At worst, the prophets could have been simply deported back to Phoenicia. That no disruption of the Phoenician/Israelite alliance took place was an issue she wouldn't have allowed herself to explore. That her father and the father of her children might have conspired in letting Elijah have his way, would have been her undoing.

In the end, she would have had to put it all behind her and concede that maybe what had happened was that the whole affair had gotten out of hand. Maybe Elijah had tried to do the right thing, and maybe there was a flash of fire - but under duress and the stresses of the long day - he went berserk. When the crowd fueled with religious fervor rioted, Ahab couldn't have stopped them.

She remembered sending her vengeful vow to Elijah:
"I will make your life as the life of one of them"[45]

But in all this, she seemed to have forgotten about *Divine Justice*. As always, it's the final word.

For starters, everybody died! *Divine* memory wouldn't forget her tears and that such was the need for Elijah's correction, that the vow was to stand - impressed - into the Scriptures: *"As it is written of him."*

No one was going to get off the hook. Elijah, as would Jezebel and all the rest, were to see consequences for both their virtues and for those issues which needed correction.

Secondly, Elijah, despite his stature, was to be labeled:
"The least person in the kingdom of heaven."[46]

Thirdly, in knowing he'd transgressed *Holy Writ*, he would anguish:

"Oh Lord, take away my life; for I am not better than my fathers [his past incarnations]"[47]

Records which Cayce termed, *Akashic* records, would keep track. Though justice would prevail, a final resolution could only come about through forgiveness. But all were in too deep to pull themselves up by themselves.

In her embittered state, she would forget – in being like ourselves - and begin complaining: "How could both the gods of her people and Yahweh have been so unfair to Jezebel?" *Why me* was what she was really asking. The specifics of her questions might long have been forgotten, but not her anger.

Nor her need for revenge.

But the *Divine's* help was predicated upon the outcome of but one option: If she were given the opportunity, could she quell her anger - though justified - and in striving for forgiveness, begin listening for a *still small voice*.

The Voice that would urge her to let go and let God.

Queen Athalia

Marcherus now contained, as you recall, not only the three major players of the Elijah saga, but those who lived the events of 1st and 2nd Kings. These were the two captains and the hundred soldiers killed by Elijah, Jezebel's prophets, and possibly *All Israel* who backed Ahab against Bar Hadad and witnessed Elijah's acts on mount Carmel.

Another had been *Athalia*.

She'd been the daughter of Ahab and Jezebel and became queen of Jerusalem.[48] It was her feisty son, *Ahazia*, whom Jehu had butchered. She had lost her husband, Joram (of the same name as her brother), just a year previous.

A few years later, she was assassinated herself.

There is some question on her family status as the Book of the Chronicles parts with secular history's chronicle and lists her as:

"Athalia the *daughter* of Omri."[49]

The scholarly *Encyclopaedia Judaica* stands tall in the opinion that she was indeed Ahab and Jezebel's daughter and that Omri had been her grandfather. Most side with the encyclopedia. It may be that the title designated her as being a member of the *dynasty* of the slighted king, who like Herod the Great's family had a complicated genealogy, but was also the most able political force of the time.

Assessing Athalia's position seems like an insignificant issue and something for the biblical historian to ponder. However, while *nit picking* must not get in the way of Spiritual meaning, historical accuracy needs to be asserted, lest human thinking and actions go awry. Upon a closer look, the passage leads to conjecture opening a heightening of positive contemplation.

The scribe's motivation might have been to absolve Josiah:

"And like unto Josiah was there no king before him, who turned to the Lord with all his heart and with all his soul and with all his might, according to all that which is written in the Law of Moses."[50]

That the scribe maintained a *lying-pen* is seen in a quick look at Josiah's record on human rights abuses. As to falsifying Athalia's parentage, the intent stands as obvious in its portraying Judah's kings as being free from the blood of foreigners. If Athalia had been Ahab's sister, she'd not have had a Phoenician bloodline to pass on to Jerusalem's Davidic line. This would keep everything lined up in maintaining Josiah's own Deuteronomic vision of ethnic purity.

Isaiah, you recall, blessed Phoenicians as *"the honorable of the earth."* They're men and women mariners sailed (as I would well like to remember) making love all over the globe. As Jezebel's daughter, Phoenicia's multi-racial bloodline - the bloodline of humanity - would have coursed throughout the lineage of David, which followed her: African blacks, American natives, Europeans, Vikings, Orientals and Asiatics. This was the lineage, which would lead - unbroken - to Jesus, Joseph, Elizabeth, John, and Mary. I find it meaningful that the gene pool of the world's people, at least symbolically, was contained in that linkage.

It became the *Blood* of Christ:

Athalia married: "Joram the son of Jehoshephat, King of Judah."

(2nd Kings 8:16)

Ahaziah was the fruit of that union. Upon his murder and that of his grandmother, Athalia, his son ascended the throne:

"Joash the son of Ahaziah king of Judah"

(2nd Kings 13:1 - 14:3)

The good name of Omri and the *House of Ahab* stand vindicated in Joash: "And Joash did that which was right."

He was followed by Amaziah:

"He did that which was right"

Then, another doing right: "Uzziah"

The Gospel of Matthew (1:9) continues:

"Uzziah begot Jotham; Jotham begot Ahaz; Ahaz begot Hezikiah...Mattthan begot Jacob;

And Jacob begot Joseph the husband of Mary, of whom was born Jesus, who is called the Christ."

The Test

Though Ahab and Jezebel's children were raised as Israelites (they had been given Hebrew names) Athalia, in learning from her mother, would have danced. Returned as Salome, the daughter of Herodias, she'd surely retain the skill. She'd also retain an intense desire to get Elijah. The deaths of her *funny uncles*, would have been traumatic to her as a *little girl*.[51]

"And the daughter of Herodias entered and danced, and she pleased Herod and the guests who were with him; and the king said to *the little girl*, Ask me whatever you wish, and I will give it to you.

And he swore to her, Whatever you ask me, I will give you, as much as half my kingdom.

She went out and said to her mother, what shall I ask him?"[52]

Herodias, momentarily, maintained a silence. The *voice* began to speak. But bad habits - being what they are - led her inner mind to a bloody flashback:

"O Baal answer us. But there was no voice nor any that answered. And they cut themselves upon the altar."

Self-castration occurred among such disciples. Origen and those of later Christian sects repeated it. Such was their devotion:

"And when it was noon, Elijah mocked them and said, Cry with a loud voice...

And they cried with a loud *voice* and they cut themselves after their custom with daggers and lances, until their blood gushed out upon them."[53]

As the *voice* of Mother Nature's prophets had fallen on deaf ears, no *voice* - not even the *Voice* of Jesus - would answer for John. In a millisecond, that heard, wouldn't be the still *small* voice of forgiveness, but the *Loud Voice* of vengeance:

"THE HEAD OF JOHN THE BAPTIST...

And immediately [Salome] entered hesitantly to the king, and said to him, I do wish in this very hour that you might give me on a tray the head of John the Baptist."

The ball was now in Herod's corner. Only he could issue a thumbs up or down. As above, so below all awaited, with equal bated breath, to see how Herod was to serve *The Work:*

He might have made similar promises of *half my kingdom* to officers facing war and he wanted his word seen as irrevocable, or he might have thought so after a few drinks. Domestic tranquility would have been another issue. Herodias humiliation at having her direct order remanded would exact a high cost.

An heir was desperately needed.

That cute kid on the dance floor wasn't going to convince the Romans she could cut the mustard as a queen. Another explanation is that political circumstances forced him aside, as they had forced Ahab to stand aside in letting Jezebel's prophets die.

Ultimately, his motives must remain - like those of *ourselves* - between himself and the *creative forces* he worshiped as his inner God. Hopefully, Herod repent-fully chose, like Elijah, to acquiesce the lessons of the karmic wind which:

"Returns again according to its circuits."[54]

Josephus presumably, in not knowing of Chuza, didn't mention the birthday scandal, reporting the event as purely political. He noted Herod:

"Thought it best, by putting John to death, to prevent mischief he might cause, and not bring himself into difficulties, by sparing a man who might make him repent of it when it should be too late."[55]

And added:

"Now some of the Jews thought that the destruction of Herod's army came from God, and that very justly, as a punishment of what he did against John that was called the Baptist"

Josephus, you recall, was no friend of the Herods. Except for them, he might have been king himself. He had a legitimate complaint in John's execution. However, his bias saw Herod's marriage and the encroachment of Tiberius' borders upon a cemetery as major crimes. Herod's fondness for stone animal sculptures, which were displayed on the palace grounds, was likewise a scandal. (Ahab had a similar taste, though for ivory animals and he kept them indoors in his famed *ivory palace*.) Josephus' judgments further vilify Herod and may appear in Luke 3:19 as:

"All the evil things he was doing."

In acting as the evidence suggests, Herod might have comforted in this advice given to those who pursue *The Work*.

"Blessed are you when men hate you and discriminate against you and reproach you and publish your names as bad for the sake of the son of man."   (Luke 6:22)

Had Herod not so acted, then may God have rested his soul.

The Vineyard

Herod survived and served *The Work* in orchestrating a successful peace between Rome and the Persians. At the death of Emperor Tiberius, the infamous Gaius Caligula came to power. This began an unusual turn of events. Though Herod was content to rest on his laurels, Herodias pushed him to *upgrade* his title to King. The issue centered over the appointment of her young brother, Agrippa, as king of Judea. You recall the man, *of the grape,* and his fondness for wine. Fortunately for him, so had his *drinking buddy*, Caligula. Upon his promotion, Caligula gave Agrippa the kingdom. This so enraged Herodias that, as in the case of John, questions of karmic causation needs to be scrutinized.

Her anger with Elijah/John had its justification and any serious look at Jezebel's suffering must gain history's sympathy. However, like Ahab, she had one inexcusable flaw.

The problem, you'll remember, was in the treatment of another *man of the grape* named Naboth. He owned a vineyard. Ahab wanted to purchase the land and convert it into a vegetable garden. Upon Naboth's refusal, Ahab grew depressed. The event occurred shortly after Quagar and may indicate his suffering a delayed stress reaction. He had witnessed, as the coalition's commander, the loss of twenty-five thousand:

"And Ahab laid down on his bed and turned away his face and would eat no food."[56]

Jezebel fabricated a note accusing Naboth of treason. The court, thinking the evidence came from the king, executed Naboth. By law, the land became Ahab's. He might have been innocent. Unfortunately, it seems he simply looked the other way, as he had on Mount Carmel. In so great a king treating one of his subjects so shabbily, the *Word of the Lord* spoke through Elijah. While litanies of the *lying* pen's slander are included, one prediction was clear:

"In Ahab's son's days will I bring the evil upon his house."[57]

Elijah and Ahab part.

So predictable a split might normally explain Jezebel's action as simple revenge. In *Biblical Cases*, I gave her some bad press. It might have been a *guy thing* in my thinking. I figured once she saw the man she had been conditioned to worship become so sick, she *snapped,* and for the first time, saw him for what he was: a human being *like ourselves*. And as a human being, he was capable of collusion with Elijah and her father. He was also capable of putting his insatiable sexual drive not only over her - a priestess of Venus - but over that of national security. She suspected Samaria's harem strumpets led to his slipping away from his troops and the embarrassing entrapment by Bar Hadad.

Scoundrels, cheats, adulterers, all these guys were alike! She'd fix em. Insane, she stole Ahab's ring and pressed its image on what became Naboth's death warrant. The scandal would drive a wedge between Ahab and Elijah. If she got caught, who'd dare prosecute the queen mother?

However, in rethinking the situation, her act might have had a more rational motivation. While Ahab's debilitating mental breakdown might have jogged her thoughts, if his illness was known by Israel's enemies, they might seek an incursion. Time was of the essence. Jezebel, in being an astute student of political reality took charge. Had she not been a woman, Machiavellian politics would be known today as, Jezebellian politics.

The emergency demanded action. Naboth's turn down of Ahab's very generous offer, indicate his vintner's focus on wine, not only blurred his vision of patriotic duty, but blurred the realization of what he should have known was an offer, that he couldn't refuse!

It was a lesson he wouldn't forget.

Ahab recovered.

However, with Elijah out of the picture, his psychic intelligence community lay in shambles and an ever watchful Bar Hadad knew of Ahab's stealth (see 1 Kings 22). When war came, Ahab's strategies would be of little avail: The enemy was not to be Assyria, but the thankless Bar Hadad:

"And the king of Israel disguised himself and went into the battle. But the king of Aram Bar Hadad commanded the thirty-two captains of his chariots, saying, Fight neither with small nor great, save only with the king of Israel."[58]

Mortally wounded, when an arrow pierced a joint in his armor's breastplate, Ahab made the ultimate sacrifice. Despite the excruciating pain, which would have dropped a lesser man or seen him seek the rear, Ahab firmly faced his fate. Refusing to abandon his troops, he gave his all, to insure his men would not lose heart and lose Israel:

"The king was standing in the chariot facing the Arameans, and died that evening; and the blood ran out of his wound.

Now the rest of the acts of Ahab and all that he did and the ivory palace that he built and all the cities he built, behold they are written in the Book of the Chronicles of the Kings of Israel.

So Ahab slept with his fathers."[59]

After Ahab's death, Jehu justified his killing Ahab's sons as fulfilling Elijah's prophesy - the sins of Ahab were being passed on. But obviously, Jehu did not act like Jesus or as presumed in Herod. They chose to benefit God, rather than themselves. Had Jehu truly been anointed by Elisha, as Josiah had claimed, I think Jehu would have been forewarned, in personally judging Ahab and bringing *evil* or *offenses* upon Abab's children by his own hand. Elisha's advice would have been like that of Cayce and Jesus:

"Let mercy and justice be thy watchword rather than judgment upon others. For 'judge not that ye be not judged'...Do not judge thyself. Let God's mercy and love rule thee."[60]

Never forget:

"It is impossible but that offenses should come; but woe to him by whose hand they come."[61]

Jehu's judgment saw himself suffering offenses of his own making. Had he *let God's mercy and love rule*, Ahab's positive policies of gender, racial and religious toleration might have lived on. Samaria would be remembered today as *Camelot* and the Middle East and the world would be a far happier place.

God attended to Ahab. His Godliness was rewarded and his unGodliness saw *offenses* in his ruined Scriptural reputation, Herod's demeaning title of *Tetrarch,* no children, and his land lost to Naboth.

Predictably, Naboth had returned as Agrippa.

The final *offense* began when the couple reached the crazed Caligula's court. A major good side to Herod's karma, like Ahab's, was money. Not all karma is bad. The greedy Caligula was expected to bestow the kingship for flattery and cash. He would not be the first emperor to accept a bribe and Herod, as a master diplomat, knew the game of flattery.

He also knew that in the political arena, age and treachery wins out over youth and enthusiasm.

Still, as Josephus noted, Herod had trepidations about the transaction and only did so to appease Herodias' need to be queen. Herod's trepidation proved well founded, as Caligula had miraculously received a note from Naboth/Agrippa, accusing the Herods of treason. (The message was sent after the Herods sailed, but got there before them.)

Caligula, in believing the charges, banished Herod to Gaul and gave his kingdom to a man who had learned a lesson.

"And thus did God punish Herodias for her envy at her brother, and Herod also for giving ear to the vain discourse of a woman."[62]

Josephus, as seen here, is sometimes politically incorrect to quote in today's age of gender sensitivity. However, he illustrates how secular history can underline and reinforce biblically derived theories of a cause and effect *active presence of God* intent on helping humans modify their misbehaviors. Fortunately, Josephus also reveals the reactions of *psi components*, or free-willed souls, when touched by this forgiving presence:

"But when Caligula was informed that Herodias was Agrippa's sister, he made her a present of what money was her own, and told her that it was her brother who prevented her being put under the same calamity with her husband."

In Naboth/Agrippa's forgiveness of Herodias, the law of karma was put to rest between them. Such forgiveness, might have finally opened her ears and triggered a profound spiritual step in the right direction: "But she made this reply: 'The kindness which I have for my husband, hinders me from partaking of the favor of thy gift; for it is not just that I, who have been made a partner in his prosperity, should forsake him in his misfortunes.' Hereupon Caligula was angry at her, and sent her with Herod into banishment, and gave her estate to Agrippa."

Her step illustrates how history and the Bible reveal reincarnation as a Spiritual process, which helps fallen souls return to the grace of heaven.

This is the lesson at hand.

Naboth/Agrippa became a better person, though he was no friend to the earliest Christians. While not having the experience and intellect of Herod, in ruling from his heart, he was greatly beloved, though his reign was short. His son, Agrippa, shows this growth. He judged Saint Paul and after the trial, felt him not guilty.

A Real _____ !

Saint Augustine, said Christianity existed before Jesus. In that context, the word Christian seen here does not necessarily designate a specific denomination. The term has historically held a broad meaning.

Cayce saw Christianity as a universal state of mind, or consciousness, which was one with God. He labeled it the *Christ Consciousness*. A Moslem might prefer the term *Paradise* and an Easterner, *Samadhi*, or *Absolute Oneness with God*. The world's faithful have many equally as valid words, which bear repeating, in describing THE WORD.

Allah; Christ; God; I Am; Jehovah; Krishna; Lord; Love: Spirit; Yaweh...

"Hear, O Israel; the Lord our God is one Lord."

Agrippa II was both the last Herod and the last of the Jewish kings (I suspect he might have been Joash). Their successes and failures are best remembered as mirroring our human condition. They were human beings *like ourselves* and in judging them, we judge only our humanity. We are children of God and, though we inhabit the earth, we are not of the earth. Forgiveness frees us from returns and opens the way to God's universe. God's universe is called Heaven and we need never leave it! Richard Wagner termed it the *Holy Land of choice:*

"The home of desire I leave behind,
Illusion forever avoid.
The open door of return and being I close forever.
Yearning for regions of peace,
The Holy Land of choice,
Released from the path of return,
So wanders the wise one forth."
　　　　　(Finale: Die Gotterdammerung) [63]

The Transfiguration

Through successive lives, we are transfigured and evolve. Free will always allows us choice. Bible history makes this clear in closing the case of the human being - *like ourselves* - Elijah/John.

"And after six days Jesus took Peter and James and his brother John, and brought them up to a high mountain alone.

And Jesus was transfigured before them, and his face shone like the sun and his clothes turned white like light.

And there appeared to them Moses and *Elijah.*" [64]

Elijah, appearing as his spiritual self, came forth only after John's death. Where once he had stood as *the least person in the kingdom*, he now stands with its highest. While heaven was an option, his *Holy Land of choice* was saintly *business as usual* in the realm of humanity. Choosing *The Work*, he continued in helping Moses and Jesus *prepare the way*:

"And behold, two men were speaking with [Jesus], Moses and Elijah...Who appeared in glory and spoke concerning his departure which was to end in Jerusalem." [65]

Some traditions[66] honor Elijah returning as the fun loving painter, Raphael. His *delightful* Work heralds the high renaissance and may reveal visual insights he gained as John. Cayce noted a circa 1935 c.e. presence in Virginia Beach.

During Elijah's circa 30 C.E. presence in Galilee, the disciples asked:

"Why then do the scribes say that Elijah must come first?

Jesus answered saying to them, Elijah will come first, so that everything might be fulfilled.

But I say to you, Elijah has already come...

Then the disciples understood that what he had told them was about John the Baptist."[67]

Richard Wagner had Herodias returning as *Kundry* in his opera, *Parcifal*:

"You were Herodias."

In repentance, she sought forgiveness through Jesus:

"Now I try, from *world to world* to find Him again."[68]

Forgiven, she surely walks among us in regions of spirituality, Elijah and countless Judeo-Christian/Islamic generations have sought not to confront. As a healer, with the credentials of having once been a priestess of Venus, she might be, in a world now ready to accept her wisdom, a Dr. Virginia Johnson of Masters & Johnson sex clinic fame, or perhaps a Dr. Ruth Westheimer. If not, then Jezebel's equally as astute political skills could have enabled her to become a renowned leader, such as Great Britain's Margaret Thatcher, or the first lady of a great nation such as the United States.

Kevin Ryerson, at this writing, is one of the more respected of presently living psychic practitioners. He, to the best of anyone's knowledge, is not a *Levite.* Thus, there were no objections raised in his addressing an Atlantic University function.

While in trance he said of *Biblical Cases*:

"I think the precise parallels of the karmic dynamics are absolutely correct. The parallels are too precise to be coincidental."

He went on that some of those recorded in the Bible had returned and might be traced through conventional methodologies of history and transpersonal study.

One was Ahab.

Ryerson alluded to a contemporary figure, which like Ahab possessed a personal experience in the horror of combat. Like Ahab and Herod, he did not always get the best *press*. Another similarity was his family wealth. And yet another was his quick mind. Though not a builder, he possessed the two king's qualities of *stealth* and was once director of the American Central Intelligence Agency. As a diplomat, he served as ambassador to the United Nations. His political skills were such that he became president of the United States and orchestrated a consensus of international and Middle Eastern unity, against a common aggressor, that had been matched only by Ahab at Quagar and Herod at Galilee!

Unlike them, he's been able to peacefully retire, though he still pilots fast boats, and has an aircraft carrier named after him. He parachuted from an airplane on his 80th birthday. Living as Odysseus might have desired, he's surrounded by a nurturing wife and a family of numerous grandchildren and their feisty parents. One includes a down to earth kind of guy. In overcoming a thirsty habit, similar to that of a certain *man of the grape* of the past, he held his dad's old job.

As with all politicians, there were detractors and supporters. He was personally attacked from the "Scribes and Sadducees" of the day's political left, with a vehemence that no American President has felt: not even Jefferson. In contrast, he was supported, and even beloved, by the less vociferous but just as fervent "silent majority" of the more conservative Pharisees. With such extremes, it will take some time before his legacy can be more objectively evaluated. Many agreed with his successes in African aid, close ties with India, and the secure keeping of our "homeland." The maintenance of the Iraqi liberation, will keep him more kindly remembered. A successful democracy in that region, though imperfect, will encourage more nations to take the same route. This will surely help in making straight the highway of our God.

But either way, by and large, most will probably agree President Bush believed he did his best, as all of us should strive to accomplish in our lives, in going about what he felt was his *Father's* business.

May God guide the leaders of our world to wise decisions.

My prediction is that Middle Eastern peace will come about, not so much because of the arms of the "Mighty Men," but through the softer efforts of the liberated women. Like here, they'll cherish their new freedom and any modern day Jehu's thinking they can get around a return of Jezebel's wrath, should they try turning back the clock on her sisters, will wind up looking just as foolish as was the original.

Our first President put it this way:

"Liberty, when it begins to take root, is a plant of rapid growth."

Such speculation suggests the future value of *Biblical Cases of the Reincarnation Type.* They illustrate the upward evolution of souls through the just laws of a forgiving and sometimes *tough Love* - allowing for the correction of mistakes and the rewarding redemption's of real persons whether Archangels and Angels, the devil, the demons and the souls of men and women whether Republicans, Democrats, Greeks, Barbarians, the Unwise, the Wise, Sadds, Chicks, Arameans, Christians, Jews, Moslems, Buddhists, Hindus, Heathens, Baptists, Blackbeards...

The Transfiguration
Raphael's work embodies Elijah's redemption. Theories that the painter had been John the Baptist in a past life, suggest such paintings are autobiographical.

They have been featured for this reason.

Notes

1. 2nd Kings 22:2
2. John 3:8
3. Ecclesiastes 1:6
4. Antiquities XVII-8 all
5. Matthew 2:22
6. Luke 23:14-15
7. Luke 13:32
8. (2175)
9. 1st Kings 16:30
10. Mark 6:18
11. Antiquities XVIII-5:1-3
12. Mark 6:18
13. Matthew 11:18
14. Song of Solomon 4:10
15. Mark 6:20
16. Matthew 11:6
17. 1000-14
18. Lamsa (1936)
19. (254-109)
20. (5056)
21. (2520-1)
22. See Stevenson (1966)
23. 1st Kings 18:3
24. Luke 8:3
25. (275-5)
26. 1st Kings 20:8-16
27. 1st Kings 20:20
35. 1ST Kings 19:4
36. Matthew 26:39
37. Matthew 26:42
38. Head & Cranston p. 170
39. See Cohen (1977)
40. See Lamsa (1936)
41. 2nd Kings 9:30
42. 2nd Kings 9:31
43. 2nd Kings 9:33
44. Antiquities VII-13:2
45. 1st Kings 19:2
46. Matthew 11:11
47. 1st Kings 19:4
48. See 2nd Kings 11
49. 2nd Chronicles 22:2
50. 2nd Kings 23:25
51. 1st Kings 18:19
52. Matthew?
53. 1st Kings 18:26-28
54. Ecclesiastes 1:6
55. Antiquities XVIII-5:2
56. 1st Kings 21:4
57. 1st Kings 21:29
58. 1st Kings 22:31
59. 1st Kings 22:35-40
60. (262-109)
61. Luke 17:

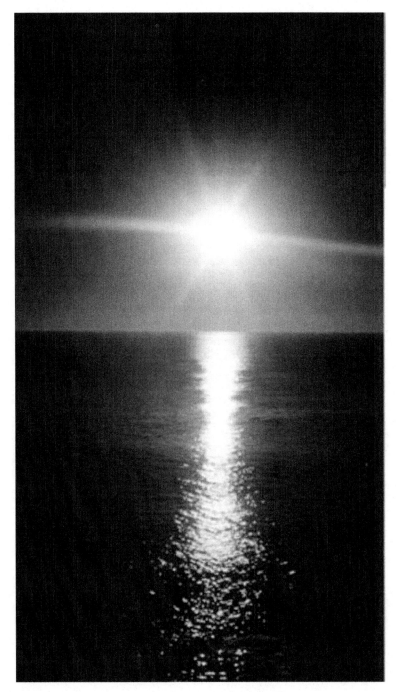

A Star to Steer Her.

The Arrival.

Chapter 19

Appendix

Table 1

**Tabulations of Biblical Statements
Direct Statements of Jesus Identifying John The Baptist as Elijah in the Aramaic Bible
(Biblical Past-life Motifs are Underlined)**

1. For this is he of whom it is written, behold I send my messenger before your face to <u>prepare the way</u> before you.
(Matthew 11:10)

2. For all the prophets and the law prophesied until John.
And if you wish to accept it, he is Elijah who was to come.
He who has ears to hear, let him hear.
(Matthew 11:13-15)

3. But I say to you Elijah has already come, and they did not know him, and they did to him whatever they pleased...
Then the disciples understood that what he had told them was about John the Baptist.
(Matthew 17:12-13)

4. He said to them, Elijah does come first to prepare everything; and as it is written concerning the Son of man that he will suffer much and be rejected
But I say to you that Elijah has come, and they did to him whatever they pleased, as it is written of him.
(Mark 9:12-13)

5. This is he of whom it is written, behold I send my messenger before your face to <u>prepare the way</u> before you.
(Luke 7:27)

6. He was a lamp which burns and gives light; and you were willing to <u>delight</u> in his light for a while.
(John 5:35)

Table 1-A

Tabulations of Biblical Statements
Direct Statements of Jesus Identifying John the Baptist as Elijah in The Jerusalem Bible:
(Biblical Past-life Motifs are Underlined)

1. He is the one of whom the scriptures says:
   Look, I am going to send my messenger before you;
   He will <u>prepare the way</u> before you;
   (Matthew 11:10)

2. And he, if you will believe me, is the Elijah who was to return.
   If anyone has ears to hear, let him listen!
   (Matthew 11:14-15)

3. He replied Elijah is to come to see that everything is once more as it should be; however, I tell you that Elijah has come already and they did not recognize him but treated him as they pleased...
   The disciples understood then that he had been speaking of John the Baptist.
   (Matthew 17:12-13)

4. He said Elijah is to come first and to see that everything is as it should be; yet how is it that the scriptures say about the Son of Man that he is to suffer grievously and be treated with contempt?
   However, I tell you that Elijah has come and they have treated him as they pleased, just as the scriptures say about him.
   (Mark 9:12-13)

5. He is the one of whom scripture says:
   See, I am going to send my messenger before you:
   He will <u>prepare the way</u> before you.
   (Luke 7:27)

6 John was a lamp alight and shining and for a time you were content to <u>enjoy</u> the light that he gave.
   (John 5:35)

Table 1-B

Tabulations of Biblical Statements
Direct Statements of Jesus Identifying John The Baptist as Elijah (Elias) In The King James Bible:
(Biblical Past-life Motifs are Underlined)

1. For this is he of whom it is written, Behold I send my messenger before thy face, which shall <u>prepare the way</u> before thee.
(Matthew 11:10)

2. For all the prophets and the law prophesied until John
And if you will receive it, this is Elias, which was for to come.
He who has ears to hear, let him hear.
(Matthew 11:13-15)

3. But I say unto you, that Elias is come already and they knew him not, but have done unto him whatever they listed...
Then the disciples understood that he spake unto them of John the Baptist. (Matthew 17:12-13)

4. And he answered and told them, Elias verily cometh first, and restoreth all things; and how it is written of the son of man, that he must suffer many things, and be set at naught.
But I say unto you, that Elias is indeed come, and they have done unto him whatsoever they listed, as it is written of him.
(Mark 9:12-13)

5. This is he of whom it is written, Behold I send my messenger before thy face, which shall <u>prepare the way</u> before thee.
(Luke 7:27)

6. He was a burning and a shining light: and ye were willing for a season to <u>rejoice</u> in his light.
(John 5:35)

Table 2

Twenty Cases Suggestive of Reincarnation in the Scriptures

1. Adam - Enoch - Melchizadek - Joseph - Joshua - Jeshua - David - Jesus the Christ.
2. Ahab - Herod Antipas.
3. All Israel, and the Prophets of Baal - The Leading Men of Galilee and the Guests who witnessed John the Baptist's head brought in on a tray.
4. Athalia - Salome.
5. Bar Hadad - Aretas of Arabia.
6. Elijah the Tishbite - John the Baptist.
7. Ethbaal - Emperor Tiberius.
8. Eve - Mary, Mother of Jesus.
9. Jehu - Josiah - Archelaus.
10. Jezebel - Herodias.
11. Joash - Herod Agrippa II
12. Joram - Pharaoh Necho.
13. The Prophet Jonah - Saint Peter, Whom Jesus Addressed as *Son of Jonah*.
14. Kings Crucified by Joshua - Officials Crucifying Jesus.
15. Naboth - Herod Agrippa .
16. Obadiah - Zechariah, father of John the Baptist.
17. Omri - Herod the Great.
18. Rahab (Rachel) the Harlot, female featured in Joshua – Mary Magdalene, the disciple Jesus loved.
19. The Captains and Their Fifty Killed by Elijah - The Captains and security personnel present at the Baptist's execution.
20. The Widow of Zarapeth, who cared for Elijah – Elizabeth, The Widowed Mother of John the Baptist

Table 3
Summary of Behavior and Statements Concerning John The Baptist's Identification With Elijah

List of Abbreviations:

Ant..Josephus	2nd K.. 2nd Kings	Rv...Revelation
Dt...Deuteronomy	Lk...Luke	War...Josephus
Is... Isaiah	Mk...Mark	( )...Cayce
Ja...James	Ml...Malachi	EJ.Encyclopaedia Judaica
Jo...John	Mt...Matthew	JB....Jerusalem Bible
1st K..1st Kings	Qo...Ecclesiastes	KJB...King James

1. The Words of Jesus Placing John as Elijah:

For this is he of whom it is written.	(Mt 11:10)
He is Elijah who was to come.	(Ml 1:13-15)
Elijah has already come.	(Mt 17:12-13)
Elijah does come first to prepare.	(Mk 12-13)
This is he.	(Lk 7:27)
You were willing to delight in his light	(Jo 5:35)

These direct statements, of the New Testament's highest authorities, offer convincing testimonies recognizing John the Baptist as Elijah returned. No counterclaims were found.

2. Statements of Old Testament Prophets Regarding The Return of Elijah to Proclaim The Presence of The Messiah:

The voice that cries in the wilderness.	(Is 40:3-5)
He shall prepare the way.	(Ml 3:1-3)
Behold, I will send you Elijah the prophet.	(Ml 4:5-6)
For all the prophets and the law prophesied until John.	(Matthew 11:13)

Isaiah's stature, as a major predictor of the Messiah, must reflect this same importance to his prediction of Elijah's return. Thus one cannot happen without the other - and unless Elijah comes first to prepare the way - the Messiah cannot make his appearance. The importance of the book of Malachi's strategic placement, as the last prediction of the Old Testament, underlines this critical point. Elijah must come first. As he appeared before Jesus, the verses do not refer to a second coming. If John the Baptist was not Elijah then Jesus was not the Messiah! The scripture cannot be broken. (Jn 10:35)

3. **The Significant Appearance of The Angel Gabriel and The Announcement of Elijah's Return:**

And he will go before them with the spirit and power of Elijah to turn the hearts. (Lk 1:13-17)

Lamsa (1957) notes that the term "angel," in ancient times, could refer also to helpful humans. That Luke describes strong fear among those concerned, indicates Gabriel may have been perceived as an apparition. That the angel is given the honor of announcing the birth of Jesus, indicates his high rank among such beings. Luke's use of the *Biblical Past-Life Motif* turn the hearts, from Malachi's verse, further evidences John's previous identity. If it is a given that all humans are spirit in nature, Gabriel's use of the term, as applied to Elijah, cannot logically be construed to limit the prophet's reappearance to anything less than a full spirit, mind, and body appearance. If John the Baptist appeared only in the spirit of Elijah - as was Elisha's case - then Jesus and the other Biblical authorities would surely have stated it as such.

4. Zachariah's Prophecy of John's Future as, The One Who Will Prepare The Way:

For you will go before the face of the Lord to prepare his way. (Lk 1:76)

That the Old Testament's last male human prophecy predicts Elijah's return, and the New Testament's first male human prophecy confirms the event, indicates the great care with which the gospels construct the narrative. (The *BPM* confirms the prophecy as it identifies Elijah's presence.)

5. **Commentaries of The Four Gospels Identifying John The Baptist as Elijah Returned:**

The *voice* which cries in the wilderness.   (Mt 3:3)
The *voice* which cries in the wilderness.   (Mk 1:3
The *voice* which calls in the wilderness.   (Luke3:4)
The *voice* of one crying in the wilderness. (Joh1:23)

Certainly, a significant consideration is seen in such unvarying agreement, on the issue of John the Baptist's past-life identity. ("The voice which cries in the wilderness" is the "BPM" of Isaiah's verse 40:3 which precedes the more well known statement *prepare the way*.) Such uniformity in the Gospels is unique. Not all major events are equally mentioned. Examples of variance can be seen in the accounts of the Magi and Christ's nativity. (Mark and John mention neither and Luke leaves out any reference to the Magi.)

6. Elijah Was an Ordinary Human Being Like Ourselves:

Even Elijah who was a weak man like ourselves. (Ja 5:17)

This insight noted by James, from the unique position as the brother of Jesus, may indicate an insight derived directly from the master. It, therefore, may have specific authority in making clear the point that Elijah, despite the circumstances of his dramatic death, is still no different than other humans; that is, all have the same potentials including reincarnation. If it were not so, others, of equal or higher authority would surely have stated their disagreement.

7. Prenatal Response Felt by Elizabeth in Mary's Presence:

The babe in my womb leaped with great joy. (Lk 1:44)

The unborn forerunner (Elijah) prophetically recognizes the unborn Messiah. His response transferred to his mother. She, as the mother of the precursor, then identifies the mother of the Christ. Instances of an unborn's affecting its mother, in responses that were unique to the previous personality, were noted by Stevenson (1987), though in far less dramatic ways. He cited cases where appetite changes, which reflected the tastes of the former incarnate, took place among the expectant mother!

8. John The Baptist's Birth into the Family of a Pious Jerusalem Priest:

There was in the days of Herod, king of Judea, a priest whose name was Zacharias, of the order of Abijah. (Lk 1:5)

O Jerusalem, Jerusalem, murderess of the prophets and stoner of those who are sent to her! (Mt 23:37)

Worship outside Jerusalem, in Elijah's time, had been outlawed by its priests, and prophets were persecuted. This might have prompted Jesus to remind the region of its shameful past of religious intolerance. The Anthropologist, Antonia Mills (1990), in replication studies of Stevenson's noted instances of children claiming a past life as a Hindu or Moslem. Some experienced family friction when, in their present lives, they were reborn into a family of the opposite faith. This seems similar to Elijah/John's situation. This should be a forewarning of the potential consequences of sectarian over-zealousness. The Baptist's birth into a hostile sect might have been to remind him of a karmic lesson on the value of cooperation. Here, his past religious rivals prove to be every bit as pious, as individuals as his past religious allies. Deeds and not creeds should therefore be the standard in choosing those with whom one would associate.

9. The Significance of the Name *John* as it May Relate to the Name *Elijah*:

You will call his name John. (Lk 1:13)

But his mother said to them [the neighbors], not so; but he shall be called John. (Lk 1:60)

Luke notes the unusual choice of the name, which was in conflict with the expectations of the family's neighbors. Its choice may reveal yet another method of identifying the past life of a Biblical personality. Though the special name could have been singled out for a variety of reasons, the selection might have been based on a system of encodement to conceal arcane knowledge. This would protect the relationship of the two names' meaning from possible interference by later redactors. Practitioners of the Cabala - a mystical oral tradition of Judaism (familiar also to the Freemasons of the American Revolution) - concede that every Hebrew letter has a corresponding numerical, astrological and other more esoteric significance. (Hironimus, 1989)

Thus, a word or name could convey additional meaning to an initiate. George Washington was known to have used a Hebrew letter/number coding system to communicate secrets with his officers. Most, if not all, were fellow Freemasons. Thomas Jefferson, considered the father of modern cryptology, may have learned the craft from his training in the order (Hironimus, 1989). As the Cabalist's tradition is still one of secrecy, unfortunately the matter must end here.

10. The Restoration of Zecharias' Voice, and His Public Identity of John The Baptist as Elijah Returned:

And you boy, will be called the prophet of the highest; for you will go before the face of the Lord to prepare his way.

(Lk 1:76)

While this verse of the long venerated Benidictus adds to the evidence of John's past life identity, it also reveals a similarity to a common occurrence found in spontaneous cases. Stevenson (1987) noted many cases where families suffered when public knowledge became a factor. Here, it is an emotional parent - rather than a young child or media reporter - who makes a disclosure. As a result, Zecharias is forced to send his family into hiding, according to Cayce, to escape the king's inquisition.

Appendix

11. Statements in The Edgar Cayce Material Identifying John The Baptist as Elijah Returned:

Yet he was Elijah. (1158-6)

Elijah, - who was the foreigner, who was the cousin, who was the Baptist. (1010-17)

These are noted, as examples of published transpersonal guidance, to demonstrate the *readings* initial contribution in choosing the personalities for study.

12. John The Baptist's Early Identification With Elijah:

By dealing with that of which it berated it's brother for his dress, it may be seen how that the law carries through. (1000-14)

John was weaned at six years of age. (2175-6)

From the periods of twelve years to that of seventeen...John went to Egypt for the preparation there. (2175-6)

These statements may reveal, as in spontaneous cases, that individuals claiming a past life remembrance, often do so at an early age. Cayce identified 1000-14 as having been John's sister. She had teased him over his camel skin clothing. She probably did so before he reached age six. But surely, no later than twelve when, according to the readings, he went to Egypt. (His sister returned as a Norfolk woman and early advocate of Cayce. She had sought him over an allergy to animal skins. She learned, "how that the law carries through." The Gospels do not record such a sister. However, Lamsa (1936) mentions Middle Eastern women, having only daughters, are often referred to as childless.)

Stevenson (1960, p. 54) noted, "the evidence for Edgar Cayce's clairvoyance regarding current features of living persons and their affairs seems to me extremely strong and that for the veridicality of his life readings extremely weak." He adds that the *life readings*, such as those exhibited here, are *extremely interesting*. The problem in proving them is another matter. Thus, if obscure facts of history - such as those shown in the Josephus literature and other sources - reveal a reading's congruency, it still remains to be proven that Cayce had not read them (highly unlikely) or received the information from some other means than the paranormal.

When no other verifications can be made, then of course one must accept - or reject - them as a matter of personal belief. Here, it has been maintained that the readings' accuracy is generally valid in all their 10,000 categories. However, this case does not stand or fall on that assumption. Enough evidence from its other sources have been presented to reach conclusions. Nevertheless, I find it interesting that the readings offer a parallel to modern cases, seen in the participants young ages.

13. John as an Essene:

The leaders of the peoples in Carmel - the original place where the school of the prophets was established during Elijah's time...were called then Essenes; and those that were students of what ye would call astrology, numerology, phrenology, and those phases of that study of the return of individuals - or incarnation. (5749-8)

The Essenes also as we call a sect of ours were excused from this [Herod's] imposition. These men live the same kind of lives as do those whom the Greeks call Pythagoreans. (Ant XIV- 10:4)

Mary and Elizabeth were members of the Essenes you see and for this very reason Zacharias kept Elizabeth in the mountains and the hills.
(5749-8)

In the school as had been undertaken by Elijah in Carmel.
(5065-1)

Beware of the leaven of the Pharisees and the Sadducees.
(Mt 16:16)

These may represent some of the difficult to verify congruencies between the readings and history, which had interested, but concerned, Stevenson. That, as infants, both Jesus and John were able to survive Herod's severe policies, may be explained by their mothers membership in the less scrutinized order.

Elijah would seemingly be attracted to the Essenes, as he had founded their predecessors - the *Sons of Prophets*. The Essenes' penchant for secrecy, and both boys' educational and travel experience may explain why so little was recorded of Jesus and John's youth.

That Jesus criticized only the teachings of Pharisees and Sadducees may indicate his having been an Essene himself. Though he never mentions them, it would not seem logical that he would denounce, not only his own sect, but that of his mother and John. Charlesworth (1988), a distinguished advocate of historic approaches, notes a general concession among scholars, to the high probabilities, that John was an Essene. Sequestered Dead Sea scrolls may help to confirm Cayce's numerous notations that Jesus was also a member.

14. The Unusual Similarity in the Extraordinary Competence of John The Baptist's and Elijah's Rhetoric:

Then went out to him Jerusalem and all of Judea and the whole country around Jordan. (Mt 3:5)

Appendix

Many others came to crowd about him, for they were greatly moved by hearing his words. (Ant XVIII-5:2)

Then Elijah came near to all the people and said...And all the people answered and said, you have spoken well. (1ST K 18:21-24)

And, behold, a prophet drew near to Ahab king of Israel and he said to him. (1st K 20:13)

For Herod was afraid of John, because he knew that he was a righteous and holy man, and he guarded him; and he heard that he was doing a great many things, and he heard him gladly. (Mk 6:6)

The Baptist, like Elijah, ranks among the greatest of speakers, This may indicate a learned behavioral skill of Elijah retained by John.

15. The Unusual Similarities in the Clothing and Physical Presence of John The Baptist and Elijah:

Now this John's clothes were made of camel's hair and, he had leather belts around his waist. (Mt 3:4)

He was a hairy man and girt with a girdle of leather about his loins. And he said to them, it is Elijah the Tishbite. (2nd K 1:8)

A figure John The Baptist, rough with the strong characteristics of a man, with the hair not too long but ruffled with a beard, with a staff resting across the limb; being seated upon the rocks, and the dress of camel's skin or hair with a girdle binding same about the body.
(275-5)

While the clothing may reflect the similar apparel of a typical hermit or prophet, I found no other personality in the Scriptures that was so uniquely identified with this peculiar dress and appearance.

16. The Unusual Similarity in the Extraordinary Survival Skills of John The Baptist and Elijah in Wilderness Areas:

His food was locusts and wild honey. (Mk 1:6)

And the ravens brought him bread and meat in the morning and bread and meat in the evening; and he drank from the brook.
(1st K 17:6)

Essene monastics would hardly seem the types to possess the nuances of wilderness survival and impart them as learned skills to John the Baptist. Elijah, of course, did, and John's mastery may be another example of learned behavior resulting from a past-life memory.

17. The Unusual Circumstance of John The Baptist and Elijah Abstaining From Wine and Strong Drink:

He will not drink wine and strong drink. (Lk 1:15)

He shall abstain from wine and strong drink. (Numbers 6:3)

Lamsa (1936) notes John's trait was like that of a Nazarite and devotees such as Samson and Samuel. The EJ mentions nomadic Rechabites and Kenazites also practiced such austerity. Members of the three sects seem to have reflected this and other similar behaviors of Elijah - including killing over religious differences. If he belonged, his never drinking wine may be explained. In contrast, Jesus created wine from water (see Jo 2:1-11) as *the first miracle* and his disciples drank wine at the last supper (See Jo 22:1-23). Of the Gospels' "holy men", only John's temperance is singled out. This may echo a past-life habit learned as Elijah.

18. The Unusual Similarity of John The Baptist and Elijah Presented as Celibates:

Q. Did I take the vows of celibacy?

A. They didn't take the vows of celibacy! Not to have children during those periods was considered to be ones not thought of God!

(2175-6)

This did not prevent her [Mary] from being, then, a material person, nor one with the faculties and desires for material associations, as indicated in the lack of celibacy. Is this indicated in any condition in the book, or man's relationship to God? Nowhere is this indicated!

(2067-11)

He [Jesus] said to them, this saying does not apply to every man, but to whom it is given.

For there are eunuchs who were born so from their mother's womb; and there are eunuchs who were made eunuchs by men; and there are eunuchs who made themselves eunuchs for the sake of the kingdom of heaven. To him who can comprehend, this is enough.

(Mt 19:11-12)

Marriage and the parenting of children, particularly sons in patriarchal Palestine, would seem the more common expectation. Though the recipient of Cayce's answer was female (2175 was identified as John the Baptist's nurse), and the answer possibly only directed toward her gender, celibacy for men would still seem extremely rare.

Normally, it is never in good taste to pry into the sexual preferences of individuals - especially those of saints. The mention here is only in noting a linked behavioral trait, of extreme rarity, though Chronicles credits Elijah with a daughter.

Luke describes the sexually active Zechariah and Elizabeth (evidenced in John's birth) as two who were:

"Righteous before God, and walked in all his commandments, and in the righteousness of the Lord without blame." (Lk 1:6)

This saintly statement - coupled with the words of Jesus and Cayce - makes clear that neither advancing age, nor a call to spiritual endeavor, need be accompanied with a corresponding call to celibacy. That sex is seen here as a happy, healthy and spiritually rewarding human expression commands an acknowledgment of appreciative thanksgiving.

19. Similar Geographic Locations of John the Baptist's and Elijah's Actions:

The Lord has sent me to Beth-el. (1st K 2:2)
These things happened in Bethany at the Jordan. (Jo 1:28)
The Lord has sent me to Jordan. (1st K 2:6)
He went throughout the country around Jordan. (Lk 3:3)

Both concentrated their activities in the northern areas. These ranged roughly from the Mt. Carmel range along Phoenicia's border to the Sea of Galilee, down the Jordan and across to the Jezreel plains. The territories conformed to similar regions ruled by both Ahab and Herod Antipas. While geography may or not be a reincarnation factor, spontaneous cases often feature investigations where past and present personalities incarnated within the same general geographic and political boundaries' (See IS, 1987)

20. John The Baptist's Inquest by the Temple Police:

And he confessed and did not deny it; but he declared, I am not the Christ. (Jo 1:20)
And they said, He is crazy. (Mt 11:17)

Like David, who once feigned insanity to escape danger, "so he changed his behavior' (see 1S 21:13-15). John the Baptist might have practiced the same ploy to confuse his adversaries. While seemingly not in keeping with the expected behavior of an Essene holy man, his actions might yet reveal another indicator of Elijah, whose wiles, are still noted in Jewish folk tradition

(EJ, 1972).

21. John The Baptist's Humiliating Denial of His Past-Life Identity as Elijah:

Are you Elijah? And he said, I am not. Are you a Prophet?
And he said, no. (Jo 1:21)
And when it was noon, Elijah mocked them. (1st K18:27)

Elijah, in dealing with the prophets of Baal, publicly humiliated them. In the presence of both his disciples and followers, John was forced to lie.

Like his sister experienced in the 20th century, he knew humiliation himself. "It may be seen how that the law carries through." The *BPM*, "I am the voice of one crying in the wilderness," (Jo 1:23) assures the reader of John's identity, though he had to publicly deny it.

22. John The Baptist's Limited Paranormal Gifts in Public:

John did not perform a single miracle. (Jo 10:41)

Let this boy's soul return to him again.

And the Lord heard the voice of Elijah; and the soul of the boy returned into him again. (1st K 17:21-22)

And Elijah answered...If I am a prophet of God, then let fire come down from heaven and consume you. (1st K 1:10)

Our Lord would you be willing that we command fire to come down from heaven and consume them, just as Elijah did?

He turned and rebuked them, saying you do not know of what spirit you are. For the son of man did not come to destroy lives, but to save.
(Lk 9:54-56)

John undoubtedly was in command of paranormal abilities. His use of telepathy in recognizing Jesus as the Messiah demonstrates this. In contrast with Elijah's, the obvious loss might be attributed to their misuse in the past.

23. The Baptism:

Then Jesus came from Galilee to the Jordan to John, to be baptized by him. (Mt 3:13)

Jesus came from Nazareth of Galilee, and was baptized in the Jordan by John. (Mk 1:9)

Jesus also was baptized. (Lk 3:21)

I saw and testified that this is the Son of God. (Jo 1:34)

In a similar ritual, on Mount Carmel, Elijah poured water on the sacrifice. Then fire came down from heaven. He turned the hearts of humanity toward a higher level of spiritual consciousness. In the same process, as John the Baptist, Elijah prepared the way for yet another step in humanity's turn toward its creator, the way of the Christ. The Messiah, as the sacrifice, was prepared and - as recorded in all four Gospels - the *fire* from heaven returned:

"And the Holy Spirit descended on him, like a dove, and a voice from heaven, saying You are my beloved son; with you I am pleased."
(Lk 3:22).

Appendix

24. John the Baptist's Unusual Link, With Herod Antipas:

And behold, a prophet drew near to Ahab king of Israel and said to him, Thus says the Lord... (1st K 20:13)

And he heard that he was doing a great many things and he [Antipas] heard him [John] gladly. (Mk 6:20)

That the two were so closely drawn together, may indicate a karmic linkage experienced from a previous life. Such evidence may increase the strengths of their individual cases. Certainly an independent study of the linked lives of Ahab and Antipas is warranted.

25. John The Baptist's Unusual Link With Herodias:

And Elijah said to them, Seize the prophets of Baal.

(1st K 18:40)

Then Jezebel sent a messenger to Elijah. (1st K 19:2)

But Herodias was bitter towards him, and wanted to kill him.

(Mk 6:19)

That Herodias was so strongly motivated to contemplate killing John, circumventing her husband's intentions and common political sense, may indicate her extreme behavior was driven by karmic causes. The strong evidence linking her to a past life as Jezebel strengthens both the Baptist's and the Tetrarch's cases. In fact, the whole interrelationship of the three reflect probabilities that would seem far beyond those of mere chance.

26. The Executions:

And Elijah brought them down to the Brook Kishon and slew them there. (1st K 18:40)

If I do not make your life as one of them. (1st K 19:2)

And his head was brought in on a tray, and given to the girl and she took it to her mother. (Mt 14:11)

Elijah did not offer Jezebel's prophets an opening to share in the God of Israel's covenant. Acting on his own will - and not God's - he mercilessly slew them. Her curse stood in the Scriptures:

"As it is written of him." (Mk 9:13).

Jesus did not intercede - such was the import to the world in learning Divine disagreement with Elijah's religious intolerance. Elijah, as John, suffered his own self-created consequence.

27. John The Baptist's and Elijah's Similar Narcissistic Behaviors Under Stress:

The children of Israel have forsaken thy covenant and thrown down thine altars and slain thy prophets. (1st K 19:10)

There is one coming after me whose shoes I am not good enough to untie. (Mk 1:7)

Are you the one who is to come or are we to expect another. (Mt 11:3)

Through Elijah's acts (though tarnished), the children of Israel returned to the Covenant, rebuilt the altars, and most certainly, were not killing God's prophets. In a like manner, John the Baptist had performed an extraordinary feat of great impact. Yet both denigrate their achievements. They might have done so, while under stress, to glean extra praise from their respondents. (Elijah had spent *forty days* getting to Mount Horeb and John was in custody.)

The *DSM* of the American Psychiatric Association notes that the sufferer of a narcissistic personality disorder often, "requires constant attention and admiration, e.g., keeps fishing for compliments" (1989, p. 351). Like those shown here? Rosenhan & Seligman (1989) add that in a relationship, the afflicted may vacillate between limits of over-idealization and devaluation of the other person. Thus John's description of Jesus as one whose shoes he was unworthy to untie, coupled with the later question casting doubt on his identity suggests such a vacillation.

28. The Marked Similarities in the Bible Translations:

The one who ties a knot is not more able than the one who can untie it. (1st K 20:11) Aramaic)

The man who puts on his armour is not the one who can boast, but the man who takes it off. (1st K 20:11) JB

Let not him that girdeth on his harness boast of himself as he that putteth it off. (1st K 20:11) KJB

This challenge of Ahab to Bar Hadad stands as the motto of today's Israeli army. In modern jargon it might read, "don't count your chickens before they're hatched!" Idiom, metaphor, and all the elements of human language changes. But - *The Word* - does not:

"The thing that has been is that which shall be; and that which has been is that which shall be done; and there is nothing new under the sun." (Qo 1:9)

29. Birthmarks and violence:

His head was brought in on a tray. (Mt 14:11)

And Jezebel painted her eyelids with kohl [a type of mascara worn by fashionable women of the time]. (2nd K 9:30)

A certain man drew his bow toward Ahab at a venture and smote the King of Israel between the joints of the breastplate.

(1st K 22:34)

    They slew Ahaziah, in his chariot.   (2nd K 9:27)
    Pharaoh smote Josiah at Megiddo.   (2nd K 23:29)

In spontaneous cases, when the previous personality died a violent death, the one claiming that identity often reveals a birthmark in the same location as the decedent's fatal wound. Elijah suffered no such injury and John would not be expected to exhibit an unusual birthmark. In a future study to see if links with Raphael exist - the wise researcher might do well in searching out evidence of a birthmark on the back of Raphael's neck! Lamsa (1964) points out that Phoenicians, who embraced reincarnation, believed their new bodies would resemble that left behind. He cited this in Jezebel's glamorizing herself in facing death. (Had she chosen, she probably could have escaped in disguise, or cited diplomatic immunity to gain safe passage home. Her brave choice of defiance, in the face of tyranny, demands recognition.) Herodias was no doubt an attractive person. A future investigation may reveal that facial make-up about her eyes, was an unusual feature of her appearance.

I found no evidence that Antipas had a birthmark, located where an arrow struck between the joints of Ahab's breastplate. I do not know if such a mark would appear in a contemporary incarnation this far removed and I have yet to call up enough *chutzpah*, to contact the former or present president. If Pharaoh Necho's mummy is in good condition with its wrappings removed, and reveals a variety of birthmarks or deformities, indicating multiple wounds from a past life, a link with Ahazia might be indicated. The intricate detail of Pharaoh Necho's statuette, is an eye opener.

Further evidence supporting the Jehu/Josiah connection may be seen in this verse:

    He who kills with the sword must be killed with the sword.

(Rv 13:10)

30. The Need for Elijah's Return:

And his disciples asked him, Why then do the scribes say that Elijah must come first?

Jesus answered, saying to them, Elijah will come first, so that everything might be fulfilled.   (Mt 17:10-11)

That all this people may know that thou art the Lord God and that thou has turned their perverse heart back again. (1st K 18:37)

He shall turn the heart of the father to the children and the heart of the children to their fathers... (Ml 4:6)

And he will go before them with the spirit and power of Elijah to turn the hearts of parents to their children. (Lk 1:17)

That a major scriptural prophecy was upheld, in Elijah's return as John the Baptist, apparently proved reason enough to satisfy the "why" of the disciple's question. Elijah came again to perform a similar task in calling humanity to turn once more toward a greater realization of its' spiritual identity. Through his past-life experience he brought the skills of an organizer, orator, and leader to insure the success of the precursor's mission. His choice was no random event. He was called, despite his liabilities, because he was the most qualified. *Like ourselves*, he was an imperfect human being. But, to who else can the Divine turn? And likewise, to who else can human beings - *like ourselves* - turn?

Therefore become perfect. (Mt 5:48)
God hath need of thee. (4083-1)

31. The Transfiguration:

And behold, two men were speaking with him, Moses and Elijah, who appeared in glory and spoke concerning his departure which was to end in Jerusalem. (Lk 9:30-31)

What meaneth the interpreter of the experience...what saw they the disciples for who appeared with him? Moses; that to those present meant a definite undertaking...and Elijah (or *John the Baptist*); representing that they too the disciples would become as messengers to a waiting world. (262-87)

That Elijah (or *John the Baptist*) is shown worthy to stand with Jesus and Moses indicates his mission's success. That Elijah appears only after John the Baptist's death adds to the overall pattern in nuance of detail and timing supporting their reincarnation linkage. As both Luke and Cayce indicate, John, Moses, and Jesus joined to plan the final strategy of the Messiah's Jerusalem ministry. Thus it is seen that many processes of divine decision-making are universal and take place:

As in heaven so on earth. (Mt 6:10)
Hear, O Israel: the Lord our God is one Lord. (Dt 6:4)

Chapter 20

Some Closing Remarks

The Elijah Lesson

Though flawed, Elijah's accomplishment on Mount Carmel was still an extraordinary achievement. For, backsliding in growth, humanity's spiritual evolution lay trapped in the worship of earth's energies. These were seen as the nature gods, or Ballim. He awakened Israel's (and ultimately the World's) return to greater awareness, so that the journey forward could begin anew. For the soul's destiny is oneness with its Creator. No force outside itself, whether benign or frightening, can deter this process. So, through a sequence of increasing levels of awareness, as Wilber (1981) notes, individuals return from matter to body, to mind, to soul, to spirit, as human inner divinity is realized.

The call forward, as it often leads one to realms of the unknown, is fearful. This is so, as unknowns are, by their nature, nearly always fearful. This leads to a temptation for stagnation or regression to more known levels of awareness. The Israelites succumbed to this lure in their embracement of Baal and the perceived comforts of group identification with nature. The more individual or egoic thinking processes, developing then and reaching their zenith today, was such a fearful step that Elijah's use of "fire from heaven," either in myth or reality, was necessary. The fear it created was more frightening than the anxieties suffered in appeasing earth's energies. While some might have regressed to even more primitive levels, most were forced forward. The new consciousness placed collective humanity somewhere between its past identity - as a creation of nature - and the future realization of its spiritual oneness with the Universe.

It's no accident that sexuality, environmental issues, and religious tolerance are major factors being redressed in today's new consciousness. As these rough places are made smooth, the *highway for our God* will straighten.

Plato

Plato, as you recall, concluded that each individual's circumstance is determined by their personal thoughts and deeds. He noted God was not responsible for humanity's plight, saying, "Heaven is guiltless." Such a premise might see the coming of a being with the attributes of a Jesus as an irrational act of the Divine. For, why would God choose to personally manifest in a human form and experience horrendous pain for events in which it had no responsibility? Certainly such capable servants as Buddha, Esther, Socrates and countless saints and sages, as we have seen, would have volunteered to teach earth-bound souls the new covenant of forgiveness of sin, as an option in the soul's return to heaven.

So why God personally?

The explanation, which maintains my faith, is this Einstein-like insight of simplicity and beauty that Jesus, the *Genius of Galilee*, offered to Nicodemus. The insight explains Divine motivation:

"For God so loved the world."   (John 3:16)

Ian Stevenson M.D.

Inevitably, Dr. Stevenson's Work will become better known. It has the potential for a Nobel Peace Prize. As each of the peoples of the world community begins to re-evaluate their collective scientific and sacred teachings, an opportunity for an age of heightened spiritual activity presents itself.

Science

Science is invited to look within the traditions of its own best practices as exhibited by Doctor Stevenson. Paranormal research has long been recognized as a legitimate discipline by the American Association for the Advancement of Science.

The contributions of science are acknowledged and utilized here. However, feelings, values, and humanities inner search for meaning are not quantifiable. As science can only quantify, meaning lays outside the scientist's limited resources. Any expert understands that - as a given in the discipline - conclusions based on incomplete data run the risk of ultimate invalidation as new facts are discovered. Thus, generalizations consigning human beings to positions of helpless creations of random events of evolution and environment, if backed by claims of scientific proof, run risks of error in being formulated on partial facts alone.

Fundamentalist Theology

Fundamentalist theology is also invited to review its best foundations and broaden its considerations. While no one's sincerity is questioned, those who would use fragmented one-line Biblical statements to theorize the after-death experience as one of eternal damnation for most, and salvation for a few, are reminded this unduly tests, and even insults, the concept of *Divine-Love*. They are asked to grasp the totality of the Bible's 774,746 words and initiate the more holistic contextual proofs - which involve history - as is commonly used in modern inquiry.

Birth Control

As co-creators with God, we share a part in maintaining this planet's environment. While God's resources are infinite, the Earth's are not. This requires then, a careful consideration as to how nature's treasures are to be utilized. Given the gains of modern technology, human populations can grow far beyond that which the planet is capable of sustaining. Thus some means of containing the number of souls, who might incarnate at any given time, is clearly necessary. Reincarnation makes clear that human bodies, (best termed as Homosapian) were created as terrestrial clothing for the soul. A parallel could be made to spacesuits worn by astronauts. Conscientiously practiced birth control, previous to the soul's being so clothed, would seem a moral environmental practice. Cayce noted we most often enter our human bodies at birth (see Puryear, 1980).

Homophobia

This is a touchy subject. Eight separate readings calmly confirmed that a variety of physical, psychological, and karmic causes lead to homosexuality. While some cases were reversible, sinfulness was never an issue - save for the sin of denial (see Puryear, 1980). As to karmic causes, reading 311-3 noted males may return as females and, likewise, females can return as males. This recalls Saint Jerome's fearful retort: "we may have no fear that we who are now men may afterwards be born women".

It should remind us that the soul's adapting to the powerful new sexual drives and social situations, confronted in such incarnations, requires some effort. Those criticizing these situations might keep in mind their own potentials for finding themselves - born again - as a member of the opposite sex.

We reap what we sow!

As to the prohibitions in the Bible, the isolated quips seem grounded in the narrow and mean minded "lying pens" of the *house of Josiah*, and reveal, not the word God, but the words of the highly homophobic culture he ruled. One would do better in seeking the *House of the Lord's* standard - of unconditional love - as to how the issue should be addressed. Recall, as well, that Saint Paul was very clear in maintaining that his issues and opinions on most matters covering social conventions reflected his personal opinions and were not at all to be construed as *Divine* directives.

Animals

We should love and respect such beings. Most concepts of reincarnation, though sects of Hindu's disagree, discount the possibilities of human returns as animals. Such possibilities might once have existed (see Wilber, 1981 and Puryear, 1980); and I'm sure my first incarnation was as a playful porpoise. However, such experiences are no longer necessary.

Humanity has progressed.

Animal evolution continuously evolves (they seem to physically reincarnate) and will continue to do so, long after we've departed.

Hopefully, we get to take our pets with us.

In my opinion, our bodies were created outside the norms of earthly evolution. Their purpose is to allow us a way to work and play with earth's energies. The Biblical Adam and Eve might have been the first to try them out. All went well until, in developing forgetfulness, they lost track of their spiritual identities. The experience brought pain in the remembrance that they were cosmic creatures trapped on the earth. Eden was no longer to be seen as home. Its escape would require *Work*. The message of Genesis, for me, is that while we, as humans, inhabit the earth, we are not of the earth. As extraterrestrials, our home lies elsewhere.

I'll miss this place.

The Pythagoreans

This statement by Josephus may best sum up what I have hoped to convey as being the correct attitude to be held toward those who properly apply their spiritual gifts:

"We have thought it proper to relate these facts to our readers concerning [the psychic abilities] of Essenes, however strange soever they be, and to declare what hath happened among us, because many of these Essenes have, by their excellent virtue, been thought worthy of this knowledge of divine revelations." (Antiquities, XV.10:5)

While both scientists and religionists have been respectfully asked to look a little deeper into their own and each others' traditions, likewise my own camp of mystics must make the same effort in appreciating the complexities of life's realities in the coming millennia. The dismissing of thousands of years of human experience and hard-won knowledge cannot be swept aside, simply with an unexamined Cayce affirmation or the machinations of the latest *New Age* guru. Our world is a three-dimensional entity, demanding the mastery and integration of spirit, mind, and the physical to achieve wisdom.

The practical application of this integration, which will be so necessary in the future, might be seen in the past example of a later-date Pythagorean, Dr. Benjamin Franklin. As a foremost scientist, astrologer, publisher, and major architect of the United State's Constitution, his *voice* warrants resurrection:

"When I see nothing annihilated and not a drop of water wasted, I cannot suspect the annihilation of souls, or believe that God will suffer the daily waste of millions of minds ready made that now exist, and put Himself to the continual trouble of making new ones. Thus, finding myself to exist in the world, I believe I shall, in some shape or other, always exist; and, with all the inconveniences human life is liable to, I shall not object to a new edition of mine, hoping, however, that the errata of the last may be corrected."

Hope

His grasp of the spiritual nature of humanity, seen in this brief passage, is no doubt reflected in the Constitution's uniqueness as the longest lived of active political documents. The value, then, of an individual utilizing an integrated approach of mind, body and soul can be seen in his contribution. Benjamin Franklin's example, among many like-minded beings, still inspires us today and adds a sense of hope, that through such understandings, humanity will achieve a future state of consciousness where each may, "because of their excellent virtue been thought worthy of this knowledge of divine revelations."

It is my sincere hope that this information, seen from within science, Judeo-Christian and Islamic traditions, will offer an opportunity for the adherents of all faiths (both East and West) to engender new responses and new hopes.

Chapter 21

Suggested Reading, Bibliography, and Index

1. American Psychiatric Association. (1987). Diagnostic and Statistical Manual of Mental Disorders (3rd ed.) (revised). Washington D.C: Author.
2. The Edgar Cayce Readings. (1971, 1993, 1994, 1995, 1996). Virginia Beach: The Edgar Cayce Foundation.
3. Charlesworth, James H. (1988). Jesus Within Judiasm. New York: Anchor Reference Library. Doubleday.
4. The Jefferson Bible, The life and Morals of Jesus of Nazareth (1989) Church, Forrest (Ed) Boston: Beacon Press.
5. Cohen, Abraham (1977). The Psalms. London-Jerusalem- New York: The Soncino Press.
6. De Anima (1947). Mckeon, Richard (Ed). Introduction to Aristotle. New York: Modern Library.
7. Donaldson, James & Roberts, Alexander (Editors) Ante-Nicene Christian Library (1867). Edinbourough: Clark.
8. Einstein, Albert (1950). Out of My Later Years. New York: Philosophical Publishing Co. (also see) The World As I See It. (1949) p. 26. New York: Philosophical Library.
9. Encyclopaedia Judaica (1972) Jerusalem: Keter Publishing
10. Gardner, Joseph L. (Ed.) The Reader's Digest Atlas of the Bible. (1981) Pleasantville, N.Y: Reader's Digest Association.
11. Head, Joseph & Cranston, S.L. (Eds.) Reincarnation: The Phoenix Fire Mystery. (1977) New York: Julian Press/Crown Publishers, Incorporated.
12. Herzog, Chaim & Gichon, Mordechai (1978). Battles of the Bible. New York: Random House.
13. Hironimus, Robert (1989). America's Secret Destiny, Spiritual Vision and the Founding of a Nation. Rochester, Vermont: Destiny Books.
14. Hoeller, Stephan A. (1989). Jung and the Lost Gospels. The Theosophical Publishing House: Wheaton,Ill.
15. Hoener, Harold W. (1980). Herod Antipas. Grand Rapids, Michigan: Zondervan Publishers.
16. Holy Bible, From Ancient Eastern Manuscripts (1957). George M. Lamsa (Trans.). Philadelphia: A.J. Holman Co.

17. Holy Bible, King James Version (1983). Grand Rapids, Michigan: Zondervan Publishers.
18. The Jerusalem Bible (1966). Alexander Jones (Ed). Garden City, N.Y: Doubleday.
19. Josephus, Flavius (Trans.) William Whiston (1865). The Life and Works of Flavius Josephus. Phila: David Mckay.
20. Jung, Carl G. (1959) Collected Works. New York: Pantheon
21. Jung, Carl G. (1963) Memories, Dreams, Reflections. New York: Pantheon
22. Keller, Werner. (1981). The Bible as History. New York: William Morrow and Company Inc.
23. Kranjenke, Robert Wm. (1976) The Psychic Side of the American Dream. Virginia Beach: A.R.E. Press
24. Lamsa, George. (1936). Gospel Light. Philadelphia: A.J. Holman Company.
25. Lamsa, George. (1964). Old Testament Light. Englewood Cliffs N.J.: Prentice-Hall.
26. Lamsa, George. (1971). Idioms in the Bible Explained. St. Petersburg Beach Fl: Aramaic Bible Society.
27. Millar, Fergus (1993) The Roman Near East 31 BC - AD 337: Cambridge. MA Harvard University Press.
28. Mills, Antonia (1990). Moslem Cases of the Reincarnation Type in North India: Part I & II: Analysis of 26 Cases. Journal of Scientific Exploration, (4) 2 171- 202.
29. New Catholic Encyclopedia. (1967). Washington D.C.: Catholic University of Amer4ica.
30. Padover, Saul K. (1970) Jefferson, A Great American=s Life and Ideas. New York: Penguin Books
31. Pagels, Elaine (1975). The Gnostic Paul. Harrisburg PA: Trinity Press.
32. Pagels, Elaine (1979). The Gnostic Gospels. New York: Random House.
33. Pagels, Elaine (1988) Adam, Eve, and the Serpent. New York: Random House.
34. Pagels, Elaine (2003) Beyond Belief, The Secret Gospel of Thomas. New York: Random House.
35. Pike, Albert (1871) Morals and Dogma of the ancient and Accepted Scottish Rite of Freemasonry Charleston S.C.
36. Pike, James A. (1968) The Other Side. Garden City N.Y: Doubleday & Co.

37. Plato. Dialogues of Plato (1932). New York: Random House.

38. Puryear, Herbert (1980) Sex and the Spiritual Path. Virginia Beach: A.R.E. Press.

39. Puryear, Herbert (1982) The Edgar Cayce Primer. Toronto: Bantam Books.

40. Quest, Linda Gerber PhD (1969) The Politics of Hope An analysis from the Edgar Cayce Readings. Virginia Beach: A.R.E. Press

41. Rosenhan, David L. & Seligman, Martin E. (1989). Abnormal Psychology. New York: N.W. Norton & Co, Inc.

42. Sachar, Abram Leon (1965). A History of the Jews. New York: Knoph.

43. Sanderfur, Glenn (1988). Lives of the Master. Virginia Beach: A.R.E. Press.

44. Snaith, Norman H. (1954). And Kings. In N.B. Harmon (Ed.). The Interpreters Bible, Vol.3. New York: Abingdon Press.

45. Stearn, Jess (1967). Edgar Cayce: The Sleeping Prophet. New York: Doubleday.

46. Steiner, Rudolph (1967). (Trans.) George Blake The Last Address of Rudolph Steiner. London: Rudolph Steiner Press.

47. Stevenson, Ian (1974). Twenty Cases Suggestive of Reincarnation. Charlottesville, VA: University Press of Virginia.

48. Stevenson, Ian (1987). Children Who Remember Previous Lives A Question of Reincarnation. Charlottesville, VA: University Press of Virginia.

49. Stevenson, Ian (1997). Where Reincarnation and Biology Intersect. Westport, CT: Praeger Publishers.

50. Sugrue, Thomas Joseph (1942). There is a River, The Story of Edgar Cayce. Virginia Beach: A.R.E. Press.

51. Teeple, Vernon (1982). The Historical Approach to the Bible. Evanston, Ill: Religion and Ethics Institute.

52. VanHoose, L. Edward (1992). Biblical Cases of the Reincarnation Type. P.O. Box 595 Virginia Beach, 23451: L. Edward VanHoose

53. Wilbur, Ken (1981). Up From Eden: A Transpersonal View of Human Evolution. Garden City N.Y.: Anchor Doubleday.

54. Wilson A.N. (1997). Paul The Mind of The Apostle. New York: W.W. Norton & Co. Inc.

General Index of Events, Places, and Topics

Alexandria, 32, 36, 100, 120, 122, 128, 136, 141, 172.
America (United States), 16, 31-5, 37, 42, 45, 49, 67, 75, 77, 83, 93, 99, 107, 111, 114-7, 132, 134, 141, 155, 161, 173, 183, 204, 204, 208, 217, 234, 236-9, 252.
Angels, 8, 64, 123, 143-4, 224, 227, 240.
Aramaic, 20, 101-2, 131, 161, 191, 212, 216, 245, 260.
Association for Research & Enlightenment, 6, 57, 59, 63, 166.
Assyria, 101-2, 161-2, 164, 179-80, 205-6, 220, 227, 234.
Athens, 71, 85, 105-6, 120-2, 128, 136, 204.
Atlantic University, 7, 47, 57, 59, 61, 71, 83, 141, 151, 173, 238, 280.
Atlantis, 156.
Baltimore, 1, 4-5, 60, 106, 133-4, 166.
Barbarians, 49, 123, 125, 127, 130, 209, 227, 240.
Bias, 28, 51, 79, 109, 150, 157, 166, 168, 171-2, 205, 209, 225, 232.
Birthmarks, 70, 176, 183, 193, 195, 197, 203, 260-1.
Born Again, 11-12, 17-19, 26, 59, 63, 69, 71, 74-75, 87, 97, 117, 137, 140, 170, 185-6, 199-200, 204, 266.
California, 6, 8-9, 60, 133, 155
Catholic, 15, 20, 90, 107, 125, 127, 133, 144-5, 147.

Christianity, 6, 15, 41, 48, 52, 71-2, 90, 103, 109, 122, 125-6, 129-30, 140, 171, 177, 204, 236-7.
Church Councils, 15-16, 143-5, 156, 216.
Communism, 19, 82, 170, 217.
Constantinople, 16, 143-5, 158, 204.
Creationism, 65-6, 68, 169.
Creeds, 17, 93, 97, 130, 143, 252.
Demiurge (Satan), 134, 158.
Devil, 134, 143-4, 240, 270.
Egypt, 53, 102-3, 114, 120, 128-29, 157-8, 164 179, 194, 200, 202-3, 216, 253.
Essenes, 78-80, 90, 97, 100, 102, 105. 126, 129, 140, 180-4, 215-17, 254, 267.
Fraud, 70, 76, 159, 178, 196, 199, 203-4, 216-7, 221.
Galilee, 40, 42, 162, 210-11, 223, 238-9, 248, 257-8, 264.
Gender, 60, 74, 109, 118, 163, 193-5, 199, 209, 235, 256, 268.
Gnostics, 49-50, 105, 125-30, 133, 160.
Golan Heights, 219-20.
Gospel, 14-15, 20, 22-3, 40, 52, 89, 99-01, 110, 126-30. 133, 152, 173, 177, 183-5, 188, 208, 215, 230, 253, 250, 253, 256, 258.
Greeks, 39, 49-0, 71-2, 79, 102, 105-8, 114, 122-3, 125-7, 129, 140, 146, 209, 211, 216, 227, 240, 254.

Heaven, 17-20, 25, 31, 36, 50, 61, 72, 84, 75, 84-5, 97, 105-7, 109, 112, 132, 137, 154, 162, 171, 180, 189, 205, 207, 221-2, 228, 236-7, 256, 258, 262-4.

Hebrews, 38, 78, 89, 92, 106, 216.

Hell, 18, 49, 66, 79, 104, 106, 120, 129, 132-3, 142, 184, 200.

History, 13-15, 25, 28-3\1, 35, 40, 42, 47-8, 51-2, 61-4, 70, 77, 79-84, 81-2, 100, 103, 114, 116, 125, 129, 131, 141, 144, 150-4, 156-7, 161-2, 179, 189-90, 199, 204-5, 209, 214, 216-17, 229, 233, 236, 239, 253-4, 265.

Holy Spirit, 16, 22-3, 31, 51, 141-9, 145-6, 179, 258.

Inquisition, 19, 48, 144, 206, 252.

Israel, 6, 25-8, 38-9, 40-41, 70, 99, 102, 123, 139-40, 160-4, 177-80, 190, 199, 204, 206, 211, 215, 218-20, 224, 226-9, 231, 234-5, 237, 248, 255, 259-263.

Islam, 28, 45, 54-5, 72, 104, 127, 154, 158, 170-1, 190, 195, 202, 238, 268.

Jerusalem, 24, 52-4, l03-4, 136, 158, 160-4, 172, 178, 181-4, 190-1, 200, 211-12, 218-20, 230, 238, 246, 249, 251, 254, 262.

Judea, 89, 110, 178, 181, 184, 210-11, 233, 251, 254.

Judaism, 52, 72, 102-3, 129, 177, 252, 255.

Karma, 41-2, 92, 109, 203, 213, 221-2, 235-6.

Materialism, 50, 65-6, 68, 77, 80-4, 169.

Masons / Free Masons, 33, 75, 107, 111, 113-4, 131, 252.

Megiddo, 200, 261.

Memory, 18, 75-6, 80, 125, 159, 166, 181-3, 193, 196, 218, 228, 255.

Neo-Platonism, 72, 79, 81, 129

New Age, 48, 61, 128, 133, 150, 154, 267.

Nicea / Nicene Creed, 15-6, 99, 139, 141.

Opera, 185, 238.

Orthodox, 61, 90, 104, 127, 132-3, 135-45, 170.

Paranormal, 30, 71, 89, 127, 147, 149, 153, 159, 161, 193, 196-7, 219, 253, 258, 264.

Pharisees, 78, 80, 97, 128, 140, 239, 254.

Philosophy, 47, 49, 83, 110 112, 114.

Politics, 17, 83, 99, 105, 114-5, 170, 214, 132-4, 234.

Pre-existence, 50, 66-9, 72-3, 76, 79-80, 83, 90-2, 97, 113, 116.

Princeton University, 15.

Prophecy, 23, 30, 123, 176-7, 180, 250, 262.

Protestant, 16, 20, 90, 93, 145.

Parapsychology and Psychology, 7, 19, 77, 126-7, 217.

Pyramid, 11, 33, 114, 156, 159.

Pythagorean, 3, 5, 72-3, 79-80, 84-5, 105, 107-9, 126, 129, 140, 143-4, 170, 177, 186, 216, 254, 267.

Quagar, 179, 220, 233, 239.

Reincarnation (Major Mentions), 1-3, 6, 11-15, 17-21, 23, 28-9, 32-4, 37, 40-2, 47-53, 55, 57, 59, 60-5, 67-74, 76, 78-85, 87, 90-2, 94, 97, 99, 110-2, 114-6, 126, 132-3, 138, 140-8, 153, 159, 163, 169-2, 176-7, 183-7, 188, 196-7, 199, 204-6, 208, 210, 217, 236, 240, 247-8, 251, 257, 261-2, 265-6.

Religion, 7, 11-2, 15-6, 19-20, 27, 38, 41-2, 48, 50, 55, 65, 71-2, 74, 82, 99, 105-6, 108, 110-1, 117, 126, 129, 138, 144, 151-2, 162, 166, 170-1, 179, 183, 194, 198, 270.

Resurrection, 13-14, 16-8, 54, 79, 95, 267.

Rome, 14-5, 16, 25, 79, 94, 96-7, 102-5, 120, 127, 129, 131, 134-7, 139, 146, 162, 189, 195, 210-13, 227, 233.

Rosicrucian, 114-5.

Sadducees, 77-8, 80-4, 97, 129, 133, 140-1, 170, 173, 193, 206, 239-40, 254.

Saints, 15, 17-8, 20, 22-3, 30-1, 34, 38, 42, 44, 49-50, 55, 63, 71-2, 78, 84, 87-9, 93-7, 99, 108, 117, 126-30, 133, 135, 141-4, 162, 172, 177, 183, 190, 195-6, 211, 236-7, 248, 256-7, 264-6.

Samaria, 53, 162, 181, 204-5, 217-20, 234-5.

Satan (Demiurge), 135-6.

Science, 5, 12-4, 21, 29, 47-0, 61, 64, 68, 70-2, 77, 82, 112, 141, 150, 217, 264, 268.

Scribes, 25, 113, 133, 160-1, 164-5 209, 212, 219-20, 226, 238, 243, 261, 264.

Sermons, 33, 36, 41, 51, 100, 113, 116, 132, 144, 154, 116, 166, 188, 223.

Soul, 1-3, 12, 14, 17-20, 24-6, 34-5, 39-40, 42, 52, 64, 66-8, 71-5, 77-8, 80-2, 87, 92, 97, 100, 107-9, 113-4, 122, 139-44, 153-5, 157-8, 165, 169-4, 204, 216-7, 209-0, 230, 232, 236, 240, 244-5, 250, 267-8.

Therapeutae, 100, 102, 105, 126, 140.

Tibet, 182, 217.

Translation, 15, 20, 53, 91, 102, 161, 171, 191, 207, 219, 260.

Unitarian, 113-4, 138.

United States (of America), 16, 31-5, 42, 45, 49, 83, 107, 116-7, 132, 161, 204, 236-9.

University of Virginia, 48, 69, 112-14.

Virginia, 5-8, 26, 32, 49, 57-60, 69, 111-13, 116, 133, 148-9, 151-3, 168, 201

Major Mentions of Personalities:

Ahab, 25-6, 42-3, 59, 99-102, 104, 115, 148, 152, 155, 161-3, 170, 178-180, 183, 199-200 205-7, 211-214, 216-218, 223-5, 228-35, 239-40, 248, 255, 257, 259-61.
Ahaziah, 53, 102, 179-200, 223, 230, 261.
Aretas of Arabia, 213-14, 248.
Athalia, 100, 102, 223, 229-31, 249.
All Israel, 163, 211, 219, 227, 229, 248.
Alexander the Great, 81-2, 84, 92, 102, 107, 115, 128.
Aristotle, 72, 77-8, 80-82, 84- 5, 107, 114-5, 121, 128 153, 172.
Archelaus, 148, 210-11, 216, 248.
Saint Augustine, 71, 236.
Bar Hadad, 213, 218-20, 229, 234-35, 248, 260.
Captains, 41-2, 111, 158, 168, 229, 234, 248.
Chuza, 218, 232.
Dalai Lama, 41, 172, 182.
Edgar Cayce, 3, 6, 18, 20, 29-31, 33-4, 44, 47, 52, 54-7, 62-4, 68, 70, 73-4, 78, 80, 84, 108, 114, 128-9, 130, 140, 148-50, 154-7, 159, 165, 171, 177, 182, 194, 196, 203, 209-10, 212, 215-16, 218, 228, 235, 237-8, 249, 252-4, 256-7, 262, 265, 267.
Elijah the Prophet, 20-28, 34, 38-43, 49, 52, 54, 63, 70, 74, 95, 99-103, 119, 144, 148-9, 160, 166-67, 171, 176-7, 179, 182-4, 191, 193-7, 199, 204, 211, 214-17, 220, 223-4, 227-9, 231-5, 237-9, 241, 245-63.
Elisha, 179, 188-90, 214, 235. 250.
Elizabeth, 22, 30-1, 34, 37, 57, 148, 172, 177-8, 182, 196, 215, 230, 248, 251, 254, 257.
Emperor Augustus, 25, 103, 189-90, 211, 227.
Emperor Caligula, 104, 233, 235.
Emperor Constantine, 16-17, 103, 126-7, 136-9, 141-2.
Emperor Nero, 90, 92, 131, 134-7, 157, 234.
Emperor Tiberius, 44, 148, 211-12, 216, 232, 248.
Albert Einstein, 12, 18, 30, 67-8, 72-5, 77, 84, 87, 93, 114, 154, 172, 217, 264.
EthBaal, 148, 179, 212, 227, 248.
Benjamin Franklin 32-33, 37, 67-8, 83, 87, 93, 108, 111, 128, 169, 172-3, 174-5, 267-8.
Gandhi, 44, 67-8, 70, 86, 172.
Saint Helena, 137-9.
Herod Agrippa I, 46, 104-5, 110, 134, 233, 235-7 248.
Herod Agrippa II, 104, 110, 134, 137, 148, 237, 248.
Herod Antipas, 25-7, 40, 42-6, 79, 112, 117, 136, 148, 181-2, 193, 206, 210-14, 220-24, 231-2,

235-40, 243, 248, 255, 257-9, 261.
Herod the Great, 25, 103, 131, 146, 152, 168, 179, 183, 221, 233, 248, 251, 254.
Herodias, 27, 40, 43, 45-6, 114, 146, 193, 213-4, 179, 216, 221-4, 227, 231-3, 235-6, 238, 248, 259-61.
Ireanaeus, 133-4, 144, 155.
Saint James, 34, 94, 97, 190-1, 237, 249, 251.
Thomas Jefferson, 36, 50-3, 68, 107, 105-6, 110-5, 130, 137, 140, 152.
Jehu, 29, 56, 102-3, 148, 159-4, 178-9, 199-2, 205-6, 209, 211, 213, 229, 235-6, 240, 248, 258, 261.
Jeremiah the Prophet, 7, 52, 55, 68, 87, 161-63, 172, 189.
Saint Jerome 142-4 161, 195. 265.
Jesus the Christ, 9, 12, 20, 26, 28, 31, 34, 39, 41-3, 48-50, 54, 59, 63, 67, 69, 72, 74-5, 78-80, 83, 87-90, 92-3, 95-7, 99-103, 105-6, 108-11, 113, 115-7, 119, 128-9, 135-7, 139-40, 146, 148-9, 162, 170-7, 180-182, 185-91, 195-7 199, 203, 207-13, 215-8, 220-3, 230-1, 235-8, 245-251, 254, 256-64.
Jezebel, 25-6, 28, 38 41-3, 58, 81, 100, 115, 148, 152, 162, 179, 199-200, 212, 214, 221, 223-35, 238, 240, 248, 259-61.
Joash, 230, 237, 248.
John the Baptist, 16, 21-8, 31, 39-49, 52, 59-60, 63-4, 70-4, 79-80, 83, 87 105, 115, 119, 114, 117-8, 129, 131, 140, 144, 150, 166, 171, 175, 180-91, 193-208, 210, 214-17, 220-4, 230-3, 237-41, 245-62, 264.
Jonah the Prophet, 95-7, 152, 155-7, 160, 248.
Joram, 28, 53, 102, 148, 159, 179, 200-3, 206, 223, 229, 248.
Josephus, 77-9, 81, 84, 97, 102-3, 129, 139, 146, 158, 180, 201, 210-17, 232-5, 246, 253, 267, 299.
Joshua, 27, 54, 149, 162, 199, 207-8, 248.
Josiah, 52-4, 148, 160-4, 179, 200, 203-9, 211-12, 229-30, 248, 261, 266.
Carl Jung, 11-12, 17, 19, 30, 74, 81, 93, 110, 114, 118-9, 122, 127-8, 172.
Justinian, 143-5, 154-8, 163, 204.
Martin L. King, 67.
George Lamsa, 20, 96, 131, 152, 158, 161, 219, 223. 250, 253, 161.
Martin Luther, 95, 118.
Mary Magdalene, The Disciple Jesus loved, 6, 100-2, 207, 248.
Mary, Mother of God, 6, 22, 31, 34, 37, 95-6, 108, 143, 149, 172, 177, 182, 193, 230-1, 248, 251, 254, 256..
Karl Marx, 80-4.
Menahem, 180.
Muhammad, 52, 152, 169-74.

Naboth, 25, 43, 148, 233-6, 248.
Nicodemus, 140, 209-10, 264.
Obadiah, 148, 182, 218, 248.
Omri, 102-3, 150, 178-1, 206, 213, 218, 229-0, 248.
Origen, 72, 129, 143, 153, 172, 231.
Saint Paul, 14-15, 30, 40, 49-51, 63, 72, 78, 84, 87, 89-5, 99, 104, 110, 112, 115-25, 127, 129-31, 134-8, 136-41, 162, 172, 236, 266.
Saint Peter, 50, 94-7, 108, 99 131, 135-6, 183, 237, 248.
Elaine Pagels, 105, 130, 138.
Pharaoh Necho, 148, 200,-3, 206, 248, 261.
Plato, 1, 12, 17, 19, 60, 71-2, 75, 77, 79-81, 84-5, 87, 107-9, 114-5, 121, 129, 143, 154, 168, 172, 181-2, 204, 207, 216, 264.
Albert Pike, 107, 121.
James A. Pike, 6, 172.
Pythagoras, 3, 5, 71-2, 79, 85, 107-8, 129, 143, 172.
Rehab (Rachel) the Harlot, 207.
Franklin Roosevelt, 7, 32-3, 37, 119, 172.
Salome, 40-1, 213. 231, 248.
B. F. Skinner, 5, 19, 39, 80, 116-7, 217.
Solomon, 7, 52, 64, 66-8, 70, 74, 87, 93, 102, 114, 116, 147, 152, 155, 161-2, 164, 167, 172, 178, 183, 199, 209-10, 214, 226.
Jess Stearn, iii, 3, 7-8, 17, 99, 103, 120, 126, 155.

Socrates, 12, 19, 71-2, 75-6, 80-1, 85, 87, 121, 140, 146-7, 151,153, 172, 216, 220, 264.
Ian Stevenson, 48, 69-71, 74-5, 80, 87, 93, 120, 146-51, 157-8, 176-7, 183-5, 193-7, 203, 205, 217, 251, 264.
Theodotus, 125-6, 129, 139.
George Washington 32, 36-7, 82, 93, 111, 117, 156, 172, 252, 220.
Valentinus, 129.
Richard Wagner, 72, 185, 237-8.
The Widow of Zarapeth, 148, 182, 248.
Zechariah, 22, 31, 177-8, 182, 196, 248, 257.

How The Bible Reveals Reincarnation
A Short Synopsis for Sharing

Reincarnation is returning to biblical study. This renewed interest has come about as a preponderance of scientific evidence suggests the precepts of mainstream theology and the materialism of the secular humanist - concerning life after death - need reexamining. Additionally, biblical and secular history shows many fine minds, majorities of ancient Judeo/Christians, and even America's founders had held the belief.

Their wisdom still lives and still imparts a timeless lesson to today: That we live in a cause and effect world of reason, purpose, free-will, and most importantly, *Divine compassion*. Thus, our present realities are more often the result of past-life acts, rather than chance factors of genetics, environment, or capricious deities.

Past study by the majority of church officials on reincarnation, though sincere, drifted away for a variety of reasons. Among these was the "Proof Context Method" (established during the *Dark Ages*") which utilized a single verse to establish a biblical point. Both secular and sectarian politics probably were among the causes as well. There was no separation of church and state back then, and all sides manipulated their agendas through religion. Fortunately, faith in the Bible's integrity remains intact as archaeology reveals old manuscripts are like today's. And as today's new information "prepares the way" to the wisdom of the old, a new opportunity exists for all faiths to engender new responses and new hopes.

Modern theology requires reading at least one verse preceding a given passage, and at least one which follows, making for three consecutive verses, before a verdict can be considered as biblical. And even then, some serious scientific consideration of linguistics, allegory, metaphor, simile, and case histories of real people, places, and events – all using the latest methods of data collection and evaluation - must be in evidence.

Reincarnation in the Bible was often dismissed, using the *proof context* method, in quoting Saint Paul.

"It is appointed for men to die once, and after their death, the judgment." But a quick look using the three-verse consideration, shows the Apostle began with the clear and straightforward proclamation, that such an appointment *to die once* will take place: "*At the end of the world!*" (See Hebrews 9:26-28) As the end of the world is yet to come, certainly reincarnation can continue, while certainly, outmoded approaches from the dark ages cannot.

That Paul preached to two audiences, and that reincarnation and resurrection are synonyms, may be another factor behind so much

How The Bible Reveals Reincarnation

confusion. He taught the basics to beginners and a deeper wisdom to those termed as "wise" Greeks. (See Romans 1:14) The wisest Greek was Socrates. He observed, on the last day of his life, that in proving a person previously existed, reincarnation could be established: "Now if it be true that the living come from the dead, then our souls must exist in the other world; for if not, how could they have been ***born again?***"

These samplings (among many) reinforce the major factor in reincarnation's return, that is, modern science. *Twenty Cases Suggestive of Reincarnation,* published by the University of Virginia in 1966, is an example. The study concludes that while humanity's future cannot be foreseen, it can be demonstrated through thousands of cases, that, as Socrates observed, human beings now alive were once dead!

Parapsychology is a science, and transpersonal psychology is that branch, which investigates ancient and modern paranormal sources, one being the Twentieth Century Christian mystic and psychic: Edgar Cayce.

Cayce was asked, while in trance: "What part of the New Testament definitely teaches reincarnation?" His response, regarding reincarnation, was the suggestion to start with the first chapter of John: "John. Six to eight, Third to fifth. Then the rest as a whole." (452 - 6) John 1:6-8 concerns John the Baptist, in every translation, including the Aramaic quoted here:

"There was a man sent by God whose name was John."

Chapters Three to Five cover a lot of territory, but prominently include the life of "the Baptist," and his critical role in the baptism of Jesus. They also include the Master's **"born again"** Socratic quizzing of Nicodemus the priest, and this closing curious remark concerning John, referring to him as the one in whom:

"You were willing to delight."

In exploring Cayce's, "the rest as whole," using any good biblical concordance will demonstrate another closing curious use of: "Delight."

It reveals the Prophet Malachi's paranormal ability in closing the Old Testament with its final prophesy, which predicted the return of a man to be "born again" in the coming New Testament. The man was Elijah.

Malachi (3:1 & 4:5-6) not only described Elijah as a "Delight," but as God's messenger who, as would John the Baptist, suddenly appear out of the wilderness to: "Prepare the way."

John the Baptist, like Elijah, was a real person whose existence secular history confirms.

The biblical Elijah appears as one of the Old Testament's grandest personalities in 1st Kings (Ch 16 - 22) and 2nd Kings (Ch 8 - 10). His story involved two historic figures. These were King Ahab and his infamous wife, Jezebel. Their dramatic three way saga started when Elijah killed the queen's priests in a dispute over sectarian religious issues, and Ahab was politically forced to side with Elijah over Jezebel in the fray.

While a "<u>delight</u>" in other areas, Elijah, as a real person, like ourselves, had a darker side. It prevailed in the killings. Nevertheless, the scribes, whom both John and Jesus cursed as "offspring of scorpions," gave the event good press and honored Elijah with being taken bodily to heaven.

Similar scribes, though of other cultures, bestowed similar eulogies upon Mithras of Persia, Romulus, the founder of Rome, and even Caesar Augustus.

But the Bible's Prophets knew better. Elijah's crime was a crime against humanity. This had to be put aright, lest future believers take the scribes' excesses as a Divine endorsement of bigotry.

Isaiah's (40:3-4) insight, noted Elijah's mistake in expressing the tearful Prophet's personal remorse as: "<u>The voice of him that cries in the wilderness.</u>" Yet Malachi still concurred with Isaiah (the Scripture cannot be broken) that Elijah, despite his sins of religious intolerance, had done such great acts - that in balance - he would remain written as the one called to: "<u>Prepare the way</u>."

It should come as no surprise that Malachi's last prophesy is confirmed by Jesus as the first prophecy of the Old Testament to be fulfilled in the New. Jesus saw this fulfillment in John the Baptist and said of him:

(1) "For ***this is he of whom it is written***, behold I send my messenger before your face to <u>prepare the way</u> before you."
(Matthew 11:10)

(2) "For ***all the prophets and the law prophesied until John***. And if you will accept it ***he is Elijah*** who was to come.

He [she] who has ears to hear, let him [her] hear."
(Matthew 11:13-15)

(3) "But I say to you that ***Elijah has already come***…Then the disciples understood that what he had told them was about John the Baptist." (Matthew 17:12-13)

(4) "But I say to you that ***Elijah has come***, and they did to him whatever they pleased, ***as it is written of him***."
(Mark 9:12-13)

(5) ***"This is he of whom it is written***, behold I send my messenger before your face to <u>prepare the way</u> before you."
(Luke 7:27)

(6) "He was a lamp which burns and gives light; and you were willing to *delight* in his light for a while."   (John 5:35)

When threatened by the Temple police (they had the power to crucify him) John denied the identity, but later acknowledged his past life in voicing what Isaiah had written of him: "***I am the voice of one crying in the wilderness**, Straighten the highway of the Lord, as the prophet Isaiah said.*"   (John 1:23)

That Elijah was "born again" as John was unanimously confirmed in each introduction of the Baptist in the remaining Gospels:

The voice which cries in the wilderness.   (Matthew 3:3)
The voice which cries in the wilderness.   (Mark 1:3)
The voice which cries in the wilderness.   (Luke 3:4)

Elijah's return to proclaim the Messiah fulfilled the Scriptures: Not all karma is bad. But there was a lot of unfinished business between him, Ahab, Jezebel, and most importantly, the misunderstanding that killing others over religious issues was Godly. That the issue is as important today as back then is seen in the headlines of our post 9-11 world!

Thus Elijah was vulnerable to Jezebel's vengeance. Bad acts bring bad ends, and in her return as Herodias, the infamous wife of Herod Antipas (Ahab returned), the error would be righted in a precise karmic consequence.

Jezebel/Herodias had Elijah/John executed, and this time, Ahab/Antipas, had to side with her in the fray. Saint Paul's popular insight (Galatians 6:7) roughly translates: "What you sow, you reap."

Today, it is more often understood as:

What goes around comes around!

(From: The Voice: How The Bible Reveals Reincarnation, By L. Edward VanHoose © All Rights Reserved ISBN # 978-1-4392-4475-3)

You may contact the author at www.captainlarry.org

or

www.reincarnationworld.com

Home at Last.

Printed in Great Britain
by Amazon